SENTENCING LAW AND PRACTICE

AUSTRALIA AND NEW ZEALAND
The Law Book Company Ltd.
Sydney : Melbourne : Perth

CANADA AND U.S.A.
The Carswell Company Ltd.
Agincourt, Ontario

INDIA
N.M. Tripathi Private Ltd.
Bombay
and
Eastern Law House (Private) Ltd.
Calcutta and Delhi
M.P.P. House
Bangalore

ISRAEL
Steimatzky's Agency Ltd.
Jerusalem : Tel Aviv : Haifa

MALAYSIA : SINGAPORE : BRUNEI
Malayan Law Journal (Pte) Ltd.
Singapore

PAKISTAN
Pakistan Law House
Karachi

SENTENCING LAW AND PRACTICE

by

C. K. BOYLE, LL.B., Dip. Crim., Barrister-at-Law
Professor of Law, University College, Galway

and

M. J. ALLEN, LL.B., LL.M., Barrister-at-Law
Lecturer in Law, University of Newcastle-upon-Tyne

London
Sweet & Maxwell
1985

Published in 1985
by Sweet & Maxwell Ltd.
of 11, New Fetter Lane, London
Computerset by Burgess & Son (Abingdon) Ltd.
Printed in Scotland

British Library Cataloguing in Publication Data

Boyle, Kevin
    Sentencing law and practice.
    1. Recidivists—England   2. Sentences (Criminal
    procedure)—England
    I. Title   II. Allen, Michael
    344.205'772   KD8406

    ISBN 0–421–34400–8

Preface

The object of this book is to give an account of sentencing law and practice in the courts of England and Wales and of those aspects of the penal administration which relate to the implementation of sentencing decisions. Sentencing is the function which most occupies the criminal courts. As the range of options increases and consequent complexity results, it is hoped that a text which offers a systematic treatment of the available options, their purposes and the principles to be considered when deciding on their application, will be of use to all those involved in the sentencing process, not excluding those who come before the courts. It is hoped that those members of the general public interested in how the courts function in this important field will also find the book of value.

The idea for this work came after the publication of our first book together, *Sentencing law and Practice in Northern Ireland*. This book is to a large extent derived from that book with major revisions to take account of both the differences in the law between England and Wales and Northern Ireland and the developments over the two years since that book was published. Most of the revision work on this book has been carried out by Michael Allen.

For ease of reference the text for the most part follows a common structure: each sentencing option is briefly described, followed by a more detailed analysis of the legal requirements; there then follows a section on combining that sentence with other measures, a section on when the sentence is appropriate and finally a section on appeal rights.

It would be surprising if this exploration of the maze of statutory provisions governing sentencing did not throw up the occasional anomaly or lacuna. For example, there is no right of appeal where an offender is dealt with by the Crown Court for breach of a community service order where the order was originally made by the Crown Court following a conviction before a magistrates' court; there is such a right of appeal in Northern Ireland. With the emphasis in recent years on measures designed to keep offenders out of prison or other penal institutions it also appears anomalous that there is no power to suspend a detention centre order or a sentence of youth custody. Again, by contrast, an order for detention in a young offenders' centre (the Northern Ireland equivalent) may be suspended. Hopefully these faults will be rectified in due course.

The most important piece of legislation in this area of late has been the Criminal Justice Act 1982 which provided a totally new legal framework of custodial sentences for offenders under 21 years of age as well as enacting changes in relation to supervision orders, partly suspended sentences, release on licence, fines, probation, compensation and community service orders. It is hoped that this book will help to explain these changes as well as all the other complexities of sentencing.

July 1985   M. J. Allen

                                                        C. K. Boyle

Contents

Table of Cases

Table of Statutes

Table of Statutory Instruments

Table of Abbreviations

[The following abbreviations are used in the text.]

A.C.O.	Attendance Centre Order
A.J.A.	Administration of Justice Act 1970
C.A.A. 1968	Criminal Appeal Act 1968
C.A.A. 1981	Criminal Attempts Act 1981
C.C.C.A.	Costs in Criminal Cases Act 1973
C.C.R.	Crown Court Rules 1982
C.D.A.	Criminal Damage Act 1971
C.J.A.	Criminal Justice Act
C.L.A.	Criminal Law Act
C.S.O.	Community Service Order
C.Y.P.A.	Children and Young Persons Act
I.A.	Immigration Act 1971
M.C.A.	Magistrates' Courts Act 1980
M.C.R.	Magistrates' Courts Rules 1981
M.H.A.	Mental Health Act
O.A.P.A.	Offences Against the Person Act 1861
P.C.C.A.	Powers of Criminal Courts Act 1973
R.T.A.	Road Traffic Act 1972
S.C.A.	Supreme Court Act 1981
T.A.	Theft Act 1968

PART I
NON-CUSTODIAL MEASURES

INTRODUCTION

By non-custodial measures is meant all methods open to the courts which do not involve sentencing the offender to detention in a penal institution. The majority of persons convicted before the courts are dealt with by non-custodial measures.

The most common mode of disposal is the fine followed by the discharge. It has been a consistent theme of penal policy in recent years to reduce the prison population and that has been encouraged by the introduction of new alternatives for sentencers, such as the community service order.

As most non-custodial measures are available for dealing with both juveniles and adults, they are treated together in this Part.

ABSOLUTE DISCHARGE

DESCRIPTION

An absolute discharge is an expedient open to a court where, following conviction, punishment is inappropriate. It differs from the order for conditional discharge, in that the offender is unconditionally released and, except for the limited consequences outlined below, he is absolved of all further liability for the offence of which he was convicted.

THE LAW

Section 7(1) of the Powers of Criminal Courts Act 1973 provides:

> "Where a court by or before which a person is convicted of an offence (not being an offence the sentence for which is fixed by law) is of opinion, having regard to the circumstances including the nature of the offence and the character of the offender, that it is inexpedient to inflict punishment and that a probation order is not appropriate, the court may make an order discharging him absolutely, or, if the court thinks fit, discharging him subject to the condition that he commits no offence during such period, not exceeding three years from the date of the order, as may be specified therein."

An order of absolute discharge may be made by any court provided the offence of which the person stands convicted is one for which the sentence is not fixed by law. It is not a punishment and where a person convicted of an offence is discharged absolutely or conditionally or a probation order is made such conviction "shall be deemed not to be a conviction for any purpose other than the purposes of the proceedings in which the order is made and of any subsequent proceedings which may be taken against the offender under the preceding provisions of this Act" (P.C.C.A., s. 13(1)).[1]

---

[1] See *Cassidy* v. *Cassidy* [1959] 1 W.L.R. 1024, D.C. In *R.* v. *Harris* [1951] 1 K.B. 107, where the defendant had previously been convicted of an offence but received a conditional discharge, this conviction was not allowed to be relied on by the prosecution to prove the defendant's bad character under s. 15 of the Prevention of Crimes Act 1871 (repealed by C.A.A. 1981). However, the prosecution were permitted to call a police officer who was in court on the day of his conviction to prove that he heard him admit that he was guilty of the offence in question or had heard a jury find him guilty. This evidence was held properly admissible as proof of the known character of the person concerned. *Harris* was applied in *R.* v. *Statutory Committee of the Pharmaceutical Society of Great Britain, ex p. the Pharmaceutical Society of Great Britain* [1981] 1 W.L.R. 886, D.C.

4

Where a person has been discharged absolutely or conditionally on a conviction of an offence under the Road Traffic Act 1972 and has been disqualified from holding a driving licence or had his licence endorsed, the conviction shall, notwithstanding section 13(1) of the Powers of Criminal Courts Act 1973, be taken into consideration in determining his liability to punishment or disqualification for any offence involving obligatory or discretionary disqualification committed subsequently (R.T.A., s. 102(2)). Certain savings are made to section 13(1) by section 13(4), for example, the offender may rely on his conviction as a bar to subsequent proceedings for the same offence.[2] Section 13(3) provides that the conviction will be disregarded for the purposes of any enactment or instrument which imposes any disqualification or disability upon convicted persons or authorises or requires the imposition of the same.[3] A conviction followed by an order for absolute discharge (or an order for conditional discharge or probation) does not constitute a conviction for the purpose of putting a suspended sentence into effect pursuant to section 23 of the Powers of Criminal Courts Act 1973 (*Tarry* [1970] 2 Q.B. 561; 54 Cr.App.R. 322). The rehabilitation period applicable for an order of absolute discharge is six months from the date of conviction under section 5(3) of the Rehabilitation of Offenders Act 1974.[4]

COMBINING AN ABSOLUTE DISCHARGE WITH OTHER SENTENCES

By its very nature an absolute discharge (or a conditional discharge) cannot be combined with any other punitive measure for the same offence. Accordingly, a fine being a punishment, may not be imposed in addition to a discharge for the same offence (*McClelland* [1951] 1 All E.R. 557). Nor may an order under section 43 of the Powers of Criminal Courts Act 1973 depriving the

[2] See also Social Security Act 1975, s. 152(2); Vehicles (Excise) Act 1971, s. 9(5).
[3] In *R.* v. *Statutory Committee of the Pharmaceutical Society of Great Britain, ex p. the Pharmaceutical Society of Great Britain, above,* it was held that the disciplinary committee, in considering whether certain of its members should be disqualified for misconduct rendering them unfit to be on the register of pharmaceutical chemists, was not prevented by s. 13(3) from acting on facts leading to convictions for which they had received conditional discharges, since s. 13(3) merely prohibited them from relying upon the convictions themselves as evidence of misconduct.
[4] But *cf. Kitt* [1977] Crim L.R. 220, where the view was taken that absolute and conditional discharges and probation orders, on the basis of s. 13 of the P.C.C.A., are not convictions for any purposes *ab initio* and thus s. 5(3) and (4) of the Rehabilitation of Offenders Act 1974 appear to be meaningless. However, it could be argued that insofar as the two provisions are inconsistent the 1974 Act must be taken to have impliedly amended the 1973 Act.

offender of property used, or intended for use, for the purposes of crime, be combined with an absolute discharge (and *semble* a conditional discharge) (*Hunt* [1978] Crim.L.R. 697).[5] Similarly it follows that a custodial sentence would be inappropriate in combination with an order for discharge. But where a person is given a discharge for one of several offences of which he is convicted, a court is free to sentence him for the other offence(s) in any manner in which it has power to do so (*Bainbridge* (1979) 1 Cr.App.R.(S.) 36).

Orders for absolute or conditional discharge may be combined, however, with ancillary orders such as orders for costs or compensation (P.C.C.A., s. 12(4)), restitution orders (P.C.C.A., s. 12(4)) or recommendations for deportation (*Akan* [1973] Q.B. 491). Although section 13(3) of the Powers of Criminal Courts Act 1973 provides that the conviction of an offender who is discharged absolutely or conditionally (or placed on probation) shall be disregarded for the purposes of any enactment or instrument which imposes any disqualification of disability on convicted persons, or authorises or requires the imposition of the same, section 102(1) and (2) of the Road Traffic Act 1972 provide that a court may exercise its powers to disqualify a person from holding or obtaining a driving licence or endorse such licence even though it has ordered that the offender be absolutely or conditionally discharged or placed on probation.

WHEN AN ABSOLUTE DISCHARGE IS APPROPRIATE

There are three conditions to be considered by a court before making an order discharging an offender absolutely (P.C.C.A., s. 7(1)): (a) that the offence is one for which the sentence is not fixed by law; (b) that it is inexpedient to inflict punishment; (c) that probation is inappropriate. An absolute discharge "may reflect the triviality of the offence, the circumstances in which it came to be prosecuted, or factors relating to the offender."[6] It will be used where, for example, the strict letter of the law has been breached but the offence is trivial and the public interest is not served by inflicting punishment on the offender (see *Smedleys Ltd.* v. *Breed* [1974] A.C. 839), where considerable time has elasped between the commission of the offence and its prosecution,[7] where the accused is morally blameless (*e.g.* *O'Toole* (1971) 55 Cr.App.R. 206), or where the

---

[5] This principle would also seem to apply to orders under s. 44 of the P.C.C.A. disqualifying offenders from driving where a motor vehicle was used for the purpose of committing or facilitating the commission of the offence in question.

[6] *The Sentence of the Court* (HMSO, 1978), para. 24.

[7] See Cross, *The English Sentencing System* (3rd ed., 1981), pp. 9–10.

offence was not serious and is an isolated one with little likelihood of the accused offending again.

APPEAL

The offender's right to appeal his *conviction* where he did not plead guilty or admit the offence charged is preserved where an order of discharge or a probation order is made (C.A.A. 1968, s. 50(1A) inserted by C.J.A. 1982, s. 66). A series of decisions of the Court of Appeal[8] had held that the terms of section 13(1) of the Powers of Criminal Courts Act 1973 which provides that a probation order or conditional or absolute discharge is deemed to be a conviction only for the purpose of the proceedings in which it was made, meant that there could be no appeal against such orders under section 9 and section 50(1) of the Criminal Appeal Act 1968, or against ancillary orders (such as a compensation order or an order to pay the costs of the prosecution) made in conjunction with them. This situation has been rectified by secton 50(1A) of the Criminal Appeal Act 1968 inserted by section 66(1) of the Criminal Justice Act 1982 which provides:

"Section 13 of the Powers of Criminal Courts Act 1973 (under which a conviction of an offence for which a probation order or an order for conditional or absolute discharge is made is deemed not to be a conviction except for certain purposes) shall not prevent an appeal under this Act, whether against conviction or otherwise." [9]

Thus an appellant may appeal either against the principal order or the ancillary order or both.

The Act also inserts a new subsection (1A) after section 108(1) of the Magistrates' Courts Act 1980 which provides:

"Section 13 of the Powers of Criminal Courts Act 1973 . . . shall not prevent an appeal under this section, whether against conviction or otherwise."

---

[8] See *Tucker* [1974] 1 W.L.R. 615; *Robinson* (1979) 1 Cr.App.R.(S.) 108; *Wilson* (1982) 4 Cr.App.R.(S.) 337.

[9] This section came into operation on January 31, 1983 (S.I. 1982 No. 1857).

CONDITIONAL DISCHARGE

DESCRIPTION

This measure differs from an absolute discharge in one respect only: a condition is imposed that the offender commits no offence for a specified period in the future. A conditional discharge differs from probation in that there is no provision for supervision during the period of the order, and in contrast to a suspended sentence, there is no statutory requirement on a court subsequently to deal with the offender for the original offence should he commit a further offence, and there is no predetermined sentence which will then normally be put into effect.

THE LAW

The power to make an order of conditional discharge is contained in section 7(1) of the Powers of Criminal Courts Act 1973. As with an order for absolute discharge, offences for which the sentence is fixed by law are excluded, and an order for conditional discharge is not a punishment, and constitutes a conviction for certain purposes only.

An order for conditional discharge may run for up to three years. Before making an order for conditional discharge the court *shall* explain to the offender in ordinary language the implication of the order; that is, if he commits a further offence during the period of conditional discharge he will be liable to be sentenced for the original offence (P.C.C.A., s. 7(3)). The Court of Appeal held in *Wehner* [1977] 1 W.L.R. 1143 that the sentencer may delegate his duty of explaining to the offender the effect of the order provided always that the court is satisfied that the explanation has been made and understood before the order is drawn up.

Section 8 of the 1973 Act sets out the procedures relevant to magistrates' courts and Crown Courts and the powers of these courts when an offender commits a further offence within the period of conditional discharge. Where a person is convicted by a court in any part of Great Britain of an offence committed during the period of conditional discharge and has been dealt with in respect of that offence, the Crown Court, if the order was made by that court, or, if the order was made by a magistrates' court, a justice of the peace acting for the same petty sessions

8

area may issue a summons against him or a warrant for his arrest
(P.C.C.A., s. 8(1) and (2)) ordering him to appear or be brought
before the court by which the order for conditional discharge was
made (P.C.C.A., s. 8(4)). Where the order was made by the
Crown Court and the person subject to it is convicted by a
magistrates' court of an offence during its currency, the magistrates' court may commit him to custody or release him on bail
until he can be¯ brought or appear before the Crown Court
(P.C.C.A., s. 8(6)).[1]

Where it is proved to the satisfaction of the court that made
the order that the person subject to the order has been convicted
of an offence committed during the currency of the order, the
court may deal with him for the original offence in any manner
in which it could deal with him if he had just been convicted by
or before the court of that offence (P.C.C.A., s. 8(7)). A Crown
Court dealing with a person where the original order of conditional discharge was made by a magistrates' court is limited to
imposing a sentence which the magistrates' court could have
imposed if it had just convicted him of the offence (P.C.C.A.,
s. 8(8)).

Where a person under 17 years of age has been made the subject
of an order of conditional discharge following conviction by a
magistrates' court for an offence triable only on indictment in the
case of an adult, any court subsequently dealing with the offender
for the original offence after he attains the age of 17 years only has
the powers which would be exercisable for an offence triable either
way which had been tried summarily (P.C.C.A., s. 9(1) as amended
by C.L.A. 1977, Sched. 12).

If an offender is sentenced for the original offence the original
order ceases to have effect (P.C.C.A., s. 7(4)), and the original
conviction will count as a conviction for all purposes.

COMBINING A CONDITIONAL DISCHARGE WITH OTHER
SENTENCES

The principles stated above (pp. 5–6) relating to absolute
discharge apply to conditional discharge.

On making an order of conditional discharge a court may, if it
thinks it expedient for the purpose of the reformation of the

---

[1] If the order for conditional discharge was made by a magistrates' court and the
person to whom it applies is convicted by another magistrates' court of any offence
committed during the currency of the order, that court may, with the consent of
the court which made the order, deal with him for the offence for which the order
was made (P.C.C.A., s. 8(9)).

offender, allow any person who consents to do so to give security for the good behaviour of the offender (P.C.C.A., s. 12(1)).[2]

There is provision for substituting a probation order with an order of conditional discharge where the probation order appears to be no longer appropriate (P.C.C.A., s. 11(1)). In such a case the offender is treated as though the original order had been one of conditional discharge (P.C.C.A., s. 11(2)).

WHEN A CONDITIONAL DISCHARGE IS APPROPRIATE

Conditional discharge is frequently used in a wide variety of cases where the possibility of punishment for the offence at a later date is thought a sufficient deterrent without any other additional measure such as a fine being necessary. It is more likely to be used where the offence is a first offence. Section 7(1) of the Powers of Criminal Courts Act states that it should be used where it is inexpedient to inflict punishment and where a probation order is not appropriate. In addition the court must have regard "to the circumstances including the nature of the offence and the character of the offender" (P.C.C.A., s. 7(1)). Thus, where there are strong mitigating circumstances punishment might not be appropriate and an order of conditional discharge may be made (see *Jagger* [1967] 3 All E.R. 545). The offender's personal circumstances, such as his age, previous good character and good work record, may result in a conditional discharge even though the offence is fairly serious.[3] A conditional discharge will also be appropriate where the offence does not merit a prison sentence but the offender does not have the means to pay a fine (*McGowan* [1975] Crim.L.R. 113; *Whitehead* [1979] Crim.L.R. 734).

APPEAL

See Absolute Discharge, above.

---

[2] In s. 7(1) of the Probation Act (N.I.) 1950 the equivalent Northern Ireland provision, the court may require the offender, or if the offender is a child (*i.e.* under 14 years of age) his parent or guardian, or if he is a young person (*i.e.* between 14 and 17 years of age) the offender or his parent or guardian, to give security for the good behaviour of the offender.

There would seem to be no reason why a court could not bind an offender over in a fixed sum to keep the peace either under s. 1(7) of the J.P.A. 1968, in the case of a Crown Court, or the J.P.A. 1361, in the case of a magistrates' court.

[3] See Cross, *The English Sentencing System* (3rd ed., 1981), p. 12; Thomas, *Principles of Sentencing* (2nd ed., 1979), p. 227.

BINDING OVER

DESCRIPTION

A recognizance is a solemn undertaking whereby a person binds himself to the performance of an obligation, *e.g.* to be of good behaviour, and acknowledges his indebtedness to pay a sum to the Crown in the event of breach of that undertaking. In addition to an offender thus binding himself, sureties or guarantors may be sought who likewise enter into a bond, in a certain sum, for the performance of the obligation undertaken by the offender. There are a variety of forms of recognizance, existing at common law and under statute, usually termed binding over, and the various forms of recognizance can be thought of as having the effect of a suspended fine.[1]

THE LAW

(a) Binding over to come up for judgment

With the exception of offences, the punishment for which is fixed by law, Crown Courts have inherent common law powers, instead of passing sentence, to respite judgment and require the convicted person to enter into a recognizance with or without sureties to come up for judgment when called upon.[2] This course may be adopted where an appeal is pending or where the circumstances of the case make it expedient and in the interests of justice.[3] The court may, in addition to a recognizance to come up for judgment, require the offender by recognizance to keep the peace and be of good behaviour. Where a person is bound over to come up for judgment he is deemed to be for all purposes a person convicted on indictment (*Jephson* v. *Barker and Redman* (1886) 3 T.L.R. 40; *Abrahams* (1952) 36 Cr.App.R. 147).

Where it is proposed to bring the convicted person up for judgment a notice must be given to him and to any sureties (*David* [1939] 1 All E.R. 782). Where the person is brought up for sentence on the ground that a recognizance entered into by him is alleged to have been broken, the court should see that the facts are as strictly proved as if the allegations were that he had committed a crime

---

[1] See Cross, *The English Sentencing System* (3rd ed., 1981), p. 14.
[2] This power was expressly recognised in the Powers of Criminal Courts Act 1973, s. 1(7) and Supreme Court Act 1981, s. 79(1), (2)(*b*).
[3] See *Archbold* (42nd ed., 1985), §5–115.

(*McGarry* (1945) 30 Cr.App.R. 187).[4] However, the issue as to whether there has been a breach is not one for a jury, but the person brought up for sentence is entitled to be heard in his own defence (*David*).[5] An order binding the offender to come up for judgment is a sentence under section 50 of the Criminal Appeal Act 1968 for the purposes of an appeal to the Court of Appeal.

(b) Binding over on condition that the offender leave the jurisdiction

The power to bind over to come up for judgment has been used as a means of ensuring that an offender leave England. In *Flaherty* [1958] Crim.L.R. 556, an offender was bound over in his recognizance in the sum of £10 to go back to Eire and not return to this country for at least three years as an alternative to a sentence of Borstal training. In *McCartan* [1958] 1 W.L.R. 933, on a reference from the Home Secretary, the Court of Criminal Appeal held that it was not possible to impose as a condition of a probation order that an offender be required to leave the country and return to Northern Ireland, because the probation could not be supervised. The correct practice is to bind him over to come up for judgment, when called upon, in lieu of sentence on condition he leaves the country; it is not proper to bind him over to keep the peace and also impose a condition that he return to his own country (*Ayu* [1958] 1 W.L.R. 1264.

In *Williams* [1982] 1 W.L.R. 1398, the Court of Appeal stated that the power to keep a defendant out of the jurisdiction on pain of imprisonment should be used very sparingly. The court was of the opinion that it would be appropriate only in exceptional circumstances, and certainly only where the defendant goes to a country of which he is a citizen or in which he is habitually resident, or where there are very special circumstances in which the receiving country is prepared to take him for his own well-being (see *Hodges* (1967) 51 Cr.App.R. 361).

In the light of *Williams* the decision in *McCartan* should be questioned. McCartan was a United Kingdom citizen born and habitually resident in Northern Ireland. It is offensive to justify his return to Northern Ireland on the basis that English taxpayers are being saved money, as was done in this case. Subject to the currency of the Prevention of Terrorism Act 1984, an offender who is a citizen of the United Kingdom should not be subject to the penalty of re-location within the country.

(c) Binding over to keep the peace or be of good behaviour

A person (including a child or young person) convicted of an

---

[4] *Ibid.*
[5] *Ibid.*

indictable offence may be ordered to enter into a recognizance, with or without sureties, to keep the peace and be of good behaviour for a reasonable time to be specified in the order and in default of so doing to be imprisoned until the recognizances are entered into or the expiration of the period during which he is required to keep the peace (*Dunn* v. *R.* (1848) 12 Q.B. 1031; *Trueman* [1913] 3 K.B. 164, C.C.A.). On breach of the conditions of a recognizance, it may be forfeited.

Magistrates' courts have a variety of powers to bind over deriving from the common law, the commission of the peace, the Justice of Peace Act 1361 and the Magistrates' Courts Act 1980, s. 115. Magistrates' courts may make orders for the purpose of preventing apprehended breaches of the peace. A magistrates' court may order any person to enter into a recognizance, with or without sureties, to keep the peace or to be of good behaviour. A person against whom such an order is made may have been brought before the court upon a complaint (M.C.A., s. 115(1)), or he may have been brought before the court following his arrest for a breach of the peace or he may be a party already before the court.

Under section 1(7) of the Justice of the Peace Act 1968 any court of record having a criminal jurisdiction has power to bind over to keep the peace and power to bind over to be of good behaviour, a person who, or whose case, is before the court, by requiring him to enter into his own recognizance or to find sureties or both and committing him to prison if he does not comply.

The following principles would appear to apply to both Crown Courts and magistrates' courts. The exercise of the power to bind over is not dependent on there being a conviction but it may be used in respect of an acquitted defendant (*R.* v. *Woking JJ., ex p. Gosage* [1973] Q.B. 448, D.C.) or an appellant whose conviction has been quashed (*Sharp* (1957) 41 Cr.App.R. 86; *Younis* [1965] Crim.L.R. 305; *Biffen* [1966] Crim.L.R. 111;), witnesses before the court (*Sheldon* v. *Bromfield JJ.* [1964] 2 Q.B. 573) or the complainant (*Wilkins* [1907] 2 K.B. 380, D.C.; *R.* v. *Hendon JJ., ex p. Gorchein* [1974] 1 All E.R. 168, D.C.).[6] Where a court proposes to bind over in

---

[6] Before the court can bind over a person he must be either a witness or a party to the proceedings. In *R.* v. *Swindon Crown Court, ex p. Pawittar Singh* (1984) 79 Cr.App.R. 137 an order binding over the applicant under J.P.A. 1968, s. 1(7) was quashed on an application for judicial review by way of *certiorari*. The applicant had been the victim of an assault. He had been at court prepared to give evidence against the assailant who was charged with inflicting grievous bodily harm on him contrary to O.A.P.A. 1861, s. 20. He did not give evidence as a plea of guilty was entered. As the applicant did not give evidence and was not a party to the proceedings he was not "a person who, or whose case, was before the court" under s. 1(7).

a substantial sum a person who has been convicted, his means and other personal circumstances should be inquired into and representations allowed in respect of them (*R.* v. *Central Criminal Court, ex p. Boulding* (1983) 5 Cr.App.R.(S) 433).

The powers under the Justices of the Peace Act 1361 "are exercisable not by reason of any offence having been committed, but as a measure of preventive justice, that is to say, where the person's conduct is such as to lead the Justice to suspect that there may be breach of the peace, or that he may misbehave" (*Veater* v. *Glennon* [1981] 1 W.L.R. 567.[7] Where a court seeks to exercise this power of preventive justice it must be satisfied on the basis of the material before it that in the absence of action there is a risk of a breach of the peace. While an order under section 115 of the Magistrates' Courts Act 1980 may only be made after a full hearing of the complaint, an order under the Justices of the Peace 1361 may be made at any time during the proceedings when the magistrates are satisfied on the basis of the material before them that in the absence of action there is a risk of a breach of the peace in the future (*R.* v. *Aubrey-Fletcher, ex p. Thompson* [1969] 1 W.L.R. 872, D.C.). If a witness or complainant is to be bound over the court, having warned him, must give him an opportunity to meet the allegations (*Sheldon* v. *Bromfield JJ.*; *R.* v. *Hendon JJ., ex p. Gorchein*; *R.* v. *Swindon Crown Court, ex p. Pawittar Singh* (1984) 79 Cr.App.R. 137) unless he consents to the order being made (*R.* v. *South West Magistrates' Court, ex p. Brown* [1974] Crim.L.R. 313, D.C.; *R.* v. *Aubrey-Fletcher*). In *R.* v. *Swindon Crown Court* the court stated that "cases where it would be appropriate to bind over the victim of an assault, particularly where the Crown had decided to prosecute the assailant for inflicting grievous bodily harm, would be rare." In the case of an acquitted defendant the court should warn him before making the order (*R.* v. *Woking JJ.*). If a complainant makes a disturbance in face of the court, the court need not warn him or give him an opportunity of being heard before binding him over (*R.* v. *North London Metropolitan Magistrate, ex p. Haywood and Brown* [1973] 1 W.L.R. 965, D.C.). Under section 7(7) of the Children and Young Persons Act 1969 where a child is found guilty of homicide or a young person is found guilty of any offence by or before any court, that court or the court to which his case is remitted shall have power:

---

[7] See *Blackstone's Commentaries* (16th ed.), Book IV, p. 251; *Lansbury* v. *Riley* [1914] 3 K.B. 229; *County of London Quarter Sessions* [1948] 1 K.B. 670; *R.* v. *Aubrey-Fletcher, ex p. Thompson* [1969] 1 W.L.R. 872, D.C.; *Everett* v. *Ribbands* [1952] 2 K.B. 198, *per* Denning L.J.

"(c) with the consent of his parent or guardian, to order the parent or guardian to enter into a recognizance to take proper care of him and exercise proper control over him."

The maximum amount for which the parent or guardian of a child or young person can be required to enter into a recognizance is £1,000 (C.Y.P.A. 1969, s. 2(13), as increased by S.I. 1984 No. 447 (art. 2(1), Sched. 1). The maximum period of a recognizance is three years or until the person becomes 18 if this is shorter. Section 120 of the Magistrates' Courts 1980, which relates to the forfeiture of the recognizances, applies to recognizances entered into under section 7(7) of the Children and Young Persons Act 1969.

The sanction in the case of a failure or a refusal to enter into a recognizance under the Justices of the Peace Act 1361 or under the Magistrates' Courts Act 1980, s. 115 is imprisonment, in the latter case for a period not exceeding six months or until he sooner complies with the order (s. 115(3)). By virtue of section 19(1) of the Powers of Criminal Courts Act, however, there is no power to imprison juveniles under the age of 17, or to order detention in a detention centre (*Veater* v. *Glennon*), nor can a magistrates' court unilaterally bind over persons to keep the peace, as the essential ingredient in a binding over order is that the person whom the justices require to be bound over acknowledges his own indebtedness to the Crown. However, where a juvenile acknowledges his own indebtedness and is prepared to enter into his own recognizance, a court may bind him over. In such a case no question of imprisonment arises; if subsequently he commits an act which amounts to a breach of the order, the remedy is to estreat the recognizance in whole or in part (*Conlan* v. *Oxford* (1983) 5 Cr.App.R.(S) 237).

(d) Breach of recognizance to keep the peace or be of good behaviour

Where it is alleged that there has been a breach of a recognizance, the recognizance may be forfeited. Where on proof that he has breached a recognizance a person is liable to be sentenced for the offence upon conviction of which he entered into the recognizance, the breach must be proved in the same way as any other allegation of fact is proved in a criminal court, and the defendant should be given the opportunity to give or call evidence (see *Pine* (1932) 24 Cr.App.R. 10; *David* [1939] 1 All E.R. 782; *McGregor* [1945] 2 All E.R. 180; *McGarry* (1945) 30 Cr.App.R. 187). Where a person who breaches a recognizance is only liable to forfeiture of the recognizance, the civil standard of proof applies (*R.* v. *Marlowe JJ., ex p. O'Sullivan* (1983) 5 Cr.App.R.(S) 279). An appeal lies to the Court of Appeal from a decision of the Crown Court that a defendant is in breach of his recognizance (*Smith* [1925] 1 K.B. 603; *McGarry*; *McGregor*).

If the breach is established the recognizance may be forfeited and the court may make an order (1) allowing time for payment; (2) directing payment by instalments; (3) discharging the recognizance or reducing the amount due thereunder (P.C.C.A., s. 31(1)). It seems that no further sentence may be passed in respect of the original offence where a person is dealt with solely by means of a bind-over (*Finch* (1963) 47 Cr.App.R. 58) although the court in forfeiting a recognizance must fix a term of imprisonment or detention under the Criminal Justice Act 1982, s. 9 not exceeding 12 months to be served in default (P.C.C.A., s. 31(2)(3) and (3A)). A person must not be committed to prison on the occasion when the recognizance is forfeited unless (i) in the case of an offence punishable with imprisonment, he appears to have sufficient means to pay forthwith; or (ii) it appears to the court that he is unlikely to remain long enough at a place of abode in the United Kingdom to enable payment of the sum to be enforced by other methods; or (iii) on the occasion when the order is made the court sentences him to immediate imprisonment, custody for life, youth custody or detention in a detention centre for that or another offence, or so sentences him in addition to forfeiting his recognizance, or he is already serving a sentence of imprisonment, youth custody, detention in a detention centre or detention for default under the Criminal Justice Act 1982, s. 9 (P.C.C.A., s. 31(3)). Where a person is sentenced to, or is serving or otherwise liable to serve, a term of imprisonment, the term fixed for non-payment of the recognizance may be ordered to run consecutively to such a term (P.C.C.A., s. 31(4)).

Where a recognizance to keep the peace or to be of good behaviour has been entered into before a magistrates' court and it appears to the court to be forfeited, the court may adjudge the person(s) bound by it, whether as principal or sureties or any of them, to pay the sum(s) in which they are respectively bound (M.C.A., s. 120(1)). The court may not declare forfeited a recognizance to keep the peace or to be of good behaviour, except by order made on complaint (M.C.A., s. 120(2)). Although a court may declare a recognizance to be forfeited, it has a discretion whether to order the person to pay the whole or part only of the sum or remit the sum (s. 120(3)). In exercising this discretion justices should take into consideration the extent to which the surety has been at fault and should take into account only his own means (*R. v. Southampton JJ., ex p. Green* [1976]. Q.B. 11; *R. v. Horseferry Road Magistrates' Court, ex. p. Pearson* [1976] 1 W.L.R. 511; *R. v. Tottenham Magistrates' Court, ex p. Riccardi* (1977) 66 Cr.App.R.

150). The onus is on the surety to show that he was not at fault and to show reasons why the penalty should not be enforced (*R.* v. *Southampton JJ., ex p. Corker* (1976) 120 S.J. 214, D.C.). There is no right of appeal under section 108 of the Magistrates' Courts Act against an adjudication of forfeiture as this does not constitute a conviction (*R.* v. *Durham JJ., ex p. Laurent* [1945] K.B. 33) but it may be challenged by way of *certiorari* (*R.* v. *Southampton JJ., ex p. Green*, above). Payment of any sum adjudged, including any costs awarded against the defendant, may be enforced, and any such sum must be applied as if it were a fine and as if the adjudication were a summary conviction of an offence not punishable with imprisonment (M.C.A., s. 120(4)). At any time, however, before the issue of a warrant of commitment to enforce payment, or before the sale of goods under a distress warrant the court may remit the whole or any part of the sum absolutely or on such conditions as it thinks just (s. 120(4)).

BINDING OVER COMBINED WITH OTHER SENTENCES

(a) Binding over to come up for sentence
This form of bind over is *in lieu* of sentence, and therefore it is wrong to impose it in addition to a sentence for the offence (*Ayu* [1958] 1 W.L.R. 1264).

(b) Binding over to keep the peace or be of good behaviour
This form of bind over may be in addition to or instead of any other sentence which the court may lawfully impose. Section 12(1) of the Powers of the Criminal Courts Act provides that a court, when making a probation order or an order for conditional discharge, may, if it thinks it expedient for the purpose of the reformation of the offender, allow any person who consents to do so to give security for the good behaviour of the offender.

WHEN BINDING OVER IS APPROPRIATE

Binding over to come up for judgment when called upon is similar to a conditional discharge and may be appropriate in similar circumstances. The period of bind over, however, may exceed the three year maximum relating to a conditional discharge where it is imposed by a Crown Court. Depending on the conditions the court sets, the recognizances may be broken by conduct which does not amount to a criminal offence.

Binding over to keep the peace or be of good behaviour on conviction of an offence, is not unusual in the case of minor domestic quarrels or neighbourhood disputes, where a court may have concern about the possibility of a continuation of the conflict which might lead to reappearances in courts. Otherwise a binding over as a sentence can be appropriate in a wide variety of circumstances.

APPEAL

There is a right of appeal to the Crown Court where a person is ordered by a magistrates' court to enter into a recognizance to keep the peace or to be of good behaviour whether under the Justices of the Peace Act 1361 or otherwise (Magistrates' Court (Appeals from Binding Over Orders) Act 1956). Where a Crown Court makes such an order following a conviction this is covered by section 50(1) of the Criminal Appeal Act 1968 which defines "sentence" to include "any order made by a court when dealing with an offender" (see *Williams* [1982] Crim.L.R. 762; but *cf. Dwyer* (1974) 60 Cr.App.R. 39 at p. 42.)

PROBATION

DESCRIPTION

Probation has been defined "as the submission of an offender while at liberty to a specified period of supervision by a social case worker who is an officer of the court: during this period the offender remains liable if not of good conduct to be otherwise dealt with by the court."[1]

Probation grew out of the use of discharges by judges and magistrates in the nineteenth century, when in addition to the normal conditions to keep the peace and be of good behaviour, an offender agreed to remain under the supervision of another individual, usually a voluntary religious worker interested in the reclamation of offenders.[2]

"Probation is not a soft option; it is a form of professional treatment within the community. It serves to protect society as well as to help the offender ... [T]hrough social casework and with the use of community resources, [it aims] ... to help the probationer to develop qualities which will enable him to adjust to the demands of society and become and to remain a happy useful citizen."[3]

The major duties of the probation service and probation officers

The major duties of the service are:

"(a) The supervision of persons subject to probation orders, supervision orders, and money payment orders.

(b) The provision of an after-care service for offenders released from penal institutions who are on licence or who request after-care on a voluntary basis.

(c) The provision of a social work service in prisons and other penal establishments.

(d) The preparation of social inquiry reports for the courts in criminal and civil cases.

(e) The provision of a marriage counselling service.

(f) The provision of a divorce court welfare service."[4]

---

[1] Report of Departmental Committee on the Probation Service (Cmnd. 1650, 1962), p. 2.
[2] See Home Office, *The Probation and Aftercare Service in England and Wales*, (HMSO, 1973), pp. 1–2.
[3] *Ibid.* pp. 5–6.
[4] *Ibid.* p. 4.

The duties of probation officers are laid down in paragraph 8(1) of Schedule 3 to the Powers of Criminal Courts Act 1973. A probation officer is under a duty to supervise probationers and other persons placed under his supervision and to advise, assist and befriend them. In relation to these duties rule 35(1) of the Probation Rules 1965 (S.I. 1965 No. 723), specifies that subject to any provision in the probation order, the officer must keep in close touch with the probationer, meet him frequently and, unless there is good reason for not doing so, visit his residence from time to time and require him to report at stated intervals. The officer must also inquire, in accordance with any directions of the court, into the circumstances or home surroundings of any person with a view to assisting the court in determining the most suitable method of dealing with his case. In certain cases the officer must also advise, assist and befriend persons who have been released from custody (see Probation Rules, r. 30(1)–(4)) or who have been remanded on bail (r. 30(4A) added by S.I. 1974 No. 1064), and must perform such other duties as may be prescribed or imposed by any enactment or instrument.

> "The probation officer's first task as a social caseworker is to win the confidence of the probationer and his family and to develop a relationship which will be a positive influence, regulating the probationer's behaviour and counteracting and modifying the ill effects of past experiences and of irremovable factors in the present. To this end the probation officer keeps in close touch with the probationer, usually both by visiting his home and by requiring the probationer to see him regularly at the probation office.
>
> If the probationer is [at school], the probation officer keeps in touch with the head teacher (but does not visit the [probationer] at school). The officer seeks to ensure that older probationers are in suitable and regular employment. He encourages the probationer to use the appropriate statutory and voluntary agencies which might contribute to his welfare, and to take advantage of the social, recreational and educational facilities suited to his age, ability and temperament."[5]

THE LAW

Section 2(1) of the Powers of Criminal Courts Act 1973 provides:

> "Where a court by or before which a person of or over seventeen years of age is convicted of an offence (not being an

---

[5] *The Sentence of the Court* (HMSO, 1969), para. 32.

THE LAW   21

offence the sentence for which is fixed by law) is of opinion that having regard to the circumstances, including the nature of the offence and the character of the offender, it is expedient to do so, the court may, instead of sentencing him, make a probation order, that is to say, an order requiring him to be under the supervision of a probation officer for a period to be specified in the order of not less than six months nor more than three years."[6]

A probation order must follow conviction and is not a substitute for it. "Instead of sentencing" in section 2(1) has been held to mean "instead of punishment" (*Parry* [1951] 1 K.B. 590). As in the case of an order of conditional or absolute discharge a conviction followed by a probation order counts as a conviction for limited purposes only (pp. 4–5). Section 13(3) specifically provides that in all three cases the conviction must be disregarded for the purposes of any enactment or instrument (*e.g.* a statute relating to pensions) which imposes or authorises any disqualification or disability upon convicted persons. An offender who successfully completes his period of probation is entitled to claim that his conviction should not form part of his criminal record (P.C.C.A., s. 13(1)).

A probation order may be made in respect of a young person or an adult. Before making the order the court must explain to the offender in ordinary language the effect of the order and any additional requirements the court is minded to impose, and that if he fails to comply with the order or commits another offence he will be liable to be sentenced for the original offence (P.C.C.A., s. 2(6)). The court must not make an order unless the offender expresses his willingness to comply with its requirements (s. 2(6)). A probation order cannot be effectively made unless the defendant has expressed a willingness to be bound by the requirements thereof (*Marquis* [1974] 1 W.L.R. 1087). For that purpose a defendant must be given a fair opportunity to make his choice whether to agree to the terms of the order (*ibid.*).

(a) The requirements of a probation order

The first requirement is that the probationer be under the supervision of a probation officer appointed for the petty sessions area in which the offender resides, for the period specified in the order, being not less than six months and not more than three years (P.C.C.A., s. 1(1)(2)).

Apart from requirements which may be imposed under sections

---

[6] The minimum period was reduced from one year to six months by S.I. 1978 No. 478, as from May 15, 1978.

3, 4A and 4B, the court may impose such other requirements on the probationer as it thinks necessary for securing the good conduct of the offender or for preventing a repetition by him of the same offence or the commission of other offences (P.C.C.A., s. 2(3)). In *Cullen* v. *Rogers* [1982] 1 W.L.R. 729 in the House of Lords, Lord Bridge stated that

> "the power to impose requirements (under s. 2(3) of the 1973 Act) must be subject to some limitation in at least two respects. First, since the making of a probation order is a course taken by the court to avoid passing a sentence, a requirement imposed under s. 2(3) must not introduce such a custodial or other element as will amount in substance to the imposition of a sentence. Secondly, since it is the court alone which can define the requirements of the order, any discretion conferred on the probation officer pursuant to the terms of the order to regulate a probationer's activities must itself be confined within well-defined limits."

The Magistrates' Courts (Forms) Rules 1968 (S.I. 1968 No. 1919), Form 68 (substituted by S.I. 1974 No. 444) contains a form of order which contains specimens of the requirements which are commonly inserted:

> "1. The accused shall be of good behaviour and lead an industrious life.
> 2. The accused shall inform the probation officer immediately of any change of address or employment.
> 3. The accused shall comply with the instructions of the probation officer as to reporting to the officer and as to receiving visits from the probation officer at home."

In a *Practice Note* in February 1952, Lord Goddard C.J. stated that the above three conditions were specimens of the sort of requirements that the court can make, and that a court might make other conditions. If other conditions are imposed they must be explained to the probationer at the time the order is made. The Lord Chief Justice went on to disapprove of the first condition as being "extremely vague" and preferred that the "well understood" condition that the offender "be of good behaviour and keep the peace," should be imposed: the condition disapproved of was not a statutory requirement ((1952) 35 Cr.App.R. 207).

Other requirements which may be included are:

(i) *Residence requirement*
A probation order may include requirements relating to the residence of the offender (P.C.C.A., s. 2(5)). Before making an order containing any such requirements the court must consider the

offender's home surroundings (s. 2(5)(*a*)) and, if the requirement relates to residence in an approved probation hostel[7] or any other institution, the requisite period of residence must be specified (s. 2(5)(*b*) as amended by C.L.A. 1977, Sched. 12). Probation hostels are run either by the probation committee with the approval of the Secretary of State or by voluntary organisations approved by him. Courts may, in certain circumstances include in an order a requirement of residence in a non-approved hostel or even a private house. In such cases the court must give notice of the terms of the order to the Secretary of State (s. 2(8)). While probation is regarded as essentially being treatment in conditions of freedom, it is recognised that

> "some offenders may be helped to respond to probation by being given initially a stable and supportive environment in which limits of conduct are implicit, where they can adjust to living with contemporaries and others, including those in authority, acquire basic ideas about social behaviour, and find and keep suitable employment."[8]

The Approved Probation Hostel Rules 1976 (S.I. 1976 No. 626), provide that residents in approved hostels must be given assistance to find jobs or undertake education or training (r. 20), facilities for private interviews with a probation officer at reasonable times (r. 21), reasonable facilities for religious practices (r. 22) and adequate free time and recreation inside and outside the hostel (r. 23). Subject to the approval of the Secretary of State, the committee managing the hostel must arrange for pocket money for residents or particular classes of them (r. 24) and must charge residents for their maintenance (r. 25).

(ii) *Requirement for medical treatment*

Where the court is satisfied, on the evidence of a medical practitioner (approved for the purposes of section 12 of the Mental Health Act 1983 by the Secretary of State as having special experience in the diagnosis or treatment of mental disorder), that the mental condition of the offender is such as requires, and may be

---

[7] "Probation hostel" means premises for the accommodation of persons who may be required to reside there by a probation order (P.C.C.A., s. 57(1) as amended by C.L.A. 1977, s. 65(4) and (5) and Sched. 12 and 13).

[8] Home Office, *op. cit.* note 2 above, p. 6. In 1927 the Departmental Committee on the Treatment of Young Offenders (Cmnd. 2831), recommended that when supervision of a young offender in the community by a probation officer would not be sufficient because he may have no home or an undesirable home, then he could be lodged in a probation hostel. However, it was not until 1970 that the Report of the Advisory Council on the Penal System recommended that probation hostels for adults should be opened. For a study of adult probation hostels see Home Office Research Study No. 52, *Hostels for Offenders.*

susceptible to treatment, but is not such as to warrant his detention in hospital, the court may, on making a probation order, include in it a requirement that the offender submit during the whole or part of the order to treatment by or under the direction of a duly qualified medical practitioner with a view to improvement of the offender's mental condition (P.C.C.A., s. 3(1) as amended by M.H.A. 1983, s. 148 and Sched. 4). The evidence of the medical practitioner may be by way of a written report (P.C.C.A., s. 3(7) as amended by M.H.A. 1983, Sched. 4). The treatment must be one of three kinds and must be specified in the order:

(a) treatment as a resident patient in a hospital within the meaning of the Mental Health Act 1983 or mental nursing home within the meaning of the Nursing Homes Act 1975, not being a special hospital within the meaning of the National Health Service Act 1977;

(b) treatment as a non-resident patient at such institution or place as may be specified in the order; or

(c) treatment by or under the direction of such duly qualified medical practitioner as may be specified in the order.

(P.C.C.A., s. 2(1) as amended by M.H.A. 1983, Sched. 4.)

No further provision as to the nature of the treatment may be made in the order (P.C.C.A., s. 2(1)). The court, before making such an order, must be satisfied that arrangements have been made for the treatment intended to be specified in the order, including arrangements for the reception of the offender where the treatment is to be under (a) above (s. 2(3)). The medical practitioner treating or directing the treatment of the probationer may, with his consent, arrange for him to receive part of the treatment at an institution or place not specified in the order (P.C.C.A., s. 3(5)). He may do this where he is of opinion that part of the treatment can be better or more conveniently given at an institution or place not specified in the order (s. 3(5)). Arrangements may even be made for treatment of the probationer as a resident patient in an institution or place which could not have been specified originally in the order (s. 3(5)).[9]

---

[9] A recent case to have attracted press attention was one arising in Huddersfield Crown Court (see *The Guardian*, December 4, 1984, and *The Times*, December 4, 1984). The accused, Horbury, aged 48 admitted three charges of gross indecency with girls aged 11 and 12 and two charges of indecently assaulting 11-year-old girls. He had a record of previous convictions for sexual offences. In mitigation counsel indicated that the accused wanted to undergo medical treatment in the form of drug therapy. Evidence was given by a consultant psychiatrist and it was ascertained that the accused was fully consenting to such treatment. After deferring sentence for two weeks, His Honour Judge Walker put Horbury on probation for three years on condition that he enter hospital and undergo minor surgery to implant the drug and that he return to hospital every three months to have the implant renewed.

(iii) *Attendance at a day centre*

Under section 4 of the Powers of Criminal Courts Act a court making a probation order had power to include a requirement that the probationer attend a day training centre specified in the order. Only four such centres were ever established in 1973/74 to deal with the socially inadequate petty recidivist as an alternative to custody. The experiment was not entirely successful and no further centres were established.[10] However, many non-statutory "day centres" have been established by probation services locally and by other organisations. Many probation orders had requirements included in them for probationers to attend such day centres. The legality of such requirements was challenged in the case of *Cullen* v. *Rogers* [1982] 1 W.L.R. 729 where the House of Lords held them to be unlawful as such centres were not recognised under section 4. This meant that requirements could only be included for attendance at day training centres recognised by the Secretary of State for the purposes of section 4. The effect of the House of Lords decision was quickly reversed by the insertion of section 4B into the Powers of Criminal Courts Act by Section 65 of and Schedule 11 to the Criminal Justice Act 1982 which also repealed section 4 of the Act. Section 4B authorises a court to require the probationer, as a condition of the order, to attend at a day centre specified in the order (s. 4B(1)). A "day centre" is defined as premises at which non-residential facilities are provided for use in connection with the rehabilitation of offenders and which:

(a) are provided by a probation committee; or

(b) have been approved by the probation committee for the area in which the premises are situated as providing facilities suitable for persons subject to probation orders.

(s. 4B(6).)

Before including a day centre attendance requirement in a probation order a court must consult a probation officer and satisfy itself that:

(i) arrangements can be made for the probationer's attendance at a centre; and

(ii) that the person in charge of the centre consents to the inclusion of the requirement.

(s. 4B(2).)

In accordance with instructions given by his supervising probation officer, a probationer may be required to attend the centre for a maximum of 60 days during the course of the probation order, and while there must comply with the instructions of the staff at the centre (s. 4B(3)). In giving instructions to attend the centre the

---

[10] See 146 J.P.N. 732.

probation officer should, as far as practicable avoid any interference with the times, if any, when the probationer normally works or attends a school or other educational establishment (s. 4B(4)).

(iv) *Attendance and participation requirement*

Schedule 11 to the Criminal Justice Act 1982 inserted a new section 4A into the Powers of Criminal Courts Act giving a new power to add requirements to a probation order. Where a court has first consulted a probation officer as to the offender's circumstances and the feasibility of securing compliance with the requirements it intends to include in the order, and is satisfied, having regard to the probation officer's report, that it is feasible to secure compliance with them (s. 4A(2)), the court may require the probationer:

(a) to present himself to a person or persons specified in the order at a place or places so specified (s. 4A(1)) on not more than 60 days (s. 4A(4)(*a*));

(b) to participate in activities specified in the order (s. 4A(1)(*b*)) on not more than 60 days (s. 4A(6)(*a*)); or

(c) to refrain from participating in activities specified in the order on a day or days so specified or during the probation period or such portion of it as may be so specified (s. 4A(1)(*b*)).

Requirements (a) or (b) may be included only with the consent of any other person whose co-operation would be involved. In giving instructions in accordance with requirements (a) and (b) the probation officer should ensure, as far as practicable that interference with the times, if any, at which the probationer normally works or attends a school or other educational establishment, is avoided (s. 4A(7)). A probationer may only be required to attend a place under (a) above if it has been approved by the probation committee for the area as providing facilities suitable for persons subject to probation orders (s. 4A(5)). An obvious requirement that might be made under (c) above is that the probationer should refrain from attending soccer matches where the offence which led to the making of the order, arose out of soccer violence.

(b) Amendment

During the period of probation, applications connected with the order are made to the supervising court, *i.e.* a magistrates' court acting for the petty sessions area named in the order:

(i) Where the probationer proposes to change, or has changed his residence from the petty sessions area named in the probation order to another petty sessions area, the court may, where the application is made by the probationer, and shall where it is made by the probation officer, amend the probation order by substituting the new or proposed petty sessions area for the one named in the order.[11] However, if the court is of opinion that the requirements contained in the order cannot be complied with unless the probationer continues to reside in the area named in the order, it shall not amend the order unless it cancels those requirements or substitutes other requirements which can be complied with (P.C.C.A., Sched. 1, para. 2(1) and (2)).

(ii) On the application of the supervising officer or the probationer, the court may cancel any of the requirements of the order or insert other requirements which it could have inserted originally under sections 2, 3, 4A and 4B of the Act. The order may be extended up to the maximum of three years but it may not be reduced. Unless the amendment is made within three months of the date of the original order, the court cannot amend the original order by inserting a requirement that the probationer shall submit to treatment for his mental condition (P.C.C.A., Sched. 1, para. 3).

(iii) Where the order contains a requirement that the probationer submit to treatment for his mental condition, the court, on application by the probation officer on the basis of a report by the medical practitioner by whom or under whose direction the probationer is being treated, may vary or cancel the requirement or extend the period of treatment beyond that specified in the order (P.C.C.A., Sched. 1, para. 4). There are five grounds upon which a medical practitioner may make a report:

   (a) that the period of treatment should be extended;
   (b) that the probationer needs different treatment;
   (c) that the probationer is not susceptible to treatment;
   (d) that the probationer does not require further treatment;
   (e) that the practitioner is for any reason unwilling to continue to treat or direct the treatment of the probationer.

(Sched. 1, para. 4.)[12]

Where it is proposed to amend a probation order otherwise than on the application of the probationer, he must be summoned to appear before the court and the court cannot amend the order unless he agrees to comply with the amended requirements, except that where the amendment

---

[11] No amendment may be made while an appeal against the probation order is pending (P.C.C.A., Sched. 1, para. (1A) as inserted by C.J.A. 1982, s. 66(3)(b)).
[12] No application may be made under para. 4 while an appeal against the probation order is pending.

involves the cancellation of a requirement, reduction of the
period of a requirement, or the substitution of a new petty
sessions area in the order, the above provisions do not apply
(P.C.C.A., Sched. 1, para. 5).

(c) Substitution

Under section 11(1) of the Powers of Criminal Courts Act an
order of conditional discharge may be substituted for a probation
order where, on application made by the probationer or probation
officer, it appears to the court having power to discharge the order
(see paragraph (f) below) that the order is no longer appropriate.
The period of conditional discharge will last until the date on which
the probation order would have expired. The offender will be
treated for all purposes, and in particular for the purposes of section
8 of the Powers of Criminal Courts Act (commission of a further
offence), as if the original probation order had been an order for
conditional discharge (P.C.C.A., s. 11(2)). If the application is made
by a probation officer it may be heard in the absence of the
probationer provided the officer produces to the court a statement
by him that he understands the effect of the order being substituted
and that he consents to the application being made.

(d) Breach

If at any time during the period of probation it appears on
information to a justice of the peace on whom jurisdiction is
conferred[13] that the probationer has failed to comply with any of the
requirements of the order, a summons or warrant may be issued by
him directing the probationer to appear before the magistrates'
court for the petty sessions area for which the justice acts (P.C.C.A.,
s. 6(1) and (2)).

If it is proved to the satisfaction of the court before whom the
probationer appears or is brought[14] that he has failed to comply with

---

[13] Jurisdiction is conferred as follows: if the probation order was made by a magistrates'
court, on any justice of the peace acting for the petty sessions area for which that court
or the supervising court acts; and in any other case, on any justice acting for the petty
sessions area for which the supervising court acts (P.C.C.A., s. 6(2)).

[14] The procedure to be followed was laid down in *Devine* [1956] 1 W.L.R. 236 as
follows: "Where a prisoner is brought before a court for breach of a probation
order, it should be put to him, when he is arraigned before the court, in the clearest
possible terms and he should be asked to say whether he admits it or not. The
terms in which the matter should be put to him are: first to say where he was
convicted and what happened to him, then to tell him how the breach is alleged to
have taken place, and, if it be by a further conviction, then to tell him the time of
the conviction and the adjudication of the court. He should next be asked to say
whether he admits those facts. If that is done, there is no further difficulty. If that is
not done, then, of course, it being a trial, albeit without a jury, the prisoner will

any of the requirements of the order, the court may[15]:

   (a) impose a fine not exceeding £400[16] (s. 6(3)(a)); or

   (b) make a community service order in respect of him[17] (s. 6(3)(b)); or

   (c) in a case to which section 17 of the Criminal Justice Act 1982 applies, make an attendance centre order (s. 6(3)(c)); or

   (d) where the order was made by a magistrates' court, deal with him for the offence in respect of which the order was made, in any manner in which it could deal with him if he had just been convicted of that offence[18] (s. 6(3)(d)); or

   (e) if the order was made by the Crown Court, a magistrates' court, instead of dealing with the probationer under its powers under paragraphs (a), (b) or (c) may commit him to custody or release him on bail until he can be brought or appear before the Crown Court (s. 6(4)).

A Crown Court before whom a probationer appears or is brought and which is satisfied that he has failed to comply with any requirements of his probation order[19] may[20]:

   (a) impose a fine not exceeding £400[21] (s. 6(6)(a); or

   (b) make a community service order in respect of him[22] (s. 6(6)(b)); or

   (c) it may deal with him for the offence in respect of which the probation order was made in any manner in which it could deal with him if he had just been convicted before the Crown Court of that offence (s. 6(6)(c)).

---

have to be asked whether he desires to give evidence or call witnesses, and the court will have to pronounce on whether they find the breach of the order has been proved. But it is desirable that the proceedings should begin by the matter being put clearly to the prisoner and for him to be asked whether he admits the allegation with regard to it."

[15] Any exercise by the court of its powers under s. 6(3)(a), (b) or (c) is without prejudice to the continuance of the probation order (P.C.C.A., s. 6(8)).

[16] The maximum amount of the fine was increased by C.J.A. 1982, s. 39 and Sched. 4 and again by S.I. 1984 No. 447, Art. 2(3), Sched. 3.

[17] No order has yet been made by the Secretary of State bringing this provision into force.

[18] Where a probationer is sentenced for the offence for which he was placed on probation, the probation order ceases to have effect (P.C.C.A., s. 5(2)). A court exercising its powers under s. 6(3)(d) may make a further probation order to run from the date of the probationer's appearance for breach (R. v. Havant JJ., ex p. Jacobs [1957] 1 W.L.R. 365).

[19] This question will be determined by the court and not by the verdict of a jury (P.C.C.A., s. 12(3)).

[20] Any exercise by a court of its powers under s. 6(6)(a) or (b) is without prejudice to the continuance of the probation order.

[21] See note 16 above.

[22] No order has yet been made by the Secretary of State bringing this provision into force.

A probationer who is required by the probation order to submit to treatment for his mental condition shall not be treated as in breach of the requirement where the complaint is that he refused to undergo any surgical, electrical or other treatment if, in the opinion of the court, his refusal was reasonable having regard to all the circumstances (s. 6(7)).

(e) Commission of a further offence

A probationer who commits a further offence while on probation is not liable to be dealt with under section 6 of the Powers of Criminal Courts Act for failure to comply with any requirement of the order (s. 6(7)); a separate procedure for dealing with this circumstance is provided by section 8.

Section 8 sets out the procedures relevant to magistrates' courts and Crown Courts and the powers of these courts when a probationer commits a further offence within the period of the probation order. Where a person is convicted by a court in any part of Great Britain of an offence committed during the probation period, and has been dealt with in respect of that offence but not in respect of the original offence, the Crown Court, if the order was made by that court, or a justice of the peace either acting for the petty sessions area for which the court acts if the order was made by a magistrates' court, or acting for the area for which the supervising court acts, may issue a summons against him or a warrant for his arrest (P.C.C.A., s. 8(1) and (2)) ordering him to appear to be brought before the court by which the order was made (s. 8(4)). Where the order was made by the Crown Court and the probationer is convicted by a magistrates' court of an offence during its currency, the magistrates' court may commit him to custody or release him on bail until he can be brought or appear before the Crown Court (s. 8(6)).

Where it is proved to the satisfaction of the court[23] that made the order or the supervising court in the case of a probation order made by a magistrates' court, that the person subject to the order has been convicted of an offence committed during the currency of the order, the court may deal with him for the original offence in any manner in which it could deal with him if he had just been convicted by or before the court of that offence (s. 8(7)).[24] A Crown Court dealing

---

[23] The procedure laid down in *Devine* [1956] 1 W.L.R. 236, in relation to breach of any requirement of a probation order must be followed (*Stuart* [1964] 1 W.L.R. 1381).

[24] A separate sentence should be passed in respect of the original offence so that the conviction of the original offence may rank as a conviction under P.C.C.A., s. 13(2) (*Webb* [1953] 2 Q.B. 390; *Stuart* [1964] 1 W.L.R. 1381). In addition, the sentence should generally be consecutive to the sentence for the later offence and should be more than nominal (*Webb*; *Stuart*).

with a probationer for a further offence committed while on probation may sentence him for the original offence, but where the original order was made by a magistrates' court it is limited to imposing a sentence which the magistrates' court could have imposed if it had just convicted him of the offence (s. 8(8)).

If the probation order was made by a magistrates' court and the probationer is convicted by another magistrates' court of any offence committed during the currency of the order, that court may, with the consent of the court which made the order or of the supervising court, deal with him for the offence for which the order was made in any manner which the court could deal with him if it had just convicted him of that offence (s. 8(9)).

(f) Discharge of probation order

A probation order may be discharged on an application made by the probation officer or the probationer (P.C.C.A., s. 5(1) and Sched. 1, para. 1(1)). Where it appears to the officer that the application can properly be made, he must apply unless the probationer does so (Probation Rules r. 39(2)). In general where the probation order was made by the court by or before which the probationer was convicted or on appeal, or by the Crown Court where a magistrates' court has committed an offender to it for sentence, or by a magistrates' court to which the offender has been remitted for sentence under section 39 of the Magistrates' Courts Act 1980, the power to discharge the order is exercisable by the supervising court (Sched. 1, para. 1(2)). However, where the court before which the probationer was convicted or the court from which the appeal is brought is the Crown Court, or where the Crown Court made the order following the offender's committal to it for sentence by a magistrates' court, and the order included a direction that the power be reserved to the Crown Court, then the power to discharge is exercisable only by that court (Sched. 1, para. 1(3)). In any other case the power must be exercised by the court by which the order was made (Sched. 1, para. 1(4)).

PROBATION COMBINED WITH OTHER SENTENCES

Where it is expedient to do so, having regard to the circumstances, including the nature of the offence and the character of the offender, the court may, instead of sentencing an offender, make a probation order (P.C.C.A., s. 2(1)). Section 7(1) states that where it is inexpedient to inflict punishment and a probation order is not appropriate, the court may discharge the offender absolutely or conditionally. The implication to be drawn from these two provisions is that probation is not a punishment (*Parry* [1951] 1

K.B. 590). In consequence a person cannot be fined and put on probation for the same offence (*Parry*; *Jones* [1968] Crim.L.R. 120). Similarly making a probation order with a custodial sentence to take immediate effect alongside the probation order is wrong in principle even where separate counts are involved (*Emmet* (1969) 53 Cr.App.R. 203; *Evans* [1959] 1 W.L.R. 26). Likewise it is wrong in principle to pass a nominal sentence on another count in order to record a conviction available to be relied on in the future for the purpose of an extended sentence. If the effective order is probation then the defendant should not be put at any risk greater than that provided by section 8 of the Powers of Criminal Courts Act, namely, of being dealt with for the original offence if he offends again within the period of probation (*Isherwood* (1974) 59 Cr.App.R. 162). However, there is no objection in principle to imposing a fine at the same time as making a probation order, so long as they are imposed in relation to different offences (*Bainbridge* (1979) 1 Cr.App.R.(S.) 36). Where an offender stands convicted by or before the court of two or more offences, the court may not make a probation order in respect of one offence and pass a suspended sentence in respect of another (P.C.C.A., s. 22(3)) even where the offender has pleaded guilty to two indictments (*Wright* [1975] Crim.L.R. 728). Where a court passes a partly suspended sentence on an offender under section 47(1) of the Criminal Law Act 1977, it cannot make a probation order in the offender's case in respect of another offence of which he is convicted by or before that court, or for which he is dealt with by that court (C.L.A. 1977, Sched. 9, para. (1)).

A probation order may be combined with an order of disqualification from holding or obtaining a driving licence (R.T.A. 1972, s. 102(1), as amended by P.C.C.A., ss. 30, 56(1), Sched. 5, para. 43, Sched 9, para. 13(*a*)).[25] In addition where disqualification has been ordered or a licence endorsed, such conviction is to be taken into account in determining the offender's liability to punishment or disqualification for an offence involving obligatory or discretionary disqualification (R.T.A., s. 102(2) as amended by P.C.C.A., Sched. 5, para. 43).[26]

A court may not make the payment of compensation a requirement of a probation order (P.C.C.A., s. 2(4)), but on making a probation order a court may order the offender to pay costs or

---

[25] This provision is expressed to apply notwithstanding anything in P.C.C.A., s. 13(3) which requires a conviction of a person put on probation or discharged to be disregarded for the purposes of the enactments relating to disqualification.

[26] This provision is expressed to apply notwithstanding anything in P.C.C.A., s. 13(1) which requires a conviction of a person put on probation or discharged to be disregarded for the purpose of subsequent proceedings.

compensation (P.C.C.A., s. 12(4)),[27] or restitution of property (P.C.C.A., s. 13(4)). In addition a court may make a recommendation for deportation (Immigration Act 1971, s. 6(3)), or an exclusion order in respect of licensed premises under the Licensed Premises (Exclusion of Certain Persons) Act 1980, s. 1(1) and (2).[28] An order under section 43 of the Powers of Criminal Courts Act for deprivation of property, is an additional punishment and cannot be combined with a probation order which is expressed to be made "instead of sentencing" the offender (see *Hunt* [1978] Crim.L.R. 697).

On making a probation order, a court may "if it thinks it expedient for the reformation of the offender" allow any person who consents to do so to give security for the good behaviour of the offender (P.C.C.A., s. 12(1)).

WHEN A PROBATION ORDER IS APPROPRIATE

The Departmental Committee on the Probation Service have suggested four conditions to be met before making a probation order:

"Firstly, the circumstances of the offence and the offender's record must not be such as to demand, in the interests of society, that some more severe method be adopted in dealing with the offender; secondly, the risk, if any, to society through setting the offender at liberty must be outweighed by the moral, social and economic arguments for not depriving him of it; thirdly, the offender must need continuing attention, since otherwise, if the second condition is satisfied, a fine or discharge will suffice; and, fourthly, the offender must be capable of responding to the attention while he is at liberty."[29]

And it has been stated that:

"The object of probation, as of all methods of treatment, is the ultimate re-establishment of the offender in the community. But probation involves the discipline of submission by the offender while at liberty to supervision by a probation officer. It thus seeks both to protect society and to strengthen the

[27] The compensation to be paid under a compensation order made by a magistrates' court in respect of any offence of which the court has convicted the offender shall not exceed £2,000 (M.C.A. 1980, s. 40).
[28] Such an order will be made where a court before which a person is convicted of an offence committed on licensed premises is satisfied that in committing the offence he resorted to violence or offered or threatened to resort to violence.
[29] Report of Departmental Committee on the Probation Service (Cmnd. 1650, 1962), para. 15.

probationer's resources so that he becomes a more responsible person. Unlike custodial treatment, which by removing the offender from his family and community tends to suspend his social and economic obligation to them, probation exacts from him a contribution, within the limits of his capacity, to their well-being."[30]

APPEAL

See Absolute Discharge at p. 7 above.

While an appeal against a probation order is pending no application may be made for substitution of conditional discharge for probation,[31] for discharge or amendment of probation orders[32] or for variation or cancellation of a requirement in an order for treatment of a mental condition.[33]

---

[30] *The Sentence of the Court*, para. 31.
[31] P.C.C.A., s. 11(1A) as inserted by C.J.A. 1982, s. 66(3)(a).
[32] P.C.C.A., Sched. 1, paras. 1(1A), 2(1A) and 3(1A) as inserted by C.J.A. 1982, s. 66(3)(b)(i) and (ii).
[33] P.C.C.A., Sched. 1, para. 4A as inserted by C.J.A. 1982, s. 66(3)(b)(iv).

DEFERMENT OF SENTENCE

DESCRIPTION

The idea of giving a specific power to courts to defer or postpone passing sentence for a limited period was one of the recommendations of the Advisory Council on the Penal System in its report on "Non-Custodial and Semi-Custodial Penalties" (HMSO 1970). The measure was adopted from the practice of the Scottish courts.

The Advisory Council thought that in addition to the existing powers of the court to postpone sentence (discussed below) there was a place in the penal armoury for this measure, "to provide an opportunity for the offender to show good behaviour, to repay money which he has acquired dishonestly or to perform some other act which would indicate ability to stay out of trouble" (para. 81). The Advisory Council Report recommended that in deferring sentence a court might impose conditions but this recommendation has not been adopted in either the English or Northern Ireland legislation creating this option.

While deferment is not itself a non-custodial measure, but rather a procedural one, it is often the first step towards the imposition of such a sentence, and thus it was thought appropriate to deal with it in this section.

THE LAW

In order to enable a court to have regard to the offender's conduct after conviction (including, where appropriate, the making by him of reparation for his offence) or to any change in his circumstances, before dealing with him, the court may defer sentence until such date as may be specified for one period of up to six months from the date on which the deferment is announced by the court (P.C.C.A., s. 1(1) and (2) as amended by C.L.A., Sched. 12). A court which defers passing sentence on an offender under section 1 may not on the same occasion remand him (P.C.C.A., s. 1(6A) as inserted by C.L.A., Sched. 12.)

The power to defer sentence is exercisable only where the defendant consents[1] and the court is satisfied, having regard to the nature of the offence and the character and circumstances of the

---

[1] If sentence is deferred without obtaining the offender's consent the court may not sentence him at the expiration of the period of deferment (*McQuaide* (1974) 60 Cr.App.R. 239).

offender, that it would be in the interests of justice to do so (P.C.C.A., s. 1(3)). Although technically, where counsel for the defendant invites the court to defer sentence under section 1, that invitation constitutes the defendant's prima facie consent for the purpose of the section, as a matter of sentencing practice the accused should be asked personally whether he consents to deferment (*Fairhead* [1975] 2 All E.R. 737).

In *Ingle* [1974] 3 All E.R. 811, the Court of Appeal rejected the argument that, because the defendant had not been brought back for sentence until after the date to which sentence had been deferred, the court had no power to pass sentence. The court does not lose jurisdiction until after sentence has been passed; but as a general principle where a sentence is deferred a defendant should be brought back on the date on which the period of deferment expires or as soon as possible thereafter.[2] The court should then deal with the offender unless there are strong reasons for not doing so. As section 1(7) of the Powers of Criminal Courts Act preserves the courts' power to bind over an offender to come up for judgment or otherwise lawfully to postpone passing sentence, the court dealing with the offender after a statutory deferment may further postpone passing sentence (although it may not use the statutory deferment again). A strong reason for further postponing sentence might be the necessity to know the outcome of the trial of other outstanding charges relating to the offender, but generally further postponements are undesirable (*Ingle*).

It is desirable that the same court which deferred sentence should pass sentence on the expiration of the period of deferment (*Gurney* [1974] Crim.L.R. 472). In *Jacobs* (1976) 62 Cr.App.R. 116, the Court of Appeal stated that where a judge defers sentence he should give instructions that the case should be re-listed before him. If he is unlikely to be available he should make a note about the case and the court officials should ensure that the judge who deals with it sees this note. Furthermore, counsel who appears for a defendant in respect of whom sentence is deferred should regard himself as bound to appear, if it is at all possible, when the defendant returns to the court for sentence (*Ryan* [1976] Crim.L.R. 508).

Where a court defers passing sentence on an offender, it may deal with him before the expiration of the period of deferment if, during that period, he is convicted in Great Britain of any offence

---

[2] See also *Anderson* (1984) 78 Cr.App.R. 251, following *Ingle*, it was held that a delay resulting from an administrative mistake on the part of the court staff did not deprive the Crown Court of jurisdiction to pass sentence thereafter. The effect of the mistake and delay was not on jurisdiction but on the sort of sentence which it would be proper to pass; as this had been taken into consideration by the judge in passing sentence, the appeal was dismissed.

(P.C.C.A., s. 1(4)). As the Crown Court is one court, the power to pass sentence for the original offence may be exercised in the location of the Crown Court where he is convicted of the subsequent offence (see *Practice Direction* [1971] 1 W.L.R. 1534, amended by *Practice Direction* [1974] 2 All E.R. 121).

Where during the period of deferment an offender is convicted in England or Wales of any offence, the court which passes sentence on him for this subsequent offence may also deal with him for the offence or offences in respect of which sentence was deferred, provided that:

(a) a magistrates' court may not so deal with the offender where the sentence was originally deferred by the Crown Court; and

(b) the Crown Court in exercising this power where sentence was originally deferred by a magistrates' court, shall not pass any sentence which could not have been passed by a magistrates' court in exercising it.

(s. 4A, as inserted by C.L.A, Sched. 12).

This provision is intended to reduce the number of court hearings although the second court is not obliged to deal with the offender for his earlier offence.

Where the court which deferred the sentence on an offender proposes to sentence him, whether on the expiration of the period of deferment or earlier by virtue of section 1(4), or where the offender fails to appear on the date specified, it may issue a summons requiring him to appear before the court, or it may issue a warrant for his arrest (s. 1(5)). In the case of a magistrates' court a deferred sentence is regarded as an adjournment of the trial under section 10(1) of the Magistrates' Courts Act 1980, so that if the offender fails to appear on the date specified, it may proceed in his absence (M.C.A., s. 11(1)) or, if certain conditions are satisfied (s. 13(1) and (2)) and the court thinks it undesirable, by reason of the gravity of the offence, to continue the trial in the absence of the accused, it may issue a warrant for his arrest (P.C.C.A., s. 1(6) as substituted by C.L.A., Sched. 12 and amended by M.C.A., Sched. 7).

When dealing with an offender following deferment of sentence a court may deal with him in any way in which the court which deferred passing sentence could have dealt with him (s. 1(8)(a), as inserted by C.J.A., s. 63). In the case of a magistrates' court, this includes the power to commit him to the Crown Court for sentence (s. 1(8)(b), as inserted by C.J.A., s. 63).[3] This provision reverses the

---

[3] This applies whether the magistrates' court is the one which originally deferred sentence or whether it is a different magistrates' court exercising its powers under s. 1(4A).

effect of *Gilby* [1975] 1 W.L.R. 924, which had held the justices had no power under section 1 of the Powers of Criminal Courts Act to commit an offender to the Crown Court for sentence following a period of deferment. Where a magistrates' court commits an offender to the Crown Court under section 1(8), section 1(8A) provides that the Crown Court may impose a second period of deferment for the same offence notwithstanding section 1(2).[4]

A deferred sentence is not supervised, but the court may request a terminal report on the offender from a probation officer on the date when it sentences him. No conditions may be attached to a deferred sentence and, accordingly, there cannot be a "breach" of a deferred sentence (*cf.* probation order).

OTHER POWERS TO POSTPONE SENTENCE DISTINGUISHED FROM A DEFERRED SENTENCE

Courts have other powers to postpone sentence which are distinguishable from the power to defer sentence.

(a) Binding over to come up for judgment

See pp. 11–12, above.

On such a bind over the offender may also be required to enter into a recognizance to keep the peace and be of good behaviour. Special conditions may also be imposed (*e.g.* to leave the jurisdiction). This power is closest in type to the power to defer sentence. However, it is not normally expected that the offender, if he keeps the conditions imposed on being bound over, will reappear before the court; whereas with the deferred sentence he must appear. The common law power is confined to courts with jurisdiction to try on indictment, whereas the deferred sentence power may be exercised by any court. In addition no conditions may be attached to a deferred sentence and the sentence may only be deferred for the purposes expressed in section 1 of the Powers of Criminal Courts Act.

(b) Postponement of sentence

Crown Courts have an inherent power to postpone sentence, or part of a sentence (*Annesley* [1976] 1 W.L.R. 106). This power may be exercised where all the material necessary to determine the full sentence is not available. In such a case the court may deal with the substantive sentence at once and postpone making ancillary orders (*e.g.* disqualification or compensation orders) until all the material is at hand.

---

[4] Inserted by C.J.A. 1982, s. 63.

(c) Remands for inquiries

Before passing sentence a court may adjourn the case to enable inquiries to be made by a probation officer, social worker or medical practitioners. Generally courts are not obliged to remand for reports but several statutes do oblige courts in certain circumstances to consider probation officer reports or medical reports (see below). If these reports are not available at the time of the trial the court will adjourn the case for inquiries to be made and remand the offender in custody or on bail.

COMBINING A DEFERRED SENTENCE WITH OTHER SENTENCES

When a court defers sentence under section 1 of the Powers of Criminal Courts Act it may make no other order by way of sentence (*Dwyer* [1974] Crim.L.R. 610). This includes the activation of an existing suspended sentence. In *Salmon* (1973) 57 Cr.App.R. 953, S. was convicted in the Crown Court in 1972 of unlawful sexual intercourse and sentenced to six months imprisonment suspended for two years. In June 1973 he pleaded guilty in the magistrates' court to stealing £8 from a meter in his mother's home. Sentence was deferred until October 1973. In July 1973, S. was brought before the Crown Court and the suspended sentence imposed in 1972 was ordered to take effect. The Court of Appeal held that the decision of the Crown Court was premature. Until the magistrates' court had dealt with S. it could not be known whether there was a "conviction" for the purposes of activating the suspended sentence, as the defendant might have been placed on probation or given a conditional discharge.

A deferred sentence may not be "split." In *Fairhead* the Court of Appeal held invalid a disqualification order on the date of conviction alongside a deferment of sentence for three months, at the end of which a suspended sentence was imposed. The proper time to make any order such as disqualification or forfeiture of weapons, etc., is when the defendant, on whom sentence has been deferred, again comes before the court (*Gilby* [1975] 1 W.L.R. 924). However, a sentencer may make a restitution order under section 28 of the Theft Act 1968, as amended by Sched. 12 of the Criminal Law Act 1977, at the time of deferring sentence.

WHEN DEFERMENT OF SENTENCE IS APPROPRIATE

A deferred sentence under section 1 of the Powers of Criminal Courts Act is appropriate

"for the purpose of enabling the court to have regard, in
determining his sentence, to his conduct after conviction
(including, where appropriate, the making by him of reparation for his offence) or to any change in his circumstances."
(s. 1(1).)

It is not available for purposes other than those specified in
s. 1(1).

In *Gilby* [1975] 1 W.L.R. 924, the justices, on convicting an
offender, deferred sentence for three months for three reasons: (1)
the court was uncertain as to the position in relation to outstanding fines; (2) to afford him an opportunity of settling
down in employment; and (3) to see what, if any, changes occurred
in relation to his domestic situation. The Court of Appeal held that
the power to defer sentence is restricted to the purposes of taking
into account post conviction behaviour (including reparation) and
change of circumstances of the offender. The second and third
reasons fell under those purposes but as to the first, if the justices
needed more information about the fines, the cases ought to
have been adjourned to enable inquiries to be made under
section 10(3) of the Magistrates' Courts Act.[5] In *George* (1984) 79
Cr.App.R.26 the Court of Appeal made it clear that deferment is
not to be used as an easy way out for a Court which is unable to
make up its mind about the correct sentence. If the principal object
is to enable a social inquiry report to be obtained deferment
should not be used but rather the case should be adjourned (see
Gilby).

In the past the Court of Appeal has set its face against adjourning
sentence in order to see whether reparation would be made. This
was described as using the court as a "money collecting agency"
(*per* Lord Parker C.J. in *West* (1959) 43 Cr.App.R. 109), or an
unseemly bargaining with the accused over sentence (*per* Salmon
L.J. in *Collins* (1969) 53 Cr.App.R. 385). However, the new power to
defer sentence does contemplate reparation or compensation being
made prior to sentence. It is clear that where a deferred sentence is
not otherwise appropriate the court should not normally hesitate to
pass sentence and then make orders for restitution or compensation.
In *George* the Court of Appeal stated that it will seldom be in the
interests of justice to stipulate that the conduct required is
reparation by the defendant. In particular any suggestion that a
wealthy offender was being given an opportunity to "buy his way

---

[5] For two cases where courts deferred sentences where there were apparently no
reasons (as provided by statute) for so doing, and for comment thereon, see
Glossop [1982] Crim.L.R. 244 and *Fletcher* [1982] Crim.L.R. 462.

out" of a deserved custodial sentence should be avoided (*Crosby and Hayes* (1975) 60 Cr.App.R. 234).

Change of the offender's circumstances will usually mean domestic or employment circumstances. The court may wish to defer sentence to await the outcome of some event, *e.g.* the defendant getting married, becoming reconciled with his family, or taking up employment. A sentence should not be deferred where it is clear that a custodial sentence will be imposed no matter what changes may occur in the offender's conduct or circumstances after conviction (*Crosby and Hayes*; *Jacobs* (1976) 62 Cr.App.R. 116). If a court simply wishes to see how an offender behaves himself after his conviction without having any particular reason for deferring sentence, it would be more appropriate to impose a probation order or a conditional discharge as this makes it clear to the offender what is expected of him and what will happen to him if he fails to comply with the order or commits a further offence during the currency of the order or period of discharge (see *George*).[6]

Where a court decides to defer sentence this decision "inevitably conveys the impression to a defendant—and we would say contains the implication—that if the report called for by the court is favourable to the defendant (even though the defendant has not achieved all that was hoped for) the court will not pass so severe a sentence as it might otherwise have imposed" (*per* James L.J. in *Gilby*, at p. 930). In *Jacobs* the Court of Appeal indicated that where sentence is deferred the offender is entitled to expect that, provided he behaves himself, he will not ordinarily be sent to prison. In *Smith (M.S.)* (1977) 64 Cr.App.R. 116, the Court of Appeal indicated that two points would be considered on appeal against a sentence imposed after a period of deferment; first, whether the sentence passed was excessive in any event and secondly, whether the judge had fairly considered the progress, if any, made by the defendant. While the court will not go into detail and try to reach conclusions of fact, it will satisfy itself that the judge in passing sentence had borne in mind the duty to see how far, if at all, the promises made by the prisoner at the time of deferment had been kept. It would obviously be wrong to send to prison someone who had fulfilled what was required of him. In *George* the Court of Appeal stated that in order to avoid misunderstandings the Court when deferring sentence, should make it clear to the defendant what the particular purposes are which the court has in mind under section 1(1) and what conduct is expected of him during deferment. The court should make a careful note of the purposes for which the sentence is

---

[6] See also Commentary to *Jacobs* [1976] 62 Cr.App.R. 116 and *Smith (M.S.)* (1977) 64 Cr.App.R. 116.

being deferred and what steps, if any, it expects the defendant to take during the period of deferment. Ideally the defendant should be given written notice of the same so that he is left in no doubt as to what is expected of him. This will make it easier for the court to deal with the offender at the expiration of the period of deferment, particularly where the sentencing Court is differently constituted from the deferring court.

When it comes to dealing with the offender at the end of the period of deferment the court should pay regard to the reason for deferring sentence and any requirements imposed on the offender. If he has substantially complied with these he may legitimately expect not to receive a custodial sentence. If he has not, the court should be careful to state clearly in what respect he has failed. A custodial sentence should not be imposed for a reason unrelated to the reasons for which sentence was deferred in the first place. Thus in *Benstead* (1979) 1 Cr.App.R.(S.) 32, a sentence of six months imprisonment was quashed where the appellant had substantially complied with the expectations of the sentencer who had deferred sentence, and who had subsequently received a favourable social inquiry report. The custodial sentence had been imposed primarily because the appellant had failed to get in touch with the police in connection with some inquiries they were making into other matters. No charges had been preferred against him as a result of those inquiries, and his whereabouts had been well known to the police throughout.

APPEAL

There can only be an appeal against the sentence when it is eventually made, but if the deferral of sentence is defective, an appeal or possibly an application for judicial review may be made on the basis that it constitutes a sentence not known to the law.

COMMUNITY SERVICE ORDERS

DESCRIPTION

Community service by offenders was introduced in an experimental way in certain probation and after-care areas in 1973. As from March 1, 1979 community service orders have been available as a mode of disposition for the courts throughout England and Wales. The C.S.O. provides a non-custodial measure whereby offenders are required to undertake unpaid community service work during their leisure hours.

In recommending the introduction of the C.S.O., the Advisory Council on the Penal System expressed the view that the proposition that some offenders should be required to undertake community service:

> "should appeal to adherents of different varieties of penal philosophy. To some extent it would simply be a more constructive and cheaper alternative to short sentences of imprisonment; by others it would be seen as introducing into the penal system a new dimension with emphasis on reparation to the community; others again would regard it as a means of giving effect to the old adage that the punishment should fit the crime; while still others would stress the value of bringing offenders into close touch with those members of the community who are most in need of help and support." (HMSO, 1970, para. 33.)[1]

The Advisory Council itself hoped that the new measure would give opportunity for constructive activity in the form of personal service to the community and create the possibility of a changed outlook on the part of the offender (para. 34).[2]

The legislative provisions for the C.S.O. are closely modelled on the probation order, but a C.S.O. is *not* a probation order, although there is provision for making the order on breach of a probation

---

[1] For an account of how community service can be used positively by using offenders to help others rather than by using community service purely as a means of punishing or rehabilitating offenders, see Richards and Maull, "Making Community Service into Service for the Community" *Probation Journal* 1982, No. 3.

[2] For an interesting account of the realities of a community service work session based on lengthy participant observation, see Vass, "A Working Sketch of a Community Service Session" *Probation Journal* 1983, No. 4.

order. Unlike probation a C.S.O. may be regarded as a penalty as it is not an alternative to a sentence. The administration of C.S.O.s is included among the duties of probation officers of the petty sessions area in which the offender is residing, and the probation committee for the area may appoint persons for those purposes (P.C.C.A., s. 14(4)).

THE LAW

Where a person over 16 years of age is convicted of an offence punishable in the case of an adult with imprisonment, the court may, instead of dealing with him in any other way, make a C.S.O. requiring him to perform unpaid work for a specified number of hours (P.C.C.A., s. 14(1) as amended by C.J.A. 1982, Sched 12). The minimum number of hours is 40 and the maximum is 120 in the case of an offender aged 16 and 240 in other cases (P.C.C.A., s. 14(1A) as inserted by C.J.A. 1982, Sched. 12).

Several conditions must be satisfied before a court may make a C.S.O. First, the offender must consent to the order being made[3] (P.C.C.A., s. 14(2) as substituted by C.J.A. 1982, Sched. 12). Secondly, the court may only make a C.S.O. where after considering a report by a probation officer or by a social worker of a local authority social services department about the offender and his circumstances and, if necessary, hearing the probation officer or social worker, it is satisfied that the offender is a suitable person to perform work under such an order (s. 14(2)). Where there is no suitable social inquiry report available (see pp. 236–239, below), the court may adjourn the case so that the suitability of the offender for community service may be assessed. If the report proves favourable and such an order is recommended, the court should not impose a custodial sentence but should make a C.S.O. as a feeling of injustice would otherwise be aroused (see *Gillam* [1981] Crim.L.R. 55; followed in *Millwood* (1982) 4 Cr.App.R. 281). Thus the decision to adjourn to obtain such a report in relation to the offender's suitability for a C.S.O. (or any other non-custodial measure) should not be made unless the court is satisfied that a C.S.O. would be

[3] This is an important requirement for three reasons: first, it helps to weed out those offenders who would probably be uncooperative if a C.S.O. were imposed against their wishes; secondly, the probation service and voluntary agencies would be unlikely to lend their support to a coercive scheme; and, thirdly, and perhaps more importantly, Art. 4(2) of the European Convention for the Protection of Human Rights and Fundamental Freedoms, and the International Labour Office Convention for the Suppression of Forced or Compulsory Labour, both prohibit the imposition of compulsory unpaid work outside an institution (see Young, *Community Service Orders* (Heinemann, 1979), p. 28).

appropriate and that it would make such an order having regard initially to the nature of the offence and other relevant circumstances (*cf. Gilby* [1975] 1 W.L.R. 924 and *Jacobs* (1976) 62 Cr.App.R. 116 in relation to deferment of sentence). However, if the judge makes it clear that in asking for a report he is not holding out any promise or expectation that a favourable report will necessarily lead to any recommended disposal being adopted, there can be no sense of injustice if he ultimately decides after mature consideration on some other disposal; but if there is something of a promise that if a particular disposal is recommended it will be adopted, then a sense of injustice will be created if it is not adopted (*Moss* [1983] Crim.L.R. 751).

Thirdly, where the offender is 17 or over, a court shall not make a C.S.O. unless satisfied that provision for him to perform work under the order can be made under the arrangements which exist in the petty sessions area in which he resides or will reside[4] (P.C.C.A., s. 14(2A)(*a*) as inserted by C.J.A. 1982, Sched. 12) where the offender is 16 the court shall not make a C.S.O. unless it has been notified by the Secretary of State that arrangements exist for 16 year olds residing in the petty sessions area in which the offender resides or will reside to perform work under such orders and it is satisfied that provision can be made under the arrangements for him to do so (s. 14(2A)(*b*)).

The hours specified in the order may not be less than 40 nor more than 120 or 240 depending on the age of the offender.[5] If orders are made in respect of two or more offences of which the offender has been convicted by or before the court, the hours may be ordered to run concurrently or consecutively, but the total number of hours shall not exceed the maximum (s. 14(3)). Where the offender is already subject to a C.S.O., a court making a further C.S.O. may make it consecutive to the existing order, but in view of section 14(1A) it is desirable that there should not be orders totalling more than the prescribed maximum in respect of the same offender (*Evans* (1976) 64 Cr.App.R. 127).

Before making a C.S.O. the court shall explain to the offender in ordinary language:

    (a) the purpose and effect of the order;

    (b) the consequences following a breach of the order; and

    (c) the court's power to review the order on the application of the offender or the supervising probation officer.

    (s. 14(5).)

---

[4] P.C.C.A., ss. 17A and 17B as inserted by C.J.A. 1982, Sched. 13 provide for the making of a C.S.O. in respect of offenders who reside or will be residing in Scotland or Northern Ireland.

[5] There is some evidence that magistrates tend to impose a greater number of hours service on unemployed offenders, see Jardine, Moore and Pease, "Community Service Orders, Employment and the Tariff" [1983] Crim.L.R. 17.

Section 14(6) provides that the offender shall be supplied with a copy of the order by the probation officer assigned to the court. Formerly this provision was regarded as mandatory; thus, until it was complied with the order was suspended and not in force, and the offender could not be dealt with under section 16 for failure to comply with its requirements (*Dugdale* [1981] Crim.L.R. 105, Preston Crown Court, His Honour Judge Kershaw). However, *Dugdale* was not followed by His Honour Judge Duckworth in *Cooper* v. *Chief Constable of Lancashire* [1984] Crim.L.R. 99 who held that the provision was directory only and was not a condition precedent to the making of such an order. Accordingly, the appellant's appeal against his conviction before Ormskirk Magistrates' Court of breaching a C.S.O. was dismissed, he having admittedly failed to do any work under the order or (despite receiving three letters from the probation service) to keep any appointments with the relevant officers (see also *Walsh* v. *Barlow* and *Thorpe* v. *Griggs, The Times,* October 9, 1984.).

An offender subject to a C.S.O. must:

(a) report to the relevant officer and notify him of any change of address; and

(b) perform for the number of hours specified in the order, such work at such times as he may be instructed by the relevant officer.

(s. 15(1).)

In allocating work to the offender the supervising officer should endeavour as far as possible, to avoid any conflict with the offender's religious beliefs and any interference with his work or attendance at school or other educational establishment (s. 15(3)).

The work required to be done under the order must normally be performed within 12 months from the date on which the order was made (s. 15(2)), but this period may be extended on application by the offender or supervising officer where this would be in the interests of justice having regard to circumstances which have arisen since the order was made (s. 15(2) and s. 17(1)). However, unless the order is revoked, it will remain in force until the offender has worked the specified number of hours (s. 15(2) as amended by C.L.A. 1977, Sched. 12).

Breach of a community service order

Upon complaint that the offender has failed to comply with any of the requirements of a C.S.O. (including failure to perform the work satisfactorily), a justice of the peace acting for the petty sessions area specified in the order, may issue a summons, or may, if the complaint is in writing and substantiated on oath, issue a warrant for his arrest (s. 16(1)). The summons or warrant will direct the offender to be brought before a magistrates' court acting for the petty sessions area specified in the order (s. 16(2)). If the magistrates' court finds that the offender has failed without reasonable excuse to comply with any of the requirements of the order (as laid down in s. 15) it may, without prejudice to the continuance of the order, impose a fine of up to £400 (s. 16(3) as amended). Alternatively, the court may:

(a) if the order was made by a magistrates' court, revoke the order deal with the offender for the original offence in any manner in which the court which made the order could have dealt with him (s. 16(3)a));

(b) if the order was made by the Crown Court, commit him in custody or release him on bail until he can be brought or appear before the Crown Court, which, in turn, may either impose a fine of up to £400 or revoke the order and deal with the offender for the original offence (s. 16(3)(b) and (5)).[6]

It has been held that the Crown Court has no jurisdiction to deal with a breach of a C.S.O. imposed by it unless the offender is first brought before a magistrates' court (nor may it amend or revoke such an order unless the offender has first appeared before a magistrates' court) (*Bethune* [1976] Crim.L.R. 316).

If the court decides to revoke the order it may deal with the offender for the original offence and pass sentence for *that offence* in light of his failure to comply with the order. A custodial sentence may well be appropriate (see *Garland* (1979) 1 Cr.App.R.(S.) 62) but only where the original offence would justify such a sentence (see *Barresi* (1981) Crim.L.R. 268). In *Simpson* [1983] Crim.L.R. 820 the court reduced the sentence of imprisonment imposed on the offender following his deliberate defiance of a C.S.O. as it appeared that the court was punishing him for the breach of the order rather than passing sentence in respect of the original offence. The court made it clear that sentence must be passed in light of the gravity of the offence and the presence of any mitigating factors, which, in this case amounted to a guilty plea and lack of previous convictions. In *Howard and Wade* [1977] Crim.L.R. 683 the Court of Appeal stated that a C.S.O. was an indulgence to the offender saving him from an immediate custodial sentence, although it was hoped that it was also an advantage to the community if the offender complied with it. Accordingly, those who broke the terms of the order (in this case for the second time, having been fined on the first occasion) could not

---

[6] Any question whether there has been a failure to comply with the requirements of s. 15 shall be determined by the court and not by the verdict of a jury (P.C.C.A., s. 16(7)).

complain if a custodial sentence was imposed when they had thrown away the advantage offered to them.

Where the offender in breach of a C.S.O. is under 21 the Court may only impose a custodial sentence where the statutory criteria in C.J.A. 1982, s. 1(4) are satisfied. The court should identify the criterion it relies on when giving its reasons under section 6(1)(b) for imposing a custodial sentence. It would appear that the only criterion which the court may rely on in such a case is that the offender is unable or unwilling to respond to non-custodial penalties. The other criteria, which require that a non-custodial penalty be inappropriate to the case because either the public requires protection or the offence is of such a serious nature as to demand a custodial sentence, would appear to be inappropriate, as if either of these was relied upon it would indicate that a C.S.O. was not appropriate in the first place. Thus, where a court seeks to impose a custodial sentence for the offence after the offender has breached the C.S.O., it must be satisfied that there is no non-custodial sentence to which the offender would be willing or able to respond. In *Gittings* [1985] Crim.L.R. 246, however, the Court of Appeal upheld a sentence of youth custody for an offender in breach of a C.S.O. without making any reference to the statutory criteria.

In sentencing the offender the court may give him credit for any substantial part performance of the order (*Paisley* (1979) 1 Cr.App.R.(S.) 196).[7]

Amendment of a community service order

Where the offender proposes to change or has changed his residence from the petty sessions area specified in the order to another petty sessions area, a magistrates' court acting for the former area may, and on the application of the relevant officer, shall, amend the order by substituting the other petty sessions area for the area specified in the order, provided that:

(a) it appears to the court, in the case of an offender of or over 17 years of age, that provision can be made for him to perform work under the C.S.O. under the arrangements which exist in the other petty sessions area; or

(b) if the offender is under 17 years of age:

    (i) that the court has been notified by the Secretary of State that arrangements exist for persons of his age who reside in the other petty sessions area to perform work under such orders; and

---

[7] See also *Anderson* (1982) 4 Cr.App.R.(S.) 252 and *Baines* [1983] Crim.L.R. 756, where the offenders were being dealt with under P.C.C.A., s. 17.

(ii) it appears to the court that provision can be made under the arrangements for him to do so.
(P.C.C.A., s. 17(5) and (5A) as substituted by C.J.A. 1982, Sched. 12.)

Under section 17(1) either the offender or the supervising officer may apply to a magistrates' court acting for the petty sessions area in the order for an extension of the duration of the order. The court will do so where it is in the interests of justice having regard to circumstances which have arisen since the order was made. Where a magistrates' court proposes to exercise its powers under section 17(1) otherwise than on the application of the offender it shall summon him to appear before the court and, if he does not appear in answer to the summons, may issue a warrant for his arrest (s. 17(7)).

There is a certain degree of overlap between this provision and section 16. An application may be made under section 17 for extension of the duration of the order, for example, on the grounds of the offender's ill health which prevented him performing the requisite number of hours of service, only for evidence to arise that the extent of the non-performance was not supported by the medical evidence. In such a case the court may treat the offender as being in breach of the order and sentence him for the original offence even though no application has been made under section 16 (*Goscombe* (1981) 3 Cr.App.R.(S.) 61). If difficulties arise which make it difficult for the offender to comply with the requirements of the order, he should notify the supervising officer and it may be possible for the order to be amended. If he simply fails to comply with the order he will find himself being dealt with under section 16 for breach of the order with the serious consequences which this may involve. In *Howard and Wade* [1977] Crim.L.R. 683 the Court of Appeal, in particular, stated that those who take employment which will create difficulties for them in complying with the order should report those difficulties to the supervising officer before accepting the job. If circumstances make it difficult or impossible for the offender to comply with the order, the court will probably deal with him more leniently if it is dealing with the offender under a section 17 application than if he is brought before the court pursuant to section 16.

Revocation of a community service order: substitution of other sentences

Where a C.S.O. is in force application may be made by the offender or the relevant officer to a magistrates' court acting for the petty sessions area specified, that having regard to circumstances which have arisen since the order was made, it would be in the interests of justice that the order should be revoked or that the offender should be dealt with in some other manner for the offence in respect of which the order was made (P.C.C.A., s. 17(2)). In such circumstances the court may:

(a) if the order was made by a magistrates' court, revoke the order or revoke it and deal with the offender for the original offence in any manner in which he could have been dealt with when the order was originally made;

(b) if the order was made by the Crown Court, commit him to custody or release him on bail until he can be brought or appear before the Crown Court.

Where a magistrates' court proposes to exercise its powers under section 17(2), otherwise than on an application of the offender, it shall summon him to appear before the court and, if he does not appear in answer to the summons, may issue a warrant for his arrest (s. 17(7)). Where an application is made under section 17 for a C.S.O. to be revoked on grounds which effectively amount to an allegation of a breach of the order, the court should take steps, by adjournment if necessary, to put the matter on a proper evidentiary basis before exercising its powers under section 17 (*Jackson* [1984] Crim.L.R. 573). Accordingly evidence should be heard in the same manner as if the proceedings had been brought under section 16.

Where a C.S.O. is in force and the offender is convicted of an offence before a magistrates' court (not being a magistrates' court acting for the petty sessions area specified in the order) and the court imposes a custodial sentence on him, and it appears to the court, on the application of the offender or the relevant officer, that it would be in the interests of justice to do so having regard to circumstances which have arisen since the order was made, the court may

(i) if the order was made by a magistrates' court, revoke it; and

(ii) if the order was made by the Crown Court commit him in custody or release him on bail until he can be brought or appear before the Crown Court which may revoke the order if it appears to be in the interests of justice so to do.

(s. 17(4A) and (4B) as inserted by C.J.A. 1982, Sched. 12.)

Where the offender is convicted of an offence before a magistrates' court acting for the same petty sessions area as the magistrates' court specified in the order (whether or not he receives a custodial sentence) an application may be made under section 17(2) for the order to be revoked or for the offender to be dealt with in some other way.[8] It is noticeable that section 17(4A) does not include a power to deal with the offender for the original offence.

---

[8] See Hines, *Judicial Discretion in Sentencing by Judges and Magistrates* (1982), §9.56.

Thus, if an offender is convicted of an offence before a magistrates' court acting for another petty sessions area and receives a custodial sentence, but the supervising officer wants him to be dealt with in some other way for the original offence, or where he is so convicted but receives some other non-custodial sentence but the officer thinks it desirable in the interests of justice that the C.S.O. be revoked or that he be dealt with in some other way, application will have to be made to a magistrates' court acting for the petty sessions area specified on the order. It is interesting to note that magistrates' courts cannot take the initiative in these matters where an offender, subject to a C.S.O., is convicted before them of another offence.[9]

In addition to its powers under section 17(4A) and (4B) there are three circumstances in which the Crown Court, if it appears to be in the interests of justice to do so, having regard to circumstances which have arisen since the order was made, may revoke the order or revoke the order and deal with the offender for the original offence:

(a) where the offender is convicted of an offence before the Crown Court;

(b) where the offender is committed by a magistrates' court to the Crown Court for sentence and is brought or appears before the Crown Court; or

(c) where the offender is brought or appears before the Crown Court by virtue of section 17(2)(b).

COMBINING A COMMUNITY SERVICE ORDER WITH OTHER MEASURES

A C.S.O. is not a probation order, and an order for community service work may not be made a condition or requirement on making a probation order.[10]

A court may deal with an offender by using a C.S.O. "instead of dealing with him in any other way" (P.C.C.A., s. 14(1)). Accordingly, a C.S.O. may not be combined with any other measure for the same offence (excluding ancillary orders). Further, it is wrong in principle and bad sentencing practice to impose a C.S.O. on the same occasion as a suspended sentence (and presumably an immediate prison sentence) even though they relate to separate counts (*Starie* (1979) 1 Cr.App.R.(S.) 172) or separate indictments (*Ray* (1984) 6 Cr.App.R.(S) 26). In *Carnwell* (1978) 68 Cr.App.R. 58, the Court of Appeal stated that a fine may not be imposed on an

[9] This compares with the comparable position in Northern Ireland which gives the court the initiative.
[10] The provision in P.C.C.A., s. 6(6)(b) for making a C.S.O. where the offender has failed to comply with the requirements of a probation order has not yet been brought into force.

offender at the same time as a C.S.O. in relation to the same offence. However, by analogy to *Bainbridge* (1979) 1 Cr.App.R.(S.) 36, a fine may be imposed at the same time as a C.S.O., so long as they are imposed in relation to different counts. Section 16(8) of the Power of Criminal Courts Act preserves the courts' powers to make an order for costs against, or impose any disqualification on, the offender and to make in respect of the offence orders for compensation (P.C.C.A., s. 35), criminal bankruptcy (s. 39), deprivation of property used, or intended for use, for purposes of crime (s. 43), disqualification from driving where the vehicle was used for the purposes of crime, and restitution under section 28 of the Theft Act 1968.

WHEN A COMMUNITY SERVICE ORDER IS APPROPRIATE

A C.S.O. may be made where the offender is convicted of an offence punishable with imprisonment. Six Court of Appeal decisions give some guidance on the considerations which a court will take into account.[11] The important considerations, not all of which may be present in each case, appear to be:

(a)   whether the offence is an isolated incident not likely to be repeated in the foreseeable future (*Brown*; *Lawrence*; *McDiarmid*; *Canfield*; but *cf. Heyfron*);

(b)   whether the offender is of generally good character (*McDiarmid*; *Brown*) or has made significant efforts to settle down and avoid further offences (*Lawrence*; *Canfield*);

(c)   whether the offender has a stable home or family background (*McDiarmid*; *Brown*; *Lawrence*; *Canfield*);

(d)   whether he has employment (*McDiarmid*), hope of employment (*Brown*), or a good record (*Canfield*);

(e)   whether the offender has responded positively to probation in relation to another offence and has undergone a favourable change of character (*Azfal*).

Even though the offence is one of violence a C.S.O. may be appropriate.[11a]

APPEAL

The normal rights of appeal apply.

Where an offender is in breach of the requirements of a C.S.O. and the order was made by a magistrates' court and he is dealt with

---

[11] See *McDiarmid* (1980) 2 Cr.App.R.(S.) 130; *Heyfron* (1980) 2 Cr.App.R.(S.) 230; *Azfal* (1981) 3 Cr.App.R.(S.) 93; *Brown* [1982] Crim.L.R. 126; *Lawrence* [1982] Crim.L.R. 377; *Canfield* [1982] 4 Cr.App.R.(S.) 94.

[11a] See *McDiarmid; Shenton* (1982) 4 Cr.App.R.(S) 294; *West* (1983) 5 Cr.App.R.(S) 206; *McDermot* [1985] Crim.L.R. 245.

under section 16(3)(*a*) he may appeal to the Crown Court against the sentence imposed. Where the order was made by the Crown Court following a trial on indictment and he is subsequently dealt with by the Crown Court under section 16(5) for breach of the order, he may appeal to the Court of Appeal under section 9 of the Criminal Appeal Act 1968. Where the order was originally made by the Crown Court on committal following a conviction before the magistrates' court and the offender is dealt with by the Crown Court under section 16(5), there is no right of appeal because of a lacuna in section 10(2)(*b*) of the Criminal Appeal Act 1968.[12]

In relation to sentences passed in substitution for C.S.O.s the following rights of appeal apply. Where the C.S.O. was made by, and is revoked by, a magistrates' court and a new sentence is substituted under section 17(2)(*a*), the offender may appeal to the Crown Court (s. 17(4)). Where the order was made by the Crown Court following a trial on indictment and it is subsequently revoked by the Crown Court and the offender is sentenced for the original offence under section 17(3), he may appeal to the Court of Appeal against that sentence under section 9 of the Criminal Appeal Act 1968. However, where the order was originally made by the Crown Court on committal following a conviction before the magistrates' court and the order is revoked and a sentence passed in substitution, there is no right of appeal because of the lacuna in section 10(2)(*b*) of the Criminal Appeal Act 1968 (see *Harding, The Times,* June 15, 1983).

---

[12] See *Harding, The Times,* June 15, 1983. If, however, a magistrates' court dealing with a breach of the order under s. 16(3)(*a*) commits him to the Crown Court for sentencing for the original offence then there is a right of appeal under C.A.A. 1968, s. 10(2)(*a*). This lacuna does not exist in the equivalent provision in Northern Ireland, see Art. 9(6) of the Treatment of Offenders (N.I.) Order 1976 and s. 9(2) of the Criminal Appeal (N.I.) Act 1980.

ATTENDANCE CENTRE ORDERS

DESCRIPTION

An attendance centre is a place where offenders under the age of 21 are required to attend for specified numbers of hours usually on a Saturday afternoon (or sometimes morning) at weekly or fortnightly intervals. The purpose of attendance centres is described in *The Sentence of the Court* as being

> "... to deal with young offenders whose future conduct may be expected to be influenced by the deprivation of leisure time involved and by the endeavours of the staff to encourage them to make constructive use of leisure time and to guide them towards worthwhile recreational activities which they can continue on leaving the centre."

This would seem to be over-optimistic. A more realistic description of aims is that given by A. B. Dunlop, in *Junior Attendance Centres*[1]:

> "No matter how time is spent at the centres, the limited nature of the requirements of the orders provoke scepticism about ascribing to the measure a reformative or therapeutic aim. Commonsense suggests that the attendance centre order's rationale is a straightforward punitive or deterrent one. Insofar as the aim is to deprive offenders of their leisure time and to substitute authority's choice of activities for those of the boys' choosing, attendance centres are punitive. ... Inasmuch as the experience of the deprivation of leisure time can be expected to influence future conduct, it can also be expected to deter offenders from further offending."

THE LAW

The law in relation to attendance centre orders is now to be found in sections 16 to 19 of the Criminal Justice Act 1982 which largely re-enacted, with some amendments, the provisions of the Criminal Justice Act 1948.

A magistrates' court or the Crown Court may make an attendance centre order (A.C.O.) in respect of an offender who is

[1] Home Office Research Study No. 60 (1980), p. 1.

under 21 years of age where it would have power[2] to pass a sentence of imprisonment or to commit the offender to prison in default of payment of any sum of money or for failing to do or abstain from doing anything required to be done or left undone, or where it has power to deal with the offender under section 6 of the Power of Criminal Courts Act for failure to comply with any of the requirements of a probation order (C.J.A. 1982, s. 17(1)).

An A.C.O. may be made by a court only:

(a) if it has been notified by the Secretary of State that an attendance centre is available for the reception of persons of his description (s. 17(1));

(b) if satisfied that the attendance centre to be specified is reasonably accessible to the offender, having regard to his age, the means of access available to him and any other circumstances (s. 17(7))[2a];

(c) if the offender has not been previously sentenced to imprisonment, detention under section 53 of the Children and Young Persons Act 1933, Borstal training, youth custody or detention in a detention centre, unless it appears to the court that there are special circumstances (whether relating to the offence or to the offender) which warrant the making of such an order in his case (s. 17(3)).

Hours of attendance

The order must specify the time at which the offender is first to attend (s. 17(9)) and the total number of hours for which he is to attend (s. 17(1)). The total number of hours should be not less than 12, except where the offender is under 14 years of age and the court considers that 12 hours would be excessive, having regard to his age or any other circumstances (s. 17(4)). The total may be more than 12 where the court considers, in the light of all the circumstances, that 12 hours would be inadequate (s. 17(5)). In such a case a total of up to 24 hours may be specified where the offender is under 17 years of age, or 36 hours where he is under 21 but not less than 17 years of age (s. 17(5)).

The time at which an offender is required to attend at an attendance centre shall be such as to avoid interference, so far as practicable, with his school hours or working hours (s. 17(8)). The

[2] But for the provisions of C.J.A. 1982, s. 1.
[2a] In the case of offenders under 14, the Home Office has recommended that an order should not be made if the offender would have to travel more than 10 miles to reach the centre or if the journey would take him more than an hour; in the case of offenders over 14 the recommended maxima are 15 miles and one and a half hours.

first time having been specified in the order, the remaining times will be fixed by the officer in charge of the centre, having regard to the offender's circumstances (s. 17(10)). An offender shall not be required to attend a centre on more than one occasion on any one day, or for more than three hours on any occasion (s. 17(11)).

A court may make an A.C.O. in respect of an offender before a previous A.C.O. made in respect of him has ceased to have effect, and may determine the number of hours to be specified in the order without regard to the number specified in the previous order, or to the fact that the order is still in effect (s. 17(6)).

Discharge and variation of an attendance centre order

An A.C.O. may be discharged on an application by the offender or the officer in charge of the attendance centre. Such an application should be made to, and the power to discharge an A.C.O. shall be exercised by, either

(a) a magistrates' court acting for the petty sessions area in which the relevant attendance centre is situated; or

(b) the court which made the order.

(s. 18(3).)

However, where the court which made the order is the Crown Court and there is included in the order a direction that the power to discharge the order is reserved to that court, the power may only be exercised by that court (s. 18(4)).

An application to vary an A.C.O. may be made by the offender or the officer in charge of the centre, to a magistrates' court acting for the petty sessions area in which the centre is situated (s. 18(5)). Where the order was made by a magistrates' court it may also be varied on an application to that court (s. 18(5)). Under this power of variation the court has power:

(a) to vary the day or hour specified in the order for the offender's first attendance at the centre; or

(b) if the court is satisfied that the offender proposes to change or has changed his residence, to substitute another attendance centre which the court is satisfied is reasonably accessible to the offender, having regard to his age, the means of access available to him and any other circumstances.

(s. 18(6).)

Where any application is made under s. 18 by the officer in charge of an attendance centre, the court may deal with it without summoning the offender (s. 18(7)).

Where an attendance centre order has been made in default of the payment of any sum of money, then:

(a) on payment of the whole sum to any person authorised to receive it, the A.C.O. shall cease to have effect;

(b) on payment of part of the sum, the total number of hours for
which the offender is required to attend the centre shall be
reduced proportionally.
(s. 17(13).)

Revocation of an attendance centre order on failure to attend or on breach of the attendance centre rules

While at an attendance centre, the young offender is the
responsibility of the officer in charge, and is required to obey orders
given by the officer. Discipline is by the personal influence of the
officer who may effect discipline by reprimanding the offender,
separating him from others attending at the centre, by giving him a
less attractive form of occupation, or by sending him home which
means an extra attendance has to be made at the centre.[3] Ultimately
the officer may apply to court for revocation of the order in cases of
more serious absenteeism or indiscipline.

Where an A.C.O. has been made and it appears on information
to a justice acting for a relevant petty sessions area[4] that the offender
has failed to attend in accordance with the order, or while attending
has committed a breach of rules made under section 16(3)[5] which
cannot be adequately dealt with under those rules, the justice may
issue a summons requiring the offender to appear at a magistrates'
court acting for the area or, if the information is in writing and on
oath, may issue a warrant for the offender's arrest requiring him to
be brought before such a court (s. 19(1)).

The magistrates' court before which the offender is brought has,
where the A.C.O. was made by a magistrates' court, power to revoke
the order and deal with the offender for the original offence
(s. 19(3)(a)). If the order was made by the Crown Court it may commit
him in custody or release him on bail until he can be brought before the
Crown Court (s. 19(3)(b)) which has power to revoke the order and
deal with the offender for the original offence (s. 19(5)).[6]

COMBINING AN ATTENDANCE CENTRE ORDER WITH OTHER MEASURES

It is not possible to combine an A.C.O. with any custodial order
on the same occasion. Nor should a probation order be made at the

---

[3] See Home Office Research Study No. 1, pp. 18–19.
[4] *i.e.* either the petty sessions area in which the attendance centre the offender is
required to attend is situated, or if the order was made by a magistrates' court, the
petty sessions area for which that court was acting (s. 19(2)).
[5] s. 16(3) provides that the Secretary of State may by statutory instrument make
rules for the regulation and management of attendance centres.
[6] Any question whether there has been a failure to attend or a breach of the rules
shall be determined by the court and not by the verdict of a jury (s. 19(7)).

same time as an A.C.O., the reason being that an A.C.O. is one of the available methods open to a court where the offender is in breach of the requirements of a probation order (P.C.C.A., s. 6; C.J.A., s. 17(1)).

WHEN AN ATTENDANCE CENTRE ORDER IS APPROPRIATE

The A.C.O. is only available for persons under 21 found guilty of an imprisonable offence or who are in breach of a probation order. In the absence of special circumstances an A.C.O. may not be made in respect of offenders who have previously served a custodial sentence.

The Advisory Council on the Treatment of Offenders in its Report on Non-Residential Treatment of Offenders Under 21, stated that the attendance centre was only appropriate for a particular type of delinquent:

"Those whose minds are still, as the Ingelby Committee put it, 'open to the effects of punishment and the influence of the attendance centre staff in teaching them to respect the law and the property of others'. The effectiveness of the attendance centre should be judged in relation to the class of offender for which it was designed; and by that standard the centres seem to have achieved a fair measure of success." (HMSO, 1962, para. 21.)

APPEAL

An A.C.O., including the imposition of an A.C.O. for breach of a probation order, is a sentence from which an appeal may be brought in the normal way.

Where an attendance centre order is revoked and the offender is dealt with for the original offence then he may appeal against the sentence imposed (a) to the Crown Court if the sentence is imposed by a magistrates' court (s. 19(6)) or, (b) to the Court of Appeal if the sentence is imposed by the Crown Court (C.A.A. 1968, s. 10(2)(b) as amended by C.J.A. 1982, Sched. 14, para. 23).

FINES

DESCRIPTION

A fine is a pecuniary penalty imposed on an offender on conviction for an offence. All courts have power to fine offenders and the fine is the most commonly imposed punishment in the courts.

THE LAW

In the Crown Court following a conviction on indictment for any offence, subject to any enactment requiring the offender to be dealt with in a particular way,[1] a fine may be imposed in addition to or in lieu of any other sentence, except where the sentence is fixed by law or where the court exercises a power which precludes it from sentencing the offender, for example, making a probation order or granting a discharge (P.C.C.A., s. 30(1)). There is no statutory limit to the amount of the fine which may be imposed (C.L.A. 1977, s. 32(1)).[2] There is similarly no limit where an offender is committed for sentence under M.C.A., s. 38 following a conviction in the magistrates' court of an offence triable either way. On committal under C.J.A. 1967, s. 56 the Crown Court is limited to the maximum fine which the magistrates' court could have imposed.

A magistrates' court is always limited in the fine it may impose by the statutory enactment empowering the imposition of the fine. A new method of determining fines for summary offences was laid down by the Criminal Justice Act 1982 (see below). In the case of a summary offence the power to impose a fine generally derives from the statute creating or consolidating the law relating to an offence, which will also specify the maximum amount of the fine and whether the power to fine is additional to or in lieu of a power to imprison or order some other form of detention. Where under any enactment a magistrates' court has power to sentence an offender to imprisonment or other detention but not to fine, then, unless an Act

---

[1] Thus a fine cannot be used in lieu of an obligatory penalty such as disqualification from driving under R.T.A., s. 93.

[2] The power to impose a fine without limit on conviction on indictment also applies to cases of committal for sentence under C.J.A. 1967, s. 62 relating to prisoners on licence and M.C.A., s. 38 relating to persons convicted summarily of indictable offences as P.C.C.A., s. 42 gives the Crown Court in such cases "power to deal with the offender in any manner in which it would deal with him if he had just been convicted of the offence on indictment before the court."

passed after December 31, 1879 expressly provides to the contrary, the court may, instead of sentencing him to imprisonment or other detention, impose a fine (C.J.A. 1982, s. 34(3)). The maximum fine which may be imposed in such a case for an offence triable either way shall not exceed "the prescribed sum" within the meaning of section 34(3) of the Magistrates' Courts Act.[3] The maximum in the case of a summary offence is £400 (s. 34(3)).

There are several provisions which apply where an offender is convicted summarily of an offence triable either way:

  (i) if the offence is "scheduled" under Schedule 2 to the Magistrates' Courts Act and the defendant has been tried summarily under section 22 of the same Act, the maximum fine which the court may impose is £1,000 (M.C.A., s. 33(1) as amended by S.I. 1984 No. 447);

 (ii) If the offence is one of incitement or attempt to commit an offence triable either way the court has power to impose a maximum fine not exceeding the maximum applicable to the substantive offence (M.C.A., s. 32(1)(b) and C.A.A. 1981, s. 4(1));

(iii) if the offence is listed in Schedule 1 to the Magistrates' Courts Act the court may impose a fine not exceeding the "prescribed sum"[4] (M.C.A., s. 32(1));

(iv) in any other case of an offence not listed in Schedule 1 to the Magistrates' Courts Act, being an offence under a "relevant enactment"[5] the court has power to impose a fine not exceeding the "prescribed sum" unless a larger fine is permitted by some other enactment (M.C.A., s. 32(2)). However, lower maxima are retained in respect of certain offences under the Misuse of Drugs 1971 (M.C.A., s. 32(5)).

The power to fine under (i), (ii), (iii) above may be exercised in addition to or in lieu of imprisonment while under (iv) the terms of the enactment will specify whether the fine is to be in addition to or in lieu of imprisonment.

---

[3] In s. 32(9) the "prescribed sum" is defined as meaning "£1,000 or such sum as is for the time being substituted by an order in force under s. 143(1)." s. 143(1) provides:

> "if it appears to the Secretary of State that there has been a change in the value of money since the last occasion when the sum or sums specified in section 32(9) were fixed, he may by order substitute for the sum or sums for the time being specified in that provision such other sum or sums as appear to him justified by the change."

The "prescribed sum" was increased to £2,000 by S.I. 1984 No. 447.

[4] See note 3 above.

[5] Under s. 32(9) "relevant enactment" is defined as "an enactment contained in the Criminal Law Act 1977 or in any Act passed before, or in the same session as that Act."

Where under any enactment a magistrates' court has power to sentence an offender to imprisonment for a period specified by the enactment, or to a fine of an amount so specified, then, except where an Act passed after December 31, 1879 expressly provides to the contrary, the court may sentence him to imprisonment for less than that period or, as the case may be, to a fine of less than that amount (M.C.A., s. 34(1)).

Where a person under 17 years of age is found guilty by a magistrates' court of an offence for which it would have power to impose a fine in excess of £400, the amount of any fine imposed must not exceed £400 (M.C.A., s. 36(1) S.I. 1984 No. 447). In the case of a child under the age of 14 the maximum fine which the court may impose is £100 (M.C.A., s. 36(2) S.I. 1984 No. 447). Where a juvenile is convicted on indictment there is no limit on the fine which the Crown Court may impose.

Where a child or young person is convicted or found guilty of an offence for which a fine may be imposed and the court considers that the case would best be met by imposing a fine (whether with or without any other punishment), it is the duty of the court to order that the fine be paid by the parent or guardian of the child or young person unless the court is satisfied

(i)   that the parent or guardian cannot be found; or
(ii) that it would be unreasonable to make an order for payment, having regard to the circumstances of the case.

(C.Y.P.A. 1933, s. 55(1) as substituted by C.J.A. 1982, s. 26.)

Such an order may be made against a parent or guardian who, having been required to attend, has failed to do so but no order may be made without giving the parent or guardian an opportunity of being heard (C.Y.P.A. 1933, s. 55(2) as substituted by C.J.A. 1982, s. 26).[6]

Where under any "relevant enactment"[7] a person convicted summarily of an offence triable either way is liable to a maximum fine of one amount in the case of a first conviction and of a different amount in the case of a second or subsequent conviction, then, irrespective of whether the conviction is a first, second or subsequent one, he will now be liable to a fine not exceeding the "prescribed sum"[8] unless the offence is one for which some other enactment provides that a larger sum may be imposed on summary conviction (M.C.A., s. 32(2)).

Where under an Act a person convicted of a summary offence[9] is

---

[6] Such orders made against parents or guardians under s. 55 are enforceable under A.J.A., s. 41.
[7] See note 5 above.
[8] See note 3 above.
[9] Other than offences under ss. 33 to 36 of the Sexual Offences Act 1956 or s. 1(2) of the Street Offences Act 1959 (C.J.A. 1982, s. 35(3)).

liable to a fine, or maximum fine, of one amount in the case of a first conviction, and of a different amount in the case of a second or subsequent conviction, he is now liable on summary conviction to a fine, or maximum fine, or an amount not exceeding the greatest amount to which he would have been liable if the conditions for the imposition of the enhanced penalty had been fulfilled (C.J.A., s. 35).[10]

The Criminal Justice Act

Apart from the provisions of the Criminal Justice Act noted above which deal with the new method of determining fines for summary offences and the abolition of enhanced penalties, the Criminal Justice Act also provided for a general increase of fines for summary offences and introduced a standard scale of fines which was also applied to existing enactments. The standard scale created by section 37 of the Criminal Justice Act is set out below; the amounts of fines on the standard scale were increased as from May 1, 1984 by the Secretary of State under powers conferred by section 143 of the Magistrates' Courts Act as amended by section 48(1) of the Criminal Justice Act (see S.I. 1984 No. 447).

level on scale	Old amount of fine	New amount of fine
1	£25	£50
2	£50	£100
3	£200	£400
4	£500	£1,000
5	£1,000	£2,000

Henceforth fines imposed by statute for summary offences will be expressed by reference to one of the levels on the standard scale. Most fines in statutes passed prior to the Criminal Justice Act have been converted to the appropriate level on the standard scale (C.J.A., s. 46).

The Criminal Law Act 1977 increased fines under many enactments. Those fines under statutes passed on or before July 29, 1977 which were not increased by the 1977 Act were in general increased to the level on the standard scale next above the amount of the existing fine. Fines of £400 or more were increased to level 5

[10] C.J.A. 1982, s. 36 deals with the situation where an Act confers power by subordinate instrument to impose an enhanced penalty for second or subsequent convictions for a summary offence, so that such an Act now has effect as if it conferred power to make a person liable to the greatest penalty to which he would otherwise have been liable.

(C.J.A., s. 38). The maximum fines which could be imposed by means of subordinate instrument were similarly increased (C.J.A., s. 40). In exercise of his powers under section 143 of the Magistrates' Courts Act as amended by section 48 of the Criminal Justice Act, the Secretary of State increased the level of many fines and financial penalties as from May 1, 1984 (S.I. 1984 No. 447).[11]

Requirements on imposing a fine

Although a fine may be imposed by the Crown Court, it is the appropriate magistrates' court which will enforce payment.

Where the Crown Court imposes a fine on any person, it may make an order

(a) allowing time for the payment of the amount of the fine;

(b) directing payment of that amount by instalments of such amounts and on such dates respectively as may be specified in the order.

(P.C.C.A. 1973, s. 31(1).)

Where the Crown Court imposes a fine on any person it must make an order fixing a term of imprisonment or of detention under section 9 of the Criminal Justice Act 1982 to be served in default of payment (P.C.C.A., s. 31(2) as substituted by C.J.A. 1982, s 69(1)).[12] The maximum period of imprisonment or detention which the court may fix, varies according to the amount of the fine:

---

[11] While the provisions of the C.J.A. 1982 were designed to simplify matters (and ultimately they may do so) they presently only serve to complicate matters. To determine the present level of a fine on the standard scale in the case of an offence contained in a statute passed before July 29, 1977 (the date of the passing of the C.L.A.) it is necessary to examine the C.L.A., ss. 30 and 31 to see whether the fine was altered by that Act; if it was, that fine was not increased by C.J.A., s. 38(1) and should be placed at the appropriate level on the standard scale. If the C.L.A. did not alter the fine it is necessary to check the level of the fine and whether it has been altered by any enactment after July 29, 1977; if so it is not increased by C.J.A. 1982, s. 38(1); and if not, it is increased by C.J.A. 1982, s. 38(1). The figure arrived at in each case for the fine is then placed at the appropriate level on the standard scale. By S.I. 1984 No. 447 the amount of fines appropriate to each level on the scale have been doubled.

[12] The court may order the term of imprisonment or detention to be served in default of payment, to run consecutively to any term of imprisonment or youth custody or term of detention under C.J.A. 1982, s. 4 or 9, which he is sentenced to serve by the court or which he is serving or otherwise liable to serve (P.C.C.A., s. 31(4) as inserted by C.J.A. 1982, s. 69(1)). For the purpose of fixing default terms each count of an indictment is treated as a separate indictment (*Savaundranayagan and Walker* [1968] 1 W.L.R. 1761, C.A.). Terms of imprisonment imposed in default may be consecutive to each other (*Savundranayagan*).

An amount not exceeding	£50			7 days
An amount exceeding	£50	but not exceeding	£100	14 days
An amount exceeding	£100	but not exceeding	£400	30 days
An amount exceeding	£400	but not exceeding	£1,000	60 days
An amount exceeding	£1,000	but not exceeding	£2,000	90 days
An amount exceeding	£2,000	but not exceeding	£5,000	6 months
An amount exceeding	£5,000	but not exceeding	£10,000	9 months
An amount exceeding	£10,000			12 months

(P.C.C.A., s. 31(3A) as substituted by C.J.A. 1982, s. 69(1) and S.I. 1984 No. 447.)

Where the offender does default on payment of the fine then the period of imprisonment or detention ultimately imposed will be reduced proportionally to the amount of the fine, if any, paid at that time (P.C.C.A., s. 31(3B) as substituted by C.J.A. 1982, s. 69(1)), but the maximum period may not be reduced to less than five days (P.C.C.A., s. 31(3C) as substituted by C.J.A. 1982, s. 69(1)). Where the Crown Court imposes the fine on committal for sentence from the magistrates' court in circumstances in which the powers of the Crown Court are limited to those of the magistrates' court, the Crown Court must impose the term to be served in default of payment of the fine even though a magistrates' court would be prevented from doing so in the first instance (P.C.C.A., s. 31(6)), but the length of term which the Crown Court may fix in such a case must not exceed the length of term which a magistrates' court eventually could have fixed (P.C.C.A., s. 31(7) as substituted by C.J.A., s. 69(1)).

The Crown Court must not commit an offender to prison or order his detention forthwith for non-payment of a fine unless:

(a) in the case of an offence punishable with imprisonment, he appears to the court to have sufficient means to pay the sum forthwith;

(b) it appears to the court that he is unlikely to remain long enough in the United Kingdom to enable payment of the sum to be enforced by other methods; or

(c) on the occasion when the order is made the court sentences him to an immediate custodial sentence for that or another offence, or he is already serving a custodial sentence or detention under section 9 of the Criminal Justice Act 1982.

Where a fine is imposed by the Crown Court, the responsibility for collection, enforcement and remission of that fine is placed upon the magistrates' court which committed the offender for trial, or the magistrates' court specified in an order made by the Crown Court (P.C.C.A., s. 32(1)) and the magistrates' court has the same powers as if the fine was imposed on conviction by it (s. 32(1)). However, a magistrates' court may not remit in whole or in part a fine imposed by the Crown Court without the consent of that Court (s. 32(4)). Where the magistrates' court commits the offender to prison or detention under section 9 of the Criminal Justice Act 1982 in default of payment, it must do so for the period specified by the Crown Court, less any reduction on account of part payment (s. 32(2)).

Magistrates' Court

In fixing the amount of a fine a magistrates' court must take into consideration the means of the offender so far as they appear or are known to the court (M.C.A., s. 35).

Unless the offender is willing to pay immediately on sentence being passed, the court may allow time for payment,[13] or order payment by instalments (M.C.A., s. 75(1)).[14,15]

On convicting an offender a magistrates' court may not issue a warrant of commitment for default in paying the fine unless

(a) the offence is punishable with imprisonment and the offender appears to the court to have sufficient means to pay the sum forthwith;

(b) it appears to the court that he is unlikely to remain long enough in the United Kingdom to enable payment of the sum to be enforced by other methods; or

(c) he is at the same time sentenced to an immediate custodial sentence for that or another offence or he is already serving a custodial sentence or detention under section 9 of the Criminal Justice Act.

(M.C.A., s. 82(1) as amended by C.J.A. 1982, s. 77 and Sched. 14.)

Where the court has power to issue a warrant of commitment it may, if expedient to do so, fix a term of imprisonment or detention under section 9 of the Criminal Justice Act 1982 and postpone the issue of the warrant until such time and on such conditions, if any, as the court thinks just (M.C.A., s. 77(2)). Except where it has power to issue a warrant of commitment forthwith but postpones doing so under section 77(2) of the Magistrates' Courts Act, a magistrates' court may not, in advance of the issue of a warrant of commitment,

---

[13] Where the court has allowed time for payment, the court may, on application by or on behalf of the person liable to make payment, allow further time or order payment by instalments (s. 75(2)).

[14] Where the court orders payment by instalments, the court, on an application made by the person liable to pay that sum, has power to vary that order by varying the number of instalments payable, the amount of any instalment payable, and the date on which any instalment becomes payable (M.C.A., s. 85A as inserted by C.J.A. 1982, s. 51(1)).

[15] Where a court has ordered payment by instalments and default is made in the payment of any one instalment, proceedings may be taken as if the default had been made in the payment of all the instalments then unpaid (M.C.A., s. 75(3)).

fix a term of imprisonment which is to be served by an offender in the event of default in paying the fine (M.C.A., s. 82(2)). If on convicting the offender a magistrates' court issues a warrant of commitment for a default in paying the fine or, having power to do so, fixes a term of imprisonment, the reason for the court's action must be entered in the register or any separate record kept for the purpose of recording particulars of fine enforcement (M.C.R., r. 65, S.I. 1981 No. 552).

Where a magistrates' court is required to enforce payment of a fine imposed by a Crown Court, or where the court allows time for payment of a fine imposed following a summary conviction or directs that the sum be paid by instalments, or where the offender is absent when a fine is imposed following a summary conviction, the clerk of the court must serve on the offender notice in writing stating the amount of the fine, the date on which payment is required, and the place or places and the time at which payment may be made, and, if payment by instalments is directed, particulars of the instalments (M.C.R., r. 46(1)).[16] No warrant of distress or commitment may be issued until after service of the notice has been effected (r. 46(1)).

Where a fine is imposed on an offender by a magistrates' court and he is not committed to prison forthwith in default of payment an order may be made placing him under supervision of a person appointed by the court (M.C.A., s. 88(1)), usually a probation officer. The order will remain in force so long as any part of the sum remains unpaid, unless it ceases to have effect[17] or is discharged by further order of the court (s. 88(2)). Where following a summary conviction a fine has been imposed on a person under 21 years old and the court does not commit him to detention under section 9 of the Criminal Justice Act 1982 forthwith in default of payment, the court subsequently may not commit him to such detention in default of payment of the sum, or for want of sufficient distress to satisfy the sum, unless he has been placed under supervision in respect of the sum or the court is satisfied that it is undesirable or impracticable to place him under supervision (s. 88(4) as amended by C.J.A. 1982, s. 77 and Sched. 14). Where a court is so satisfied and it does commit an offender to such detention it must state the grounds for its satisfaction in the warrant of commitment.

In any case where a money payment supervision order is in force

---

[16] Service of the notice is effected by delivering it to him or by sending it to him by post in a letter addressed to him at his last known or usual place of abode (M.C.R., r. 46(2)).

[17] This occurs where a transfer of fine order under M.C.A., s. 89 is made, transferring enforcement of the fine to another petty sessions area in which the offender is then residing (M.C.A., s. 88(3)).

the court cannot commit for default until it has taken such steps as
are reasonably practicable to obtain from the supervisor a report
(oral or written) on his conduct and means (M.C.A., s. 88(6)).[18]

COMBINING A FINE WITH OTHER MEASURES

Fines are frequently provided either as an alternative to or
additional to a sentence of imprisonment for the same offence (see
pp. 59–60, above). A court which imposes a suspended sentence of
imprisonment may also impose a fine, provided that the amount is
within the offender's means (*King* (1970) 54 Cr.App.R. 362). A
compensation order (P.C.C.A., s. 35(1)) restitution order (T.A.,
s. 28(1) as substituted by C.J.A. 1972, Sched. 5), criminal bankruptcy order (P.C.C.A., s. 39(1)), an order depriving the offender of
property used for the purposes of crime (P.C.C.A., s. 43(1)) or order
of disqualification where a vehicle was used for the purposes of
crime (P.C.C.A., s. 44(2)) may all be combined with a fine. A fine
may not be combined with a probation order (*Parry* [1951] K.B.
590)[19], or an absolute or conditional discharge (*McClelland* (1951)
35 Cr.App.R. 22 and P.C.C.A., s. 7(1)), or a community service
order (P.C.C.A., s. 14(1) and *Carnwell* (1979) 68 Cr.App.R. 58).[20]

WHEN A FINE IS APPROPRIATE

A fine is the most common of all punishments imposed by the
courts.

"Fines are generally used in cases where a deterrent or punitive
sentence is necessary, but either the inherent gravity of the
offence is insufficient to justify a sentence of imprisonment, or
the presence of mitigating factors justifies the sentencer in
avoiding a sentence of imprisonment."[21]

In giving consideration to the appropriate sentence, the first
question for a court to answer is whether a custodial sentence is
appropriate (*Lewis* [1965] Crim.L.R. 121). It is wrong in principle to

[18] Further consideration of the process of enforcement of fines is outside the scope of
a work concerned with sentencing, and the reader is recommended to consult a
work dealing with criminal procedure.
[19] Note, a fine not exceeding £400 may be imposed for failing to comply with the
requirements of the order (P.C.C.A., s. 6(6)(*a*) as amended by C.J.A. 1982, s. 39
and Sched. 4 and S.I. 1984 No. 447). In addition a court may impose a fine for one
offence when making a probation order, on the same occasion, for another
(*Bainbridge* (1979) 1 Cr.App.R.(S.) 36).
[20] Note, a fine not exceeding £400 may be imposed for failure to comply with the
requirements of a community service order (P.C.C.A., s. 16(3) and (5), as amended
by C.J.A. 1982, s. 39 and Sched. 4 and S.I. 1984 No. 447).
[21] Thomas, *Principles of Sentencing* (2nd ed., 1979), p. 318.

impose a fine on a person of substantial means for an offence for which a person of lesser means would be imprisoned (*Markwick* (1953) 37 Cr.App.R. 125; *Lewis*), as "one has to take great care that there should be no suggestion that there is one law for the rich and one for the poor."[22] Equally an offender should not be imprisoned because he does not have the means to pay a fine (*Reeves* (1972) 56 Cr.App.R. 366). In such a case the appropriate sentence may be a conditional discharge (*Whitehead* (1979) 1 Cr.App.R.(S.) 187) and not a suspended sentence (*Ball* [1982] Crim.L.R. 131). However, where a conditional discharge is inappropriate (*e.g.* where the offender is in breach of an earlier discharge) the court may impose a small fine with a long period in which to pay (*Ball*, where a fine of £25 with six months to pay was imposed). Where an offence which would normally attract a fine is committed by an offender of unusual affluence, it is wrong in principle to impose, in addition, a suspended sentence to bring home to him the gravity of the matter (*Hanbury* (1979) 1 Cr.App.R.(S.) 243).

Once the sentencer has decided not to impose a custodial sentence, the next issue for the court to determine is that of the quantum of the fine appropriate to the offence in question and the offender. Thus the sentencer must take into consideration both the gravity of the offence (see *Beynon* (1972) 57 Cr.App.R. 259)[23] and the means of the offender (see Commentary to *Ashmore* [1974] Crim.L.R. 375 and *Thompson* [1974] Crim.L.R. 720). In *Fairbairn* [1981] Crim.L.R. 190, the Court of Appeal made it clear that the amount of a fine should be determined in relation to the gravity of the offence and then the offender's means should be considered before fixing the fine to ensure that he will be able to pay it. Where the offender is a person of means the judge should not increase the fine above what is appropriate to the gravity of the offence although he should ensure that the fine has the effect of punishing the offender (*Messana* [1981] Crim.L.R. 506). Save in exceptional circumstances, fines should be capable of being paid within 12 months (*Knight* (1980) 2 Cr.App.R.(S.) 82; *Nunn* [1983] Crim.L.R. 690). It is incorrect to fix the level of the fine before considering the offender's means and then order payment of the sum by instalments over as long a period as may be necessary (*Rizvi* (1979) 1 Cr.App.R.(S.) 307). As an offender should not be fined a sum which he has no means of paying, it is likewise wrong to impose a fine on the basis tha someone else will pay it (*Baxter* [1974] Crim.L.R. 611; *Curtis* (1984) 6 Cr.App.R.(S.) 300.

[22] *Per* Lord Goddard C.J. in *Markwick* (1953) 37 Cr.App.R. 125 at p. 126.
[23] In this case a fine of £250 for possession of 22 pills containing pemoline, a proscribed drug, was reduced to £25 as the fine went far beyond what was appropriate for that particular offence.

In the Crown Court a fine may be imposed in addition to any other sentence which the court imposes. The general principle which emerges from the cases is that such a course may be followed where the aim is that of depriving the offender of benefits received by him from his crime (see *Savundra* (1968) 52 Cr.App.R. 637; *Lott-Carter* (1978) 67 Cr.App.R. 404; *Benmore* (1983) 5 Cr.App.R.(S.) 468. This approach should be followed only in circumstances where the court has reason to believe that a substantial amount of stolen property still remains outstanding and may be available for the use of the offender when he has completed his sentence. (see *Chatt* (1984) 6 Cr.App.R.(S.) 75; *Michel, Berry and Eade* [1985] Crim.L.R. 162). However, the court may not impose a fine as a means of depriving an offender of money in his possession believed to be the proceeds of offences which have not been charged or proved (*Johnson* [1984] Crim.L.R. 691). (Where it is clear that the offender has no means from which the fine can be paid no fine should be imposed but the sentence should be whatever is appropriate to the gravity of the offence (*Maund* (1980) 2 Cr.App.R.(S.) 289).) In fixing the term of imprisonment in such cases the practice appears to be to discount that term by a period equal to that which is fixed in default of payment of the fine (see *Savundra* and *Benmore*). This is done because of the difficulty of determining the means of the offender in such cases, whereas the amount of money involved in the offences can be determined. If he fails to pay the fine and is committed to prison in default he will not then serve a longer total sentence than would have been passed without the fine. The drawback of this approach, however, is that an offender with means is given the opportunity of buying his way out of part of his sentence.[24] Where the sentencer does impose a substantial fine in conjunction with a sentence of imprisonment, with a consecutive term in default, the combined total of the immediate sentence and the default term must not amount to an excessive sentence for the offence if that term had been imposed in the first place (see *Michel, Berry and Eade*).

For combining a suspended sentence and a fine see pp. 113–114, below.

APPEAL

The normal rights of appeal apply.

Where a parent or guardian has been ordered to pay a fine under

---

[24] This approach is criticised in the commentary to *Benmore* [1984] Crim.L.R. 243 at pp. 244–245.

section 55 of the Children and Young Persons Act 1933 he has the same rights of appeal against sentence as if he had been convicted of the offence and had the fine imposed on him (C.Y.P.A. 1933, s. 55(3) and (4) as substituted by C.J.A. 1982, s. 26).

Enforcement of a fine cannot commence until the determination of the appeal, or in the case of an appeal from a magistrates' court, where notice to abandon the appeal has been duly given by the appellant (M.C.A., s. 109(1)).

SUPERVISION ORDERS

DESCRIPTION

A supervision order has some of the characteristics of a probation order except that it is available only for children and young persons. A supervision order may be made in juvenile criminal proceedings or in care proceedings. The order will place the juvenile under the supervision of a local authority designated by the order or a probation officer. This section will only deal with criminal proceedings.

The Supervisor

A court may only designate a local authority as the supervisor either where it agrees so to act or where it appears to the court that the juvenile resides or will reside in the area of the authority (C.Y.P.A. 1969, s. 13(1)). In the case of a child up to the age of 13, a probation officer may be named as the supervisor only where the local authority so request and the officer is supervising or has supervised another member of the child's household on probation (C.Y.P.A. 1969, s. 13(2)). Where the local authority is the supervisor it will discharge its duty through the agency of social workers.

While a supervision order is in force it is the duty of the supervisor to advise, assist and befriend the supervised person (C.Y.P.A. 1969, s. 14)).

THE LAW

A supervision order may be made where a child or a young person is found guilty of any offence (C.Y.P.A. 1969, s. 7(7) and s. 34(1)(c) and S.I. 1970 No. 1882, para. 4(1) and (2)). A supervision order may be made by a juvenile court or the Crown Court but not by an adult magistrates' court (C.Y.P.A. 1969, s. 7(8)). Unless it has been discharged previously, a supervision order will cease to have effect on the expiration of three years from the date on which it was made or such shorter period as may be specified in the order (C.Y.P.A. 1969, s. 17(a)).

Section 12 of the Children and Young Persons Act 1969 (as amended by C.L.A. 1977 and C.J.A. 1982) empowers the court to include requirements in a supervision order:

(a) Residence

The supervisee may be required to reside with an individual named in the order who agrees to this requirement (s. 12(1)).

(b) Mental treatment

Where, on the evidence of a duly qualified medical practitioner, a court proposing to make a supervision order is satisfied that the mental condition of the juvenile is such as requires and may be susceptible to treatment but is not such as to warrant making a hospital order, it may include in the order a requirement that the supervisee shall submit to treatment for his mental condition for a period specified in the order (s. 12(4)). Where the juvenile is 14 or over such a requirement may not be included unless he consents to its inclusion (s. 12(5)(*b*)). The court may require the supervisee to submit to any of the following forms of treatment:

(a) treatment by or under the direction of a registered medical practitioner;

(b) treatment as an out-patient at a specified place; or

(c) treatment as a resident patient in a hospital or mental nursing home provided under the Mental Health Act not being a "special" hospital under that Act.

(s. 12(4).)

A requirement for treatment of a mental condition may not be included in a supervision order unless the court is satisfied that arrangements have been or can be made for the treatment in question and, in the case of residential treatment, for the reception of the patient (s. 12(5)(*a*)). A requirement for the treatment of a mental condition ceases automatically on the supervisee attaining the age of 18 (s. 12(5)).

Where the medical practitioner treating or directing the treatment of the supervisee is unwilling to continue to do so or is of opinion:

(a) that the period of treatment should be extended;

(b) that different treatment is appropriate;

(c) that the supervisee is not susceptible to treatment;

(d) that no further treatment is required;

he should make a written report to the supervisor (s. 15(5)). The supervisor must refer such a report to the juvenile court which may cancel or vary the order (s. 15(5)).

(c) Intermediate treatment

Intermediate treatment had its origins in the Government White Paper, *Children in Trouble* (1968), which said:

"Existing forms of treatment available to the juvenile courts distinguish sharply between those which involve complete removal from home and those which do not. The juvenile courts have very difficult decisions to make in judging whether circumstances require the drastic step of taking a child away from his parents and his home. The view has often been expressed that some form or forms of intermediate treatment should be available to the courts, allowing the child to remain in his own home but bringing him also into contact with a different environment. . . . A new legal and administrative framework will therefore be established for the development of a variety of forms of intermediate treatment for children and young persons placed under supervision by the juvenile courts. One object is to make possible the use for this purpose of facilities not provided expressly for those who have been before the courts."

Effect was given to these proposals in section 12 of the Children and Young Persons Act 1969. Schemes of intermediate treatment are prepared by local authorities who have a statutory duty to provide such schemes (s. 19(1)). In preparing such a scheme they must consult with the relevant probation committees and details of the scheme must be sent to the clerk to the justices of the appropriate petty sessions areas. The arrangements to be provided must either be approved by the Secretary of State or be of a kind approved by him (s. 19(11)). A supervision order may not include requirements for intermediate treatment unless the court making it is satisfied that a scheme is in force for the area where the supervisee resides or will reside (s. 19(12)).

There are two forms of intermediate treatment requirements which may be included in a supervision order:

(i) *Discretionary intermediate treatment*

Under section 12(2) the court may include a requirement that the supervisee comply with directions given to him by his supervisor. The supervisor in his discretion will determine the intermediate treatment, if any, suitable to the supervisee and will give directions to the supervisee accordingly. The supervisor is empowered to direct the supervisee to do all or any of the following things:

    (a) to live at a specified place(s) for a specified period(s).

    (b) to report to a specified person at a specified place on specified days;

    (c) to participate in specified activities on specified days.

    (s. 12(2).)

Typical directions might require the supervisee to reside in a community home, attend a holiday camp, participate in a youth group or undergo a useful course of training. The supervisee may be required to comply with the directions given by the supervisor for up to a maximum of 90 days (s. 12(3)).

(ii) *Court specified intermediate treatment*

Prior to the Criminal Justice Act 1982 a court only had power to include in a supervision order a discretionary intermediate treatment requirement. The Government's White Paper on Young Offenders (Cmnd. 8045, 1980) suggests (para. 49) that courts were reluctant to make supervision orders in serious or difficult cases because they had no control over the directions for intermediate treatment ultimately made by the supervisor. Accordingly, the Criminal Justice Act 1982 inserted new provisions into section 12 of the Children and Young Persons Act which empower the court to give the directions regarding intermediate treatment which the supervisor is empowered to give in the case of discretionary intermediate treatment (s. 12(3C)(*a*). The supervisee may be required to comply with the directions given by the court for up to a maximum of 90 days (s. 12(3E)). Before including such directions in a supervision order, the court must:

(a) consult the supervisor as to the offender's circumstances and be satisfied, in light of his report, that it is feasible to secure the offender's compliance with the proposed requirements;

(b) consider the requirements necessary to secure the good conduct of the offender or to prevent a repetition by him of the same offence or the commission of other offences; and

(c) obtain the consent of the offender or, if he is under 14, his parent or guardian to the inclusion of the requirements in the order.
(s. 12(3F).)

If the requirement the court intends to include would involve the co-operation of someone other than the supervisor, that person's consent must be obtained (s. 12(3G)). Requirements that the supervisee reside with a specified individual (as opposed to residing at a specified place), or submit to treatment for a mental condition may not be included in an order by virtue of section 12(3C), although they may be included by virtue of section 12(1) and section 12(4) respectively (s. 12(3G)). Such a requirement may not be combined with an ordinary intermediate treatment requirement.

(d) Night restriction order

This, in effect, is a curfew imposed on the supervisee in the hope that it may reduce the risk of re-offending.[1] Where the supervisee is

---

[1] This provision ran into considerable opposition from the probation service, the local authority associations and knowledgable bodies such as NACRO who thought it was potentially unworkable.

subject to a night restriction order he must remain for specified periods between 6 p.m. and 6 a.m. at a place, or one of several places, specified in the order (s. 12(3C)(*b*)). The place, or one of the places prescribed, must be the place where the supervisee lives (s. 12(3H)). During the hours of curfew the supervisee may leave the place specified only if he is accompanied by his parent or guardian, his supervisor or some other person specified in the order (s. 12(3M)). A night restriction order must not:

   (a)   require the supervisee to remain at a place for longer than 10 hours on any one night (s. 12(3J));
   (b)   be imposed in respect of more than 30 days in all[2] (s. 12(3L));
   (c)   be imposed in respect of any day more than three months after the date when the supervision order was made (s. 12(3K)).

Before imposing a night restriction order the court must comply with the provisions of section 12(3F) and (3G) above. Where a court imposes both intermediate treatment requirements under section 12(3C)(*a*) and a night restriction requirement under section 12(3C)(*b*) the total number of days affected by the requirements must not exceed 90. A night restriction requirement cannot be combined with an ordinary intermediate treatment requirement.

(e) Negative Requirements

The Criminal Justice Act also empowers courts to impose negative requirements on a supervisee under which he is required to refrain from participating in activities specified in the order (s. 12(3C)(*c*)). Such a requirement may operate during the whole period the supervision order is in force or on a specified day or days within that period (s. 12(3C)(*c*)). Before imposing a negative requirement the court must comply with the provisions of section 12(3F) and (3G) above.

TERMINATION OF A SUPERVISION ORDER

A supervision order shall, unless it has previously been discharged, cease to have effect on the expiration of three years from the date it was made or such shorter period as may be specified in the order, unless it was made on the occasion of the discharge of a care order in which case it may terminate on the offender's eighteenth birthday if this occurs first (s. 17).

---

[2] For these purposes a night restriction order imposed in respect of a period of time beginning in the evening and ending in the morning is treated as imposed only in respect of the day upon which the period begins (s. 12(3N)).

VARIATION AND DISCHARGE

During the currency of a supervision order in respect of a person who has not attained the age of 18,[3] a juvenile court, on the application of the supervisor or supervisee, may make an order discharging or varying the supervision order if it appears to the court to be appropriate.[4] The court may vary the supervision order either by cancelling any requirement included in it (s. 15(1)(*a*)), or inserting in it (either in addition to or in substitution for any of its provisions) any provision which could have been included in the order if the court had then had power to make it and were exercising the power, and on discharging the supervision order the court may make a care order in respect of the supervisee.[5] A juvenile court, however, may not exercise its powers under section 15 to make a care order or an order discharging a supervision order or inserting in it an authorised requirement or cancelling such a requirement except in a case where the court is satisfied that the supervisee either is unlikely to receive the care or control he needs unless the court makes the order or is likely to receive it notwithstanding the order (s. 16(6)(*a*)).

If while a supervision order in respect of a young offender who has attained the age of 18 is in force (*i.e.* an order to which s. 12(3A) applies), it is proved to the satisfaction of a juvenile court, on the application of the supervisor, that the supervisee has failed to comply with any requirement included in the order, the court may, whether or not it also makes an order varying or discharging the order, impose a fine of up to £100 or make an attendance centre order in respect of him (s. 15(2A); increased by S.I. 1984 No. 447).

While a supervision order is in force in respect of a supervisee who has attained the age of 18, a magistrates' court other than a

---

[3] If the supervisee is 17 and the order was made in criminal proceedings and it appears to the court appropriate to do so, it may proceed as if the application were in pursuance of s. 15(3) or s. 15(3), (4) and those provisions are to be adapted accordingly (s. 15(2))—(see text above).

[4] Where an application for discharge of a supervision order is dismissed, no further application for its discharge may be made under s. 15 by any person during the period of three months beginning with the date of the dismissal except with the consent of a court having jurisdiction to entertain such an application (s. 16(9)).

[5] The powers of variation conferred by s. 15(1) do not include power to insert in the supervision order, after the expiration of three months from the date when the order was originally made, a requirement in pursuance of s. 12(4), unless it is in substitution for such a requirement already included in the order (s. 15(1)). Nor do such powers include power to insert in the supervision order a requirement in pursuance of s. 12(3C)(*b*) in respect of any day which falls outside the period of three months beginning with the date when the order was originally made (s. 15(1)).

juvenile court, on the application of the supervisor or supervisee, may make an order discharging or varying the order if it appears appropriate (s. 15(3)). The court may vary the order by:

(a) inserting in it a provision specifying the duration of the order or altering or cancelling such a provision already included in it; or

(b) substituting for the provision of the order by which the supervisor is designated or by virtue of which he is selected such other provisions in that behalf as could have been included in the order if the court had then had power to make it and were exercising the power; or

(c) substituting for the name of an area included in the order the name of any other area of a local authority or petty sessions area, as the case may be, in which it appears to the court that the supervised person resides or will reside; or

(d) cancelling any provision included in the order for the purpose of facilitating the supervisor's functions or inserting in it any new provision for that purpose; or

(e) cancelling any requirement included in the order in pursuance of section 12(1) or (2).

If on the application of the supervisor it is proved to the satisfaction of a magistrates' court other than a juvenile court, that a supervisee who has attained the age of 18 has failed to comply with any requirement included in the order, the court may:

(a) whether or not it also makes an order discharging or varying the supervision order, order him to pay a fine not exceeding £100 or make an attendance centre order;

(b) if it also discharges the supervision order, make an order imposing on him any punishment which it could have imposed on him if it had then had power to try him for the offence in consequence of which the supervision order was made and had convicted him in the exercise of that power.

(s. 15(4).)

In a case where the offence in question is of a kind which the court has no power to try or has no power to try without appropriate consents, the punishment imposed by virtue of (b) above may not exceed that which any court having power to try such an offence could have imposed in respect of it and shall not in any event exceed imprisonment for a term of six months and a fine of £2,000 (s. 15(4) as increased by S.I. 1984 No. 447).

Where the supervised person has attained the age of 14, then except with his consent a court may not make an order varying a supervision order and containing provisions which insert in the supervision order a requirement as to treatment of the supervisee's mental condition under s. 12(4) or which alter such a requirement already included in the supervision order otherwise than by removing it or reducing its duration (s. 16(7)).

APPEAL

The normal rights of appeal apply.

CARE ORDERS

DESCRIPTION

A care order is an order committing a child or young person to the care of a local authority. The order transfers to the local authority the rights and duties which the parents of the subject of the order would otherwise have. A care order may be made in care proceedings, in criminal proceedings and on the discharge of a supervision order. This section will be concerned only with criminal proceedings.

THE LAW

The Crown Court or juvenile court may make a care order when dealing with a child or young person under the age of 17 found guilty of any offence which is punishable in the case of an adult with imprisonment (C.Y.P.A. 1969, s. 7(7)(a); S.I. 1970 No. 1882). A court may not make a care order unless it is of opinion:

  (a) that a care order is appropriate because of the seriousness of the offence;

  (b) that the child or young person is in need of care or control which he is unlikely to receive unless the court makes a care order.

(s. 7(7A).)

In the case of a child or young person who is not legally represented in court, a court may not make a care order unless either:

  (a) he applies for legal aid and the application was refused on the ground that it did not appear that his means were such that he required assistance; or

  (b) having been informed of his right to apply for legal aid and had the opportunity to do so, he refused or failed to apply.[1]

(s. 7A(1).)

An offender will be committed to the care of the local authority in whose area it appears to the court making the order that he resides

---

[1] A person is to be treated as legally represented in a court only if he has the assistance of counsel or a solicitor to represent him in the proceedings in that court at some time after he is found guilty and before a care order is made and "legal aid" means legal aid for the purposes of proceedings in that court, whether the whole proceedings or the proceedings on or in relation to the making of the care order (s. 7A(2)).

or, if it does not appear to the court that he resides in the area of a local authority, any local authority in whose area it appears to the court that any offence was committed or any circumstances arose in consequence of which the order is made (s. 20(2)(a)).[2]

A care order ceases to have effect (a) in the case of a young person who was 16 when the order was originally made, when he attains the age of 19 and (b) in any other case when he attains the age of 18 (s. 20(3)). Where a person subject to a care order is accommodated in a community home or a home provided by the Secretary of State and the order would cease to have effect by virtue of him attaining the age of 18, the local authority may apply to a juvenile court to extend the order until he attains the age of 19 where it is in the public interest or his interest to continue in such accommodation by reason of his mental condition or behaviour (s. 21(1)).

It is the duty of a local authority to whose care a child has been committed by a care order to receive the child into their care and, notwithstanding any claim by his parent or guardian, to keep him in their care while the order or warrant is in force (Child Care Act 1980, s. 10(1)). The local authority has the same powers and duties with respect to a person in their care by virtue of a care order as his parent or guardian would have apart from the order (s. 10(2)). In exercising their powers and carrying out their duties in relation to children in their care a local authority must give first consideration to the need to safeguard and promote the welfare of the child throughout his childhood and shall as far as practicable ascertain the wishes and feelings of the child regarding the decision and give due consideration to them, having regard to his age and understanding (s. 18(1)). Where there is a need to protect the public the local authority may exercise its powers in relation to the child to achieve this result even if the action proposed is not guaranteed to promote the welfare of the child (s. 18(3)).

In exercising their powers a local authority may place a child in a foster home, a community home, a voluntary home or allow him to remain under the charge and control of his parent or guardian or place him under the charge and control of a relative or friend (s. 21).

Charge and control of offenders
Once a care order has been made it is the local authority which

[2] A court may make an interim order lasting up to 28 days (s. 20(1)). In such a case the local authority to whose care a person is committed will be such one of the local authorites mentioned in paragraph (a) as the court or justice making the order thinks fit (whether or not the person in question appears to reside in their area) (s. 20(2)(b)).

decides on what should happen to the juvenile. Prior to the Criminal Justice Act 1982, there was some disquiet over cases where juveniles placed into care following a finding of guilty of an offence were allowed to remain at home only to offend again. This was a particular problem in the case of children under 14 where no custodial penalties are available; in such cases there was no guarantee that, if another care order was imposed, the local authority would not do the same again. Section 22 of the Criminal Justice Act 1982 inserts a new section 20A into the Children and Young Persons Act 1969 to meet this situation.

Where a person who is already subject to a care order as a result of committing an offence is convicted of an imprisonable offence, the court may add to the care order a "residential condition" restricting the power of the local authority in whose care he has been placed to allow him to be under the charge and control of a parent, guardian, relative or friend (s. 20A(1)). Such a condition may, however, be made subject to an exception in favour of a named parent, guardian, relative, or friend; otherwise the juvenile will have to be accommodated in a community home, voluntary home or boarded out with foster parents. A residential condition may be imposed for up to six months. At the end of the prescribed period the local authority will regain its full discretionary powers under the care order. If a person subject to a residential condition is found guilty of an imprisonable offence during its currency the court may replace it with a fresh residential condition (s. 20A(2)). There is no provision, however, for consecutive residential conditions to be imposed where a person is convicted of several imprisonable offences on the one occasion.

Several conditions must be satisfied before a residential condition may be added to a care order:

(a) the care order must have been made because the offender had committed an imprisonable offence (s. 20A(1));

(b) the subsequent offence must be punishable with imprisonment in the case of a person over 21 (s. 20A(1));

(c) that the court, having obtained and considered information about the circumstances, is of opinion that it is appropriate to impose a residential condition and that no other method of dealing with the juvenile is appropriate (s. 20A(3));

(d) the offender, if not legally represented, either applied for legal aid and had the application refused on the ground that it did not appear that his means were such that he required assistance, or having been informed of his right to apply for legal aid and having the opportunity to do so, he refused or failed to apply (s. 20A(4));

(e) before adding a residential condition the court must explain

to the offender the purpose and effect of the condition
(s. 20A(5)).

At any time during the currency of a residential condition the
juvenile, his parent or guardian acting on his behalf, or the local
authority in whose care he is may apply to a juvenile court for the
revocation or variation of the condition (s. 20A(6)).

Where a residential condition is added to a care order by a
magistrates' court the local authority (s. 7(7)) or the subject of the
order (M.C.A., s. 108) may appeal to the Crown Court. An
aggrieved parent or guardian may apply to the High Court for
judicial review of such a condition. Where the Crown Court
imposes such a condition the local authority has no right of appeal
but the offender may apply for leave to appeal to the Court of
Appeal.

Restriction on placing children in care in secure accommodation

Prior to the Criminal Justice Act 1982 a local authority had
complete discretion as to whether or not to send a child to a
community home, and if so, to what home it sent him. Homes
varied greatly as to the degree of control to which the residents were
subjected; a minority of homes provided secure accommodation
"for the purpose of restricting liberty." Section 25 of the Criminal
Justice Act inserted a new section 21A into the Child Care Act 1980
designed to restrict a local authority's discretion. This section in
turn has been substituted by a new section 21A by section 9 of and
Schedule 2 to Health and Social Services Adjudication Act 1983.
This new section provides that the safeguards contained in the
original section can be extended by means of regulation, to cover all
children in the charge of local authorities who might be placed in
secure accommodation. A child may not be kept in secure
accommodation unless either:

(a) he has a history of absconding and is likely to abscond from
     any other description of accommodation, and if he absconds,
     it is likely that his physical, mental or moral welfare will be
     at risk; or

(b) that if he is kept in any other description of accommodation
     he is likely to injure himself or other persons.

(s. 21A(1).)

The maximum period which a child in the care of a local
authority may be kept in secure accommodation without the
authority of a juvenile court is 72 hours, whether consecutively or
72 hours in aggregate in any period of 28 consecutive days
(s. 21A(2)(a) and Children and Young Persons Secure Accommodation Regulations 1983 (S.I. 1983 No. 652), reg. 7). A juvenile court
may authorise a child to be kept in secure accommodation for up to

three months (reg. 8). On subsequent occasions a juvenile court may authorise his containment in secure accommodation for up to six months (reg. 9).

It is the duty of a juvenile court before which a child is brought to determine whether any relevant criteria for keeping him in secure accommodation are satisfied in his case (s. 21A(3)). If it determines that any such criteria are satisfied it must make an order authorising the child to be kept in secure accommodation specifying the maximum period for which the order may last (s. 21(3)). A juvenile court may not exercise its powers under section 21A in respect of a child who is not legally represented unless either he applied for legal aid and his application was refused on the ground that it did not appear his means were such that he required assistance, or having been informed of his right to apply for legal aid and had the opportunity to do so, he refused or failed to apply (s. 21A(6)). The decision of a juvenile court may be appealed to the Crown Court.

VARIATION AND DISCHARGE OF CARE ORDERS

If it appears appropriate to a juvenile court, on the application of a local authority to whose care a person is committed by a care order or on the application of that person, it may discharge the order and on doing so it may make a supervision order in respect of him unless it was an interim order or he has attained the age of 18 (s. 21(2)). In the case of a person who has not attained the age of 18 who appears to the court to be in need of care or control, the court may not make a supervision order unless it is satisfied that, whether through the making of such an order or otherwise, he will receive that care and control (s. 21(2A)). Where an application is dismissed, then in the case of an interim order no further application for its discharge may be made except with the consent of a juvenile court, and in any other case no further application for discharge may be made by any person during the period of three months beginning with the date of dismissal except with a juvenile court's consent (s. 21(3)).

The subject of a care order may appeal to the Crown Court against the dismissal of an application for discharge of the order or against a supervision order made on the discharge of the care order (s. 21(4)).

APPEAL

Appeal lies in the normal way.

PART II
CUSTODIAL MEASURES

INTRODUCTION

Compulsory deprivation of liberty is a sanction available to courts for all classes and ages of offenders. Except in a very few cases it is a discretionary measure and the trend in penal policy has been to reduce reliance on imprisonment so far as is consistent with public safety. There are many drawbacks with imprisonment, particularly from the viewpoint of ultimately rehabilitating prisoners because of the rupture of those imprisoned with their communities. More and more the justification for imprisonment is punishment, deterrence and public interest, rather than any belief that it will help the individual subjected to it. In an important recent judgment, the Court of Appeal declared as policy for all sentencers that imprisonment should be used sparingly, and in the case of the non-violent petty offender, a term of imprisonment, if considered necessary, should be as short as possible (*Bibi* [1980] 1 W.L.R. 1193).

There are, however, different considerations with younger offenders, particularly since the Criminal Justice Act 1982 came into operation. For sentencing purposes the law distinguishes offenders by age into the following categories; (i) adult of 21 years of age or over, (ii) young offender of 17 to 21, (iii) children and young persons. The custodial measures available to the courts are limited according to the category into which the offender falls. In addition, courts of summary jurisdiction are limited in the length of the sentence they may impose.

In the Home Office publication, *The Sentence of the Court,* the aims and efficacy of custodial sentences were considered:

> "The aims of the courts in imposing custodial sentences may include the expression of public condemnation of a particular act or course of conduct; the protection of the public by the removal of a dangerous or persistent offender from among them; the prevention of future offences on the part of the convicted offender himself or other potential offenders, through the deterrent effect of being held in custody; and the reformation or improvement of the offender through pro-grammes of training or treatment.... [O]ne point that is particularly relevant ... is the growing realization in recent years that neither the experience of institution staff, nor the findings of research, nor the reaction of offenders themselves, justifies a general assumption that a custodial sentence of a certain length will enable the offender to receive effective

reformative training or treatment. This is not to say that custodial sentences can do no good, nor that the staff of penal establishments are less concerned than in the past to help those in their care. The point is that there is no evidence that the prison system does or can exert such a positive reformative influence as to justify the imposition of a longer custodial sentence than would otherwise be appropriate to the offence, or the imposition of a custodial sentence where other sentencing objectives do not require custody." (Para. 98 at pp. 29–30.)

It has been a consistent policy to seek to reduce the prison population, particularly by the introduction of new non-custodial measures and exhortations by the Lord Chancellor, Lord Chief Justice and others emphasising that shorter rather than longer sentences may prove most effective where a custodial sentence is to be imposed. In common with many other European countries the concept of prison as the sanction of last resort is increasingly being recognised as the correct sentencing policy.

IMPRISONMENT

DESCRIPTION

Imprisonment is the only custodial sentence available for mentally normal offenders of or over 21 years of age. There are five types of prison sentence which may be imposed; the ordinary fixed-term sentence of immediate imprisonment, life imprisonment the extended sentence, the suspended sentence and the partly suspended sentence.

THE LAW

Who may be imprisoned

Imprisonment is a sanction for adult offenders of 21 years of age or more. Section 1(1) of the Criminal Justice Act 1982 provides that no court may pass a sentence of imprisonment on a person under 21 years of age or commit such a person to prison for any reason.[1] The relevant time for consideration of the offender's age is when sentence is passed. However, where sentence is deferred in respect of an offender who is under the age of 21 and who attains that age during the period of deferment, the sentencing court would appear to be unable to sentence him to imprisonment as the power it has is "to deal with him in any way in which the court which deferred passing sentence could have dealt with him." (P.C.C.A., s. 1(8) as substituted by C.J.A. 1982, s. 63(d)).

Where an offender is over 21 years of age certain conditions must be satisfied before a sentence of imprisonment may be passed in respect of him. With the exception of offences the sentence for which is fixed by law (P.C.C.A., s. 20(4)), a court may not pass a sentence of imprisonment on a person who has not previously been sentenced to imprisonment unless the court is of opinion that no other method of dealing with him is appropriate (P.C.C.A., s. 20(1)). For this purpose a previous suspended sentence which has not taken

---

[1] s. 1(2) provides, however, that subs. (1) shall not prevent the committal to prison of a person under 21 years of age who is remanded in custody or committed in custody for trial or sentence.

effect is to be disregarded (s. 20(3)).[2] Where a magistrates' court passes a sentence of imprisonment, it must state the reason for its opinion that no other method of dealing with him is appropriate (s. 20(2)).

For the purpose of determining whether any other method of dealing with the offender is appropriate, the court is under an obligation: (1) to obtain and consider information about the circumstances (s. 20(1)); (2) to take into account any information before the court which is relevant to his character and his physical and mental condition (s. 20(1))[3]; and (3) to obtain a social inquiry report[4] (s. 20A(1) as inserted by C.J.A. 1982, s. 62). The obligation to obtain a social inquiry report does not apply if, in the circumstances of the case, the court is of opinion that it is unnecessary (s. 20A(2)). If a magistrates' court passes a sentence of imprisonment without obtaining a social inquiry report, it must state in open court the reason for its opinion that it was unnecessary (s. 20(3)). No consequence flows from failure to comply with section 20A(1) as a sentence of imprisonment passed in such circumstances is not thereby invalidated, although, on appeal the appeal court must obtain a social inquiry report if none was obtained by the sentencing court, unless it is of opinion that in the circumstances of the case it is unnecessary to do so (s. 20A(5)). The appeal court in determining whether it should deal with the appellant otherwise than by passing a sentence of imprisonment on him is required to consider any social inquiry report which either it or the court below has obtained (s. 20A(6)).

A magistrates' court may only impose a sentence of imprisonment where the accused is present in court (M.C.A., s. 11(3)).

Legal representation

Section 21(1) of the Powers of Criminal Courts Act provides that a court shall not pass a sentence of imprisonment on an offender who is not legally represented in that court and who has not previously been sentenced to imprisonment[5] unless either

[2] However, apart from this suspended sentences constitute sentences of imprisonment and accordingly the provisions of ss. 20, 20A and 21 apply when a court is considering passing such a sentence.

[3] Such information may be acquired from a judge's own observation of an accused during a trial which has lasted several days and in which the accused had given evidence and put his character in (see *Peter* [1975] Crim.L.R. 593).

[4] A "social inquiry report" means a report about a person and his circumstances made by a probation officer (s. 20A(7)).

[5] For this purpose a previous suspended sentence which has not taken effect is to be disregarded (s. 21(3)); but a suspended sentence is otherwise to be regarded as a sentence of imprisonment so that the provisions of s. 21 apply when a court is considering passing such a sentence.

(a) he applied for legal aid[6] and was refused it on the ground that it did not appear that his means were such that he required assistance, or (b) having been informed of his right to apply for legal aid and had the opportunity to do so, he refused or failed to apply.[7] A person is to be treated as legally represented in a court only if he has the assistance of counsel or a solicitor to represent him in the proceedings in that court at some time after he is found guilty and before he is sentenced (s. 21(2)). Where the sentencing court fails to observe the provisions of section 21(1), a sentence of imprisonment passed by it is invalid (*R.* v. *Birmingham Justices, ex p. Wyatt* [1976] 1 W.L.R. 260; see also *McQuaide* (1974) 60 Cr.App.R. 239). In such circumstances if the appeal is to the Crown Court from a decision of a magistrates' court the Crown Court is limited to the powers which the magistrates' court could have exercised in the circumstances, *i.e.* it cannot impose a prison sentence (see *Birmingham Justices* above and S.C.A., s. 48(4)). If the appeal is to the Court of Appeal from a decision of the Crown Court, it is not so limited but may exercise any powers which the Crown Court could have exercised had there been compliance with the provisions of section 21, *i.e.* it may rectify the error by itself complying with the provisions of section 21 and impose a prison sentence (see *McGinley and Ballantyne* (1976) 62 Cr.App.R. 156).

Powers of the Courts

Crown Courts

Imprisonment may be imposed for any common law offence and for a statutory offence where imprisonment is provided as a penalty. In relation to common law offences, unless a different maximum penalty is provided by statute, they are punishable with imprisonment for life. However, any punishment must not be disproportionate to the offence (*Castro* (1880) 5 Q.B.D. 490; *Morris* [1951] 1 K.B. 394; *Higgins* [1952] 1 K.B. 7). An example of a common law offence, the penalty for which has been reduced by statute, is common assault, for which the maximum penalty is one year's imprisonment (O.A.P.A., s. 47). For each statutory indictable offence, the statute normally provides for a maximum term of imprisonment on conviction of that offence. If a statute creating an indictable offence punishable with imprisonment,

---

[6] "Legal aid" means legal aid for the purposes of the proceedings in that court, whether the whole proceedings or the proceedings on or in relation to sentence (s. 21(2)).

[7] In the case of a person committed to the Crown Court for sentence or for trial, it is immaterial whether he applied for legal aid in the Crown Court, or was informed of his right to apply by that court or the court which committed him (s. 21(3)).

fails to specify a maximum term, the maximum sentence for such an offence is to be two years imprisonment (P.C.C.A., s. 18(1)). Section 4(1) of the Criminal Attempts Act 1981 provides that an attempt to commit an offence is in general punishable to the same extent as the completed offence. However, the lower maximum penalties for attempts to commit certain offences under the Sexual Offences Act 1956 have been retained (C.A.A. 1981, s. 4(5); S.O.A., s. 37 and Sched. 2). Punishment for conspiracy is generally limited to the maximum sentence available for the substantive offence contemplated (C.L.A., s. 3).[8] If two or more offences are contemplated by the conspiracy, the maximum sentence available for the conspiracy will be the same as the maximum sentence for the most serious of the contemplated offences.

Magistrates' courts

If a magistrates' court decides to impose a sentence of imprisonment, it may not sentence the offender to less than five days in prison (M.C.A., s. 132). However, where a court has power to impose imprisonment, instead of doing so, it may order the offender to be detained for up to four days in police cells or similar place certified by the Home Secretary as suitable for such detention (M.C.A., s. 134(1) and (2)). Alternatively, instead of imprisoning the offender a court may order his detention in the cells of the court or at any police station for the remainder of the day until 8.00 p.m. or such earlier hour as the court may direct (M.C.A., s. 135(1)).[9]

The maximum sentence which a magistrates' court may impose in respect of any one offence is six months (M.C.A., s. 31(1)) unless this provision has been expressly excluded by Parliament (s. 31(2)). This provision[10] reduces to six months the maximum period of imprisonment available on summary conviction of a number of offences formerly carrying longer maximum sentences. On summary conviction of an indictable offence listed in Sched. 1 to the Magistrates' Courts Act the maximum sentence available is six months provided the offence is punishable with imprisonment on conviction on indictment (M.C.A., s. 32(1)(a)). On summary conviction of incitement, or attempt, to commit an offence triable either way, an offender is liable to the same penalty to which he would have been liable on summary conviction of the substantive offence (M.C.A., s. 32(1)(b) and C.A.A. 1981, s. 4(1)(c)). Where pursuant to

---

[8] In the case of a common law conspiracy preserved by C.L.A., s. 5(2) or (3), the maximum penalty available is life imprisonment.

[9] A court shall not make an order under s. 135 if it would deprive the offender of a reasonable opportunity of returning to his abode on the day of the order (M.C.A., s. 135(2)).

[10] Formerly C.L.A., s. 27.

section 22 of the Magistrates' Courts Act the accused is convicted of an offence scheduled in Schedule 2 to the Act for which he has been tried summarily, the maximum sentence is three months (M.C.A., s. 33(1)).

In sentencing an offender to imprisonment a magistrates' court may order that term of imprisonment to be consecutive to any sentence of imprisonment which he may already be serving (M.C.A., s. 133(1)). Likewise, where a magistrates' court imposes separate terms of imprisonment for two or more offences, the court may, subject to certain maxima, order the sentences to run consecutively (M.C.A., s. 133(1)). Where a court imposes consecutive sentences for two or more summary offences the aggregate of the terms imposed must not exceed six months (M.C.A., s. 133(1)).[11] The maximum aggregate where consecutive terms are being imposed in respect of two or more offences at least two of which are indictable offences tried summarily (provided neither was tried summarily in pursuance of M.C.A., s. 22(2)) is 12 months (M.C.A., s. 133(2)).[12] For the purpose of arriving at the aggregate under section 133, a term of imprisonment imposed in default of payment of, or for want of sufficient distress to satisfy, a fine or other sum adjudged to be paid on conviction, is to be included in the calculation (s. 133(5)). However, where a person has been sentenced by a magistrates' court to imprisonment and a fine for the same offence, a period of imprisonment imposed for non-payment of the fine, or for want of sufficient distress to satisfy the fine, is not to be included in calculating the aggregate (s. 133(4)) and such a term will therefore be additional to the aggregate term.

Life imprisonment

Only an adult of 21 years or over may be sentenced to life imprisonment. Life imprisonment as a sentence may be discretionary or mandatory. A life sentence is available for a considerable number of offences, the major ones being:
*1.   murder (Murder (Abolition of Death Penalty) Act 1965, s. 1(1));
2.   procuring a miscarriage (O.A.P.A., s. 58);
3.   assault with intent to rob and robbery (T.A., s. 8);
4.   attempt to choke, strangle, or suffocate (O.A.P.A., s. 21);

---

[11] Where by statute the magistrates' court is empowered to pass a sentence in excess of six months for one of those offences then this higher maximum will constitute the overall maximum for the purposes of aggregating the terms (see M.C.A., s. 133(3)).
[12] Where by statute the magistrates' court is empowered to pass a sentence in excess of 12 months for one of those offences then this higher maximum will constitute the overall maximum for the purposes of aggregating the terms (M.C.A., s. 133(3)).

5.   violation of Biological Weapons Act 1974 (s. 1);
6.   buggery in certain circumstances (S.O.A., s. 12(1) and Sched. 2);
7.   aggravated burglary (T.A., s. 10);
8.   wounding or causing grievous bodily harm with intent to cause grievous bodily harm (O.A.P.A., s. 18);
9.   child destruction (Infant Life (Preservation) Act 1929, s. 1);
10.   conspiracy in certain circumstances (C.L.A., s. 3(2)) and common law conspiracy;
11.   using, sending, etc., explosives or corrosives with intent to cause grievous bodily harm (O.A.P.A., s. 29);
12.   arson (C.D.A., ss. 1(3) and 4);
13.   causing criminal damage with intent to endanger life (C.D.A., ss. 1(2) and 4);
14.   administering drugs with intent to facilitate an offence (O.A.P.A., s. 22);
15.   causing an explosion likely to endanger life or to cause serious injury to property (Explosive Substances Act 1883, s. 2);
*16.   genocide (Genocide Act 1969, s. 1);
17.   hijacking aircraft in flight (Hijacking Act 1971, s. 1);
18.   incitement to mutiny (Incitement to Mutiny Act 1797, s. 1);
19.   infanticide (Infanticide Act 1938, s. 1(1));
20.   kidnapping and false imprisonment (common law);
21.   manslaughter (common law and O.A.P.A., s. 5);
22.   mutiny and piracy (Piracy Act 1698, s. 8, common law and Piracy Act 1837, s. 3);
23.   rape (S.O.A., s. 1 and Sched. 2 and Sexual Offences (Amendment) Act 1976, s. 1);
24.   riot (common law);
25.   sedition and seditious libel (common law);
26.   treason in certain circumstances (common law and Treason Felony Act 1848, s. 3).
*   =   fixed by law.

For a discussion of the discretionary life sentence see pp. 264–269, below.

The imposition of a life sentence makes imprisonment for the remainder of the offender's life a theoretical possibility. However, the Home Secretary may release a life prisoner on licence at any time (C.J.A. 1967, s. 61).[13]

A sentence of life imprisonment is mandatory in the case of murder. On conviction for murder the court has a discretion to *recommend* a minimum term, which in its view should elapse before

---

[13] See "Release on Licence" below.

the executive should release that person on licence (Murder (Abolition of Death Penalty) Act 1965, s. 1(2)).[14] If a court decides to make a recommendation it should be for a period of not less than 12 years (*Fleming* [1973] 2 All E.R. 401). The Court of Appeal in Northern Ireland has held that for a recommendation to be valid it must specify a minimum number of years; the trial judge cannot make a recommendation that "life should mean life" (*Ferguson* [1980] N.I. 205). Accordingly "in cases where the trial judge considers that the convicted person ought not to be released on licence at any time, his correct course will be to state that by reason of his holding that view he makes no recommendation" (*per* Lord Lowry L.C.J. in *Ferguson* at p. 211). In cases where a judge makes a recommendation which the offender considers excessive his only means of redress is to address his submissions to the executive as a recommendation is not a "sentence" for the purposes of an appeal (*Ferguson*; see also *Aitken* [1966] 1 W.L.R. 1076, applied in *Bowden and Begley* (1983) 77 Cr.App.R. 66).

Extended sentences

An extended sentence is available in the case of a persistent offender primarily for the purpose of protecting the public rather than punishing the offender. While an extended sentence is very rarely passed it must be dealt with for the sake of completeness. The Advisory Council on the Penal System concluded that

> "the extended sentence is demonstrably inappropriate to the problem it was intended to solve and unwanted by the courts who have been empowered to use it. It should be abolished."[15]

The objects of an extended sentence are to be found in the power given to the court to pass a sentence longer than the maximum otherwise permitted by statute and the special provisions which may be utilised by the Home Secretary for release of the offender on licence[16] (see pp. 100–108 below). Thus it may be used to achieve one of two objects: to impose a sentence greater than would be justified on tariff principles; or as a means of providing for supervision of the offender after his release. In *Houldsworth* (unreported, January 17, 1972) The Court of Appeal stated:

> "An extended sentence has a dual purpose. It is designed to protect the public in two different ways: One, where necessary,

---

[14] The power to recommend a minimum term only arises where a judge is passing sentence for murder (*Flemming* [1973] 2 All E.R. 401).

[15] *Sentences of Imprisonment: A Review of Maximum Penalties* (1978), para. 115.

[16] See *Goody* [1970] 2 All E.R. 385.

by keeping a man in prison for a longer period than would
otherwise be required; the other by providing for compulsory
after care where this is desirable for a longer period than would
otherwise be the case."

In *Bourton*, [1985] Crim.L.R. 165, the Court of Appeal substituted an extended sentence of six years imprisonment for an
eight-year prison sentence passed on a man convicted of robbery,
to whom the sentencing judge said: "You appear through no fault
of your own perhaps, to be incapable of standing on your own
feet." The court was of opinion that eight years was too long
but wanted to ensure some supervision of the appellant when
released from prison and thus certified the sentence as an extended
one.

THE LAW

Where an offender has been convicted on indictment or
committed to the Crown Court for sentence under section 38 of the
Magistrates' Courts Act 1980 he will be liable to receive an
extended sentence if certain conditions are satisfied. These conditions are as follows:

(i)   the offence of which he stands convicted is punishable with
      imprisonment for a term of two years or more (P.C.C.A.,
      s. 28(1));
(ii) the offence was committed before the expiration of three
      years from a previous conviction[17] of an offence punishable
      on indictment with imprisonment for a term of two years or
      more[18] or before the expiration of three years from his final
      release[19] from prison on a sentence passed for such an
      offence (P.C.C.A., s. 28(3)(a));
(iii) on at least three previous occasions since attaining the age of
      21 the offender has been convicted on indictment of offences

[17] To count, a previous conviction must be by a court in any part of Great Britain
(P.C.C.A., s. 57(3)); a conviction in Northern Ireland cannot be taken into account
(*Wynne* (1971) 55 Cr.App.R. 384).
[18] A certificate purporting to be signed by or on behalf of the Lord Advocate that an
offence is punishable in Scotland with imprisonment or is punishable in Scotland
on indictment with imprisonment for a term specified in the certificate is evidence
of the matter so certified (P.C.C.A., s. 52).
[19] "Final release" includes a release on licence under C.J.A. 1967, s. 60 or 61 but does
not include any temporary discharge (P.C.C.A., s. 29(5)). If an offender absconds
from prison before "final release" and commits an offence he will be liable to an
extended sentence as the offence has been committed "before the expiration of
three years" from final release (*Johnson* [1976] 1 W.L.R. 426).

punishable with imprisonment for a term of two years or more[20] (s. 28(3)(*b*)); and

(iv) the total length of the sentences passed on him on those three occasions was not less than five years, and

    (a) on at least one of those occasions he was sentenced to preventative detention[21] or

    (b) on at least two of those occasions he was sentenced to imprisonment (other than a suspended sentence which has not taken effect) or to corrective training,[22] and of those sentences one was a sentence of imprisonment for at least three years, in respect of one offence, or two sentences of imprisonment each for a term of at least two years in respect of one offence;

(P.C.C.A., s. 28(3)(*c*));

(v) notice must be served on the offender at least three days before sentence is to be passed of the intention to prove a previous conviction or sentence to the court (P.C.C.A., s. 29(3)).[23]

If the above conditions are satisfied, then, if the court is satisfied by reason of his previous conduct and of the likelihood of his committing further offences, that it is expedient to protect the public from him for a substantial time, it may impose an extended term of imprisonment (P.C.C.A., s. 28(1)). In deciding whether an extended sentence is appropriate the court should pay attention to the nature of the present offence and particularly the offender's recent efforts to lead an honest and industrious life as well as his past record (*Kenworthy* (1969) 53 Cr.App.R. 311).

In imposing an extended sentence the court may impose a sentence which exceeds the maximum term authorised for the

---

[20] A person who has been convicted by a magistrates' court of an indictable offence and sentenced for that offence by the Crown Court, or on appeal from the Crown Court, to imprisonment must be treated as if he had been convicted of that offence on indictment (P.C.C.A., s. 29(2)). A conviction in respect of which a probation order was made is not a "conviction" for the purposes of this condition (*Spearpoint* [1973] Crim.L.R. 36). The same is undoubtedly true for a conviction resulting in a discharge.

[21] Preventive detention was abolished by C.J.A. 1967, s. 37(1).

[22] Corrective training was abolished by C.J.A. 1967, s. 37(1).

[23] No account may be taken of any offence or sentence for which notice has not been served (P.C.C.A., s. 29(3)). The offender should be asked by the trial judge before sentence is passed, whether he has received the notice, and whether he admits the conviction or sentences stated in it (*Concannon* [1970] 1 W.L.R. 1159). If he denies any of these convictions they must be strictly proved (*Blogg* [1973] Crim.L.R. 454).

offence if that maximum is less than 10 years but must not exceed 10 years if the authorised maximum is less than 10 years, and must not exceed five years if the authorised term is less than five years (P.C.C.A., s. 28(2)). However, a term of imprisonment may be ordered by the court to be an extended term even though it does not exceed the authorised maximum for the offence (*D.P.P.* v. *Ottewell* [1970] A.C. 642).

When an extended sentence is imposed the Crown Court must issue an "extended sentence certificate" directed to the governor of the prison and attached to the court order, stating that such a sentence has been imposed (P.C.C.A., s. 28(4)).

COMBINING AN EXTENDED SENTENCE WITH OTHER SENTENCES OF IMPRISONMENT

An extended sentence should be passed in the form of a single term and not in the form of an ordinary term plus an extended term (*Pearson* (1970) 55 Cr.App.R. 157). The extended term should be imposed in respect of a single offence and not a combination of offences (*McKenna* [1974] 1 W.L.R. 267).

It is wrong in principle to impose on the same occasion an extended term of imprisonment and a non-extended term to run consecutive thereto (*Wilkinson* (Note) [1970] 1 Q.B. 123; *Jackson* [1974] 1 All E.R. 640). By the same token it is wrong to impose on the same occasion an extended term and a longer non-extended term concurrent thereto (*Jackson*). There is no reason in principle why an extended term of imprisonment should not be imposed to commence at the expiration of an ordinary term of imprisonment (*Stewart* (Note) [1971] 2 All E.R. 905). Conversely, a sentence of imprisonment not certified as an extended term can properly be imposed and ordered to run consecutively to the unexpired portion of an extended term imposed on another occasion; but in such a case for the avoidance of doubt the consecutive sentence should be expressed "to run from the date upon, which but for the imposition of this sentence, you would be released from prison either on licence or finally" (*Jackson*). When a suspended sentence is being activated it should not be made operative consecutive to an extended term but concurrently; but it would be quite proper for the court to take into consideration the activation of the suspended sentence in considering what to certify as the extended sentence (*Wilkinson*).

Computation of sentence

The length of any sentence of imprisonment will be *reduced* by any time spent in custody before trial or sentence specifically related to that particular offence (C.J.A. 1967, s. 67(1)).[24, 25]

Remission

Remission is the cancellation of part of a term of imprisonment resulting from the good behaviour of the offender while in prison. The prisoner is then released without supervision but in the case of an extended sentence he may be released on licence (C.J.A. 1967, s. 60(3)).

In examining the rules on remission a distinction must be drawn between the sentence *pronounced* by the court and the *actual term* of imprisonment to be served. The pronounced sentence will normally take effect from the beginning of the day on which it has been passed by the court. However, the term will be *reduced* by time already spent in custody for that particular offence (C.J.A. 1967, s. 67(1)). The *actual term* of imprisonment for the purposes of computation of remission, therefore, is the pronounced term *less* any time already spent in custody for that particular offence.

---

[24] Where a defendant is indicted and remanded in custody at different times in respect of separate offences, the period spent in custody up to the time of the second remand will only operate to reduce the *pronounced sentence* passed in respect of the offence for which he was first remanded; it will not operate to reduce the *pronounced sentence* passed in respect of the offence for which he was remanded subsequently. For example, on March 1, 1984, D is indicted for theft and remanded in custody. On April 1, 1984, D is indicted for criminal damage and remanded in custody. On May 1, 1984, D is tried for theft, convicted and sentenced to 18 months' imprisonment. This *pronounced sentence* will be reduced to an *actual term* of 16 months to allow for the two months already spent in custody. On June 1, 1984, D is tried for criminal damage, convicted and sentenced to nine months imprisonment to run consecutively after the expiration of the first term of imprisonment. Although D spent two months in prison, from April 1, 1984 to June 1, 1984, remanded in custody in respect of this offence, this period will not operate to reduce the pronounced term as during the month of April, D was already in custody awaiting trial for the theft offence and during the month of May he was in prison serving his sentence for that offence.

Thus time in custody only counts towards the offence for which the defendant was first remanded. In the above example, even if D had been acquitted of the theft offence or convicted but given a non-custodial sentence, the term spent in custody during April would not operate to reduce the term of imprisonment pronounced in respect of the offence of criminal damage, but the period spent in custody in May remanded for that offence would now operate to reduce the *pronounced term* to an *actual term* of eight months.

[25] Where an offender is subsequently sentenced to imprisonment having *originally* received in respect of the offence a probation order, a community service order, an order for conditional discharge or a suspended sentence, any period spent in custody prior to the *original* disposition will not operate to reduce the term of imprisonment (C.J.A. 1967, s. 67(1)). Any period in custody immediately prior to the passing of the sentence of imprisonment *will* count towards reducing the term of imprisonment.

The rules on remission are as follows[26]:

(1) to be eligible for remission a prisoner must be serving a sentence of imprisonment for an actual term of more than five days;

(2) remission is not available where the prisoner is serving a life sentence;

(3) the prisoner must be industrious and of "good behaviour."

The maximum remission granted may be no more than one-third of the total pronounced sentence, *i.e.* the *actual term* added to any period reduced by section 67(1) of the Criminal Justice Act 1967. However, the *actual term* cannot be reduced to less than five days (r. 5(1)). Where the prisoner is one who has been released on licence and recalled to prison (other than a prisoner in respect of whom an extended sentence certificate was served) he cannot be released before the thirtieth day following his return to prison or recall (r. 5(1)). In the case of a prisoner in respect of whom an extended sentence certificate was issued when sentence was passed on him and who has been released on licence and recalled to prison, the maximum remission granted may be no more than one-third of the unexpired part of his sentence (r. 5(2)(*b*)) provided that the actual term is not reduced to less than five days.

The rules on remission are subject to any disciplinary award of forfeiture of remission; the maximum period of remission which may be forfeited as a disciplinary measure is 28 days on the authority of the prison governor (r. 50(*f*)), or 180 days on a reference to the board of visitors or Secretary of State (r. 51(4)(*f*) and (5)).

Release on licence

Release on licence, commonly referred to as "parole," differs from remission in two important respects. First, the granting of parole is discretionary, the discretion being exercised by the Home Secretary on the recommendation of the Parole Board. By contrast, remission is granted as a matter of right provided the prisoner has been of good behaviour. Secondly, remission is an unconditional release whereas a parolee is subject to conditions specified in his licence. This licence may be revoked resulting in the return of the parolee to prison to serve the unexpired portion of his sentence.

In a written answer to a parliamentary question on November 30, 1983 the Home Secretary indicated the principles on which he

---

[26] See the Prison Rules 1964 (S.I. 1964 No. 388), as amended (see 18 *Halsbury's Statutory Instruments*). For the purposes of the rules a sentence of imprisonment includes committal to prison in default of payment of a sum adjudged to be paid by a conviction (r. 5(3)(*a*): and consecutive terms of imprisonment are treated as one term (r. 5(3)(*b*)).

would exercise his discretion under the Criminal Justice Act 1967 to release prisoners on licence. Where prisoners are serving sentences of over five years for offences of violence or drug trafficking parole will only be granted when release under supervision for a few months before the end of a sentence would be likely to reduce the long-term risk to the public, or in circumstances which are genuinely exceptional. The Parole Board, however, will continue to see all the cases which it previously saw in order that each one can be reviewed individually in the light of the policies decided upon by the Home Secretary to determine whether there are any special circumstances which might qualify for consideration by Ministers. Where prisoners are serving life sentences the Home Secretary announced that he would exercise his discretion so that murderers of police or prison officers, terrorist murderers, sexual or sadistic murderers of children and murderers by firearm in the course of robbery can normally expect to serve at least 20 years in custody.

The validity of the policy announced by the Home Secretary was challenged in the Queen's Bench Divisional Court on four applications for judicial review in *R.* v. *Secretary of State for the Home Department, ex p. Findlay,* [1984] 3 W.L.R. 1159. The applicants were four convicted prisoners who, under the previous policy, could have expected to be released on licence in the near future. They argued that their expectations were shattered by the change of policy, that in adopting the new policy the Home Secretary acted unlawfully and that in the circumstances the court should declare that the policy was unlawful in that it contravened the statute. As the two judges hearing the case, Parker L.J. and Forbes J. failed to agree, the case proceeded to the Court of Appeal.

The Court of Appeal, by a majority, refused the prisoner's appeals ([1984] 3 W.L.R. 1159). On appeal to the House of Lords, the appeals were dismissed. Lord Scarman delivered the unanimous judgment of the House. He stated that it was entirely within the Home Secretary's discretion whether to refer a case to the Parole Board and that he had a complete discretion whether or not to accept the board's recommendation. While the Parole Board was qualified to consider the suitability of an individual prisoner for release, wider issues such as deterrence, retribution and public confidence in the system were factors of importance to the Home Secretary as a minister responsible to Parliament and the electorate.

"He had to judge the public acceptability of early release and to determine the policies needed to maintain public confidence in the system of criminal justice. That was why Parliament saw as necessary the duality of the parole system."

The failure to consult the Parole Board before adopting the new policy was of no significance as there was no express statutory requirement for such consultation and because of the essential duality of the parole system it was impossible to imply such a requirement into the statute. Nor was the Home Secretary improperly fettering his own discretion by the adoption of such a policy as he was not refusing to consider the cases of prisoners within the specified classes, but rather was requiring that exceptional circumstances had to exist or compelling reasons be given before such a person would be granted parole.

> "Presumption in certain cases against parole was an inevitable, and no doubt intended consequence of the policy. It would be unlawful only if it were irrebuttable, that is, if it precluded consideration of other factors. But the policy did not exclude consideration of other factors."

Further, the policy did not operate as a punishment or penalty. The sentence of the court was in law the punishment. As the policy was lawful, the disappointment of expectation could be no ground for judicial review. As the only expectation a prisoner could legitimately have was that his case would be considered on becoming eligible for parole, the prisoners had no cause for complaint as their cases had been considered in the light of the policy which the Home Secretary had lawfully adopted.

The Parole Board

Section 59 of the Criminal Justice Act 1967 set up the Parole Board to advise the Home Secretary on the following matters:

(a) the release on licence of prisoners serving determinate or life sentences and the recall of persons released on licence (s. 59(3)(a));

(b) the conditions of such licences and the variation or cancellation of such conditions (s. 59(3)(b));

(c) any other matters referred to it by the Secretary of State which are connected with the release on licence or recall of such persons (s. 59(3)(c)).

The Parole Board consists of a chairman and not less than four other members appointed by the Home Secretary (s. 59(1)), and the case of any prisoner referred to the Board may be dealt with by any three or more of its members (Parole Board Rules 1967, r. 1, S.I. 1967 No. 1685). The Board, which is at present composed of 44 members, ordinarily sits in panels of five members. The Board must include among its members:

(a) a person who holds or has held high judicial office (s. 59(7), Sched. 2, para. 1(a));

(b) a registered medical practitioner who is a psychiatrist (para. 1(b));

(c) a person appearing to the Secretary of State to have knowledge and experience of the supervision or after-care of discharged prisoners (para. 1(c));

(d) a person appearing to the Secretary of State to have made a study of the causes of delinquency or the treatment of offenders (para. 1(d)).

Local Review Committees

For every prison in which there are detained prisoners who are or will become eligible for release on licence there must be a Local Review Committee to review the cases of such prisoners and to report to the Home Secretary on their suitability for release (C.J.A. 1967, s. 59(6)(a); Local Review Committee Rules 1967, S.I. 1967 No. 1462, r. 1(1) as substituted by S.I. 1983 No. 622).

The Committee must consist of the governor of the prison and not less than four other members appointed by the Home Secretary (r. 1(2) as amended by S.I. 1973 No. 4) who must include a probation officer who is not a prison welfare officer, a member of the board of visitors of the prison and two other persons who are not probation officers or members of that board (r. 1(3) as amended by S.I. 1973 No. 4). The Committee must meet at least once a year to arrange for the review of prisoner's cases (r. 2(1) as amended by S.I. 1973 No. 4). The Committee must review the case of any prisoner referred to it by the Home Secretary (r. 5). They must review the case of a prisoner serving a sentence of two years or more (other than one of life imprisonment) at some time before he becomes eligible for release on licence and subsequently at intervals of not less than 10 months or more than 14 months from the last review (r. 6(1)).[27,28]

The Committee is not required to review a prisoner's case until after the conclusion of:

(a) any proceedings against him in respect of a criminal offence or any offence against discipline;

(b) any period of cellular confinement or restricted diet awarded in respect of an offence against discipline.

(L.R.C.R., r. 6(4).)

The Committee may postpone to a later date the review of a

---

[27] Where a prisoner has been released on licence under C.J.A. 1967, s. 60 and has been recalled to prison under s. 62, his case must be reviewed after an interval of not less than 10 months or more than 14 months from his recall and subsequently at similar intervals from the last review (L.R.C.R., r. 6(2)).

[28] In calculating intervals between reviews no account is to be taken of any time during which a prisoner is unlawfully at large (L.R.C.R., r. 6(2A) as inserted by S.I. 1983 No. 622).

prisoner's case if it is satisfied that it is necessary to do so (r. 6(5)). However, the committee is not required to review a prisoner's case if it appears that his sentence will expire or that (unless he forfeits remission) he will be released by reason of remission or released on licence in lieu of remission (under C.J.A. 1967, s. 60(3)) within 16 months of the last review of his case by a local review committee (r. 6(6)). Where the committee is satisfied that a prisoner desires that his case should not be reviewed on any occasion when it would otherwise be reviewed, they shall not review his case but notify the Secretary of State accordingly, and the provisions concerning subsequent reviews apply to him as if his case had been reviewed on that occasion (r. 6(7)).

Incidence of Review

Prisoners serving determinate sentences

On the recommendation of the Parole Board the Home Secretary may release on licence a person serving a sentence of imprisonment (other than imprisonment for life)[29] after he has served not less than one third of his sentence or six months of it, whichever expires later (C.J.A. 1967, s. 60(1) as amended by C.J.A. 1982, s. 33; C.J.A. 1967, s. 60(1)A as inserted by C.J.A. 1982, s. 33; and Eligibility for Release on Licence Order 1983, S.I. 1983 No. 1958).[30] The minimum period of six months is not to be reduced on account of time spent in custody on remand but the one third period is so reduced (C.J.A. 1967, s. 60(2) as amended by C.J.A. 1972, s. 64(2) and Sched. 6). In certain classes of cases, the Home Secretary may release a prisoner on the recommendation of the local review committee without referring the case to the Parole Board (C.J.A. 1972, s. 35(1)).[31] Where a prisoner (other than one serving an extended sentence) is released on licence that licence will remain in force (unless previously revoked under C.J.A. 1967, s. 62) until the date on which the prisoner would have been released on remission had he remained in prison (C.J.A., s. 60(5A) as inserted by C.L.A. 1977, Sched. 12 and amended by C.J.A. 1982, Sched. 16).

[29] Or a sentence of youth custody (inserted by C.J.A. 1982, Sched. 14, para. 18).

[30] "Because of the entitlement to remission of one third of the sentence, and the Home Secretary's direction that no inmate should be reviewed for parole unless, if it was granted, there would be a minimum of one month on licence, the reduction in the minimum qualifying period does not mean that a sentence by the courts to only 6 months will in future be eligible for parole. The minimum sentence or combination of sentence that will in practice attract earlier consideration for parole is $10\frac{1}{2}$ months from the date on which sentence was passed." (*Report of the Parole Board 1983* (HMSO, 1984), p. 1).

[31] These classes of cases are determined by the Home Secretary after consultation with the Parole Board (C.J.A. 1972, s. 35(1)).

Where a prisoner is serving a sentence certified as an extended sentence he may be released on licence in accordance with the above provisions. However, the Home Secretary, without prejudice to his earlier release under section 60(1) of the Criminal Justice Act 1967, may direct that such a prisoner, instead of being granted remission of any part of his sentence under the Prison Rules, be released on licence at any time on or after the day on which he could have been discharged from prison if the remission had been granted (C.J.A. 1967, s. 60(3)). Where a prisoner serving an extended sentence is released on licence that licence will remain in force until the date of the expiration of the sentence (C.J.A. 1967, s. 60(5A)).

Prisoners serving life sentences

If recommended by the Parole Board, the Home Secretary may release on licence a person serving a sentence of imprisonment for life (C.J.A. 1967, s. 61(1)).[32] Unlike the case of determinate sentences, there is no prescribed stage of a life sentence at which the prisoner's case must be referred to the Parole Board. The practice adopted by the current Home Secretary is that after the prisoner has served three years he will consult the judiciary for their view as to the period of years to be served in the light of the circumstances of the offence judged against the requirements of retribution and deterrence. Having obtained this advice he will decide on the date of the first referral of the prisoner's case to the Local Review Committee as the first stage of formal review.[33] The Home Secretary may not make a recommendation for release on licence except after consulting with the Lord Chief Justice and the trial judge, if available (C.J.A. 1967, s. 61(1)). If the Board do not recommend release on licence the Home Secretary has no power to authorise it and the case is usually reviewed again at a date recommended by the Board. Acceptance by the Home Secretary of the Board's recommendation for release is usual but not invariable.[34] Where a prisoner serving a life sentence is released on licence that licence will remain in force for the remainder of his life.

Procedure

Whenever a prisoner's case is due for review by the local review committee he must first be interviewed, if he is willing, by a member

---

[32] This provision also applies to a person serving a sentence of custody for life (inserted by C.J.A. 1982, Sched. 14, para. 19) and a young offender detained under C.Y.P.A. 1933, s. 53 on conviction of a grave crime.

[33] Formerly a Joint Committee of the Parole Board and the Home Office set up in 1973 performed this function but this has now been disbanded.

[34] See *Prisons and the Prisoner* (HMSO 1977), para. 112.

of the Committee other than the governor of the prison (L.R.C.R., r. 3(1)). At such an interview he must be given a reasonable opportunity to make any representations which he wishes to be considered by the Committee (r. 3(2)). A report of the interview is drawn up by the interviewer and this will be considered by the Committee when reviewing the prisoner's case (r. 3(3) and (4)). Before the Committee review his case the prisoner must be informed that he has the right to make written representations to the Committee which must be considered by it when reviewing his case (r. 4). A copy of the interview report together with the committee's report on the prisoner's suitability for release on licence must be sent to the Home Secretary (r. 3(3)). If the case is covered by section 35(1) of the Criminal Justice Act 1972 and the Local Review Committee recommend release on licence, the Home Secretary may so release the prisoner, otherwise he refers the case, together with the Committee's report to the Parole Board. The Board then deal with the case on the basis of any documents given to it by the Home Secretary together with any reports it has called for and any information, whether oral or in writing, that it has obtained (C.J.A. 1967, s. 59(4)(a)). The documents must include any written representations made by the prisoner in connection with or since the last interview conducted by the interviewing member of the local review committee (C.J.A. 1967, s. 59(5)(a)).[35] If in any particular case the Board thinks it necessary to interview the prisoner before reaching a decision, it may request one of its members to do so and it must take into account that member's report of the interview (C.J.A. 1967, s. 59(b)). While the Local Review Committee and the Board must act fairly in performing their statutory duties, the Board is under no duty to give the prisoner any reasons for refusing to release him on licence (*Payne* v. *Lord Harris of Greenwich* [1981] 1 W.L.R. 754).

On granting release on licence the Home Secretary may insert conditions in the licence with which the prisoner must comply (C.J.A. 1967, s. 60(4)). The Home Secretary must consult the Board before including conditions on release or subsequently inserting in a licence or varying or cancelling such conditions (C.J.A. 1967, s. 60(5)). However, he need not do so in every case if he has consulted the Board about a proposal to include, insert, vary or cancel a condition generally or in a particular class of case (C.J.A. 1967, s. 60(5)). The commonest condition is that the parolee accept the supervision of a probation officer or other suitable person.

---

[35] The Board is bound to consider not only the most recent written representation but also any earlier representations (*Payne* v. *Lord Harris of Greenwich* [1981] 1 W.L.R. 754).

Revocation of licences

Parole, unlike remission, is only a conditional release from prison. The essence of parole, it has been said, is that it involves serving part of the prison sentence under supervision in the community.[36] Accordingly, while a parole licence remains operative the parolee is subject to the administrative power to recall him. The Home Secretary may revoke a parolee's licence and recall him to prison on the recommendation of the Parole Board (s. 62(1)). Alternatively, he may revoke a parolee's licence and recall him without consulting the Board where it appears to him in the public interest to recall him before such consultation is practicable (s. 62(2)). A parolee recalled to prison may make written representations with respect to his recall and, on his return to prison, must be informed of the reasons for his recall and his right to make such representations (s. 62(3)).[37] Where a parolee recalled on the Board's recommendations makes representations the Home Secretary must refer the case to the Board (s. 62(4)). In addition he must refer to the Board cases of persons recalled to prison without the Board having first been consulted (s. 62(4)). Where the Board recommends the immediate release on licence of a person whose case is referred to it, the Home Secretary must give effect to the recommendation (s. 62(5)). The obligation to consult the Lord Chief Justice and trial judge under section 61(1) in the case of a person serving a life sentence, does not apply in this situation (s. 62(5)).

If a parolee during the period of licence is convicted by a magistrates' court of an offence punishable on indictment with imprisonment, the court may commit him in custody or on bail to the Crown Court for sentence (s. 62(6)). If the parolee is convicted on indictment of such an offence or is committed to the Crown Court for sentence, the court by which he is convicted or to which he is committed *may*, whether or not it imposes any other sentence on him, revoke the licence (s. 62(7)).[38] In such cases the Crown Court should consider all the facts and decide whether the offender should be returned to custody for a term not less than the remaining effective period of his licence. If so, the Court should revoke his licence and consider whether any sentence of imprisonment passed in respect of the offence should be concurrent or consecutive to the

[36] *Report of the Parole Board 1982* (HMSO, 1983), para. 6.

[37] Such reasons may be given orally; there is no statutory requirement for the reasons to be given in writing (*R.* v. *Secretary of State for the Home Department, ex p. Gunnell* [1984] Crim.L.R. 170).

[38] Any such licence is treated as revoked where (a) the offender was sentenced to imprisonment with an order under C.L.A., s. 47(1) (sentences partly suspended), and was released on licence before the expiration of any part of his sentence which he was required to serve in prison under s. 47(1), and (b) by virtue of s. 47(3) a court restores any part of the sentence held in suspense (s. 62(7A) as inserted by C.J.A. 1982, Sched. 14, para. 20).

sentence for the offence in respect of which the court has revoked the licence (para. 3, *Practice Direction* (1976) 62 Cr.App.R. 130). If the Crown Court revokes a licence granted to a prisoner serving a determinate sentence he must not again be released on licence by the Home Secretary before the expiration of one year from the date of revocation or before the expiration of one third of the period during which the licence would have remained in force, whichever is the later (s. 62(10)). If a sentence of imprisonment is passed for the offence committed while on licence, but the licence is not revoked, a court which subsequently revokes his licence cannot make the new sentence consecutive to the original sentence (para. 5, *Practice Direction*). An order revoking a licence is a sentence for the purposes of section 9 of the Criminal Appeal Act 1968 and therefore could be the subject of an appeal (*Welch* [1982] 1 W.L.R. 976).

Early Release

Section 32 of the Criminal Justice Act 1982 gives the Home Secretary power by statutory instrument to order the early release of prisoners of a certain class specified in the order (subject to certain exceptions). The order may not operate so as to allow the release of a prisoner more than six months before the time when he would be due for release under the Prison Rules (s. 32(1)). The Home Secretary may only make an order if he is satisfied that it is necessary to do so in order to make the best use of the places available for detention (s. 32(1)). The Home Secretary may not make such an order in relation to persons who are serving a sentence of life imprisonment, or imprisonment to which they were sentenced: (i) for an excluded offence[39]; (ii) for attempting to commit such an offence; (iii) for conspiracy to commit such an offence; (iv) for aiding or abetting, counselling, procuring or inciting the commission of such an offence (s. 32(2)). No person may be released under these provisions if he is subject to more than one sentence of imprisonment, and at least one of the terms that he has to serve is for an offence mentioned in head (i), (ii), (iii) or (iv) above (s. 32(3)). The order may define the class of prisoners to be released in any way, for example, by reference to the length of their sentences, or the offences of which they were convicted, or the prison in which they are detained, and may make the time at which a person of any specified class is to be released from prison depend on any circumstances whatever (s. 32(4)). Those who are granted early release are released unconditionally (s. 32(6)) with the exception of a person serving an extended sentence who will be released on licence under section 60 of the Criminal Justice Act 1967 (s. 32(5)).

---

[39] The excluded offences are listed in C.J.A. 1982, Sched. 1, Pts. I, II and III.

Temporary discharge for ill-health

Under section 28 of the Prison Act 1952 the Home Secretary may authorise the temporary and conditional discharge of a prisoner whose health makes it undesirable that he should remain in prison, where that condition is not due to the prisoner's own conduct in prison. Where a prisoner is released under this power he must comply with any conditions stated in the order of temporary discharge and must return to prison at the expiration of the stated period, and if he fails to do either, he may be arrested without warrant and taken back to prison (s. 28(3)).

Temporary release

Under rule 6 of the Prison Rules 1964 a prisoner may be temporarily released for any period and subject to any conditions for any special purpose or to enable him to engage in employment, to receive instruction or training or to assist him in his transition from prison life to freedom. The power is exercised on compassionate grounds where a prisoner's need cannot be met by the grant of letters or visits, such as visiting a near relative who is dying or to attend the funeral of one who has died.[40] Prisoners may be allowed to visit prospective employers towards the end of their sentences or long-term prisoners may be considered for the pre-release employment scheme under which they work outside for a private employer for the last six months of the sentence; and many prisoners are allowed home leave in the last few months of their sentence to help with re-adjustment on release.[41] A prisoner released temporarily may be recalled to prison at any time whether the conditions of his release have been broken or not (r. 6(3)).

COMBINING IMPRISONMENT WITH OTHER MEASURES

The measure most regularly combined with imprisonment is a fine. It is unusual for a statute creating an offence not to give a court a choice of sentencing an offender to imprisonment or to fine him, or to impose both a fine and imprisonment, for the same offence. It is, however, wrong in principle to impose on the one occasion a sentence of imprisonment for one offence and a suspended sentence for another offence (*Sapiano* (1968) 52 Cr.App.R. 674; *Butters and Fitzgerald* (1971) 55 Cr.App.R. 515). It is wrong in principle to impose a custodial sentence to take immediate effect alongside a probation order in respect of another count (*Emmet* (1969) 53 Cr.App.R. 203; *Evans* [1959] 1 W.L.R. 26). As it is wrong to impose a suspended sentence at the same time as a community service order

[40] *Prisons and the Prisoner* (HMSO, 1977), para. 73.
[41] *Ibid.* paras. 114–117.

(*Starie* (1979) 1 Cr.App.R.(S.) 172) it is equally wrong to impose an immediate custodial sentence alongside a community service order. However, there is no reason why a discharge should not be imposed in relation to one count and a custodial sentence imposed in relation to another (see *Bainbridge* (1979) 1 Cr.App.R.(S.) 36). A custodial sentence may also be combined with ancillary orders such as orders for costs, compensation, restitution, criminal bankruptcy orders, forfeiture or disqualification.

WHEN IMPRISONMENT IS APPROPRIATE

Excluding the situations where imprisonment is mandatory, the circumstances in which imprisonment is appropriate are clearly very varied. In general it may be said that imprisonment is less and less perceived as involving a reformative process, and if that purpose is the dominant factor in a particular case imprisonment increasingly is regarded as an appropriate sentence only where other methods of treatment have failed or are unavailable. Imprisonment as a punishment or for deterrence is the major use made of this sentence. It is to be noted that for many offenders where the court views imprisonment as appropriate but thinks that only a short sentence is required, the major impact of a sentence is likely to be felt in the first weeks of imprisonment. Economic and sentencing considerations, combine to encourage a "short sharp shock" approach to sentencing, assuming that a shorter rather than a longer term is appropriate in the first place. Where a longer term of imprisonment is appropriate the courts, and especially the Court of Appeal, have developed principles to guide sentencers in particular cases (see "Sentencing Principles," below, Part VI).

APPEALS

Magistrates' courts

A person convicted by a magistrates' court and sentenced to imprisonment may appeal against that sentence to the Crown Court (M.C.A., s. 108(1)). If the offender is in custody the magistrates' court may grant bail (M.C.A., s. 113(1)). The time the appellant is in custody pending determination of his appeal will count as part of his sentence (C.J.A. 1967, s. 67(1)). The Crown Court may confirm, reverse or vary the decision appealed against and may "award any punishment, whether more or less severe than that awarded by the magistrates' court whose decision is appealed against, if that is a punishment which that magistrates' court might have awarded" (S.C.A., s. 48(4)).

Crown court

Appeal lies from the Crown Court to the Court of Appeal. An appeal against a sentence of imprisonment, unless it is a sentence fixed by law, lies only with the leave of the Court of Appeal (C.A.A. 1968, s. 11(1)).

The time during which an appellant is in custody pending the determination of his appeal counts towards his sentence unless the Court of Appeal directs to the contrary (C.A.A. 1968, s. 29(1)). Where the court gives such a direction they must state their reasons for doing so (s. 29(2)). No such direction may be given where leave to appeal has been granted or where the case has been referred to the Court by the Home Secretary under section 17 of the Criminal Appeals Act 1968 (s. 29(2)).

In 1980 the Lord Chief Justice issued a *Practice Direction* ((1980) 70 Cr.App.R. 186) in the following terms:

> "In order to accelerate the hearing of those appeals in which there is some merit, single judges will, from April 15, 1980, give special consideration to the giving of a direction for loss of time, whenever an application for leave to appeal is refused. It may be expected that such a direction will normally be made unless the grounds are not only settled and signed by counsel, but also supported by the written opinion of counsel. Advice on appeal is, of course, often available to prisoners under the legal aid scheme. Counsel should not settle grounds, or support them with written advice, unless he considers that the proposed appeal is properly arguable. It would, therefore, clearly not be appropriate to penalise the prisoner in such a case, even if the single judge considered that the appeal was quite hopeless.
>
> It is also necessary to stress that, if an application is refused by the single judge as being wholly devoid of merit, the full Court has power, in the event of renewal, both to order loss of time, if the single judge has not done so, and to increase the amount of time ordered to be lost if the single judge has already made a direction, whether or not grounds have been settled and signed by counsel. It may be expected that this power too will, as from April 15, 1980, normally be exercised."

When an appellant is granted bail under section 19 of the Criminal Appeals Act 1968, the time during which he is released on bail does not count as part of any term of imprisonment under his sentence.

On an appeal against sentence the Court of Appeal may, if they consider that a different sentence should have been passed, pass such sentence or make such order as they think appropriate for the case which the court below had power to pass or make when dealing with the case, but they may not alter the sentence so that, taking the case as a whole, the appellant is more severely dealt with on appeal than he was in the court below (s. 11(3)).

SUSPENDED SENTENCE

DESCRIPTION

As the objective of the suspended sentence is to keep the offender out of prison, it might equally be considered under the heading of non-custodial measures since its distinctive feature is that a sentence of imprisonment is *imposed* on conviction but not put into immediate effect.[1] The suspended sentence is intended as a deterrent measure and differs from a conditional discharge in that with the latter there is no specified sentence hanging over the offender which will be put into effect on the commission of a further offence. Probation, in turn, differs from a suspended sentence in that no specific term of imprisonment is fixed on conviction. However, supervision during the period of suspension is possible by means of a suspended sentence supervision order.

The suspended sentence was first introduced in 1967. A development of this sentence is the partly suspended sentence introduced by the Criminal Law Act 1977.

THE LAW

Where a court passes a sentence of imprisonment for a term not exceeding two years, the court may order that it be suspended for an operational period of not less than one and not more than two years (P.C.C.A., s. 22(1)).[2] Where a court passes consecutive sentences in respect of two or more offences the court may suspend the total term provided it does not exceed two years (P.C.C.A., s. 57(2); *Coleman* [1969] 2 Q.B. 468 and *Arkle* [1972] Crim.L.R. 582). By virtue of section 57(2) they constitute a single suspended sentence for the purposes of section 23(1) (*Gall* (1970) 54 Cr.App.R. 292). Where a judge imposes two suspended sentences he should state whether, as between themselves, they are to be concurrent or

---

[1] It should be noted that there is no power to suspend a detention centre order or a sentence of youth custody. By contrast, in Northern Ireland an order for detention in a young offenders' centre may be suspended. This would appear to be a serious omission in the legislation in England and Wales. This omission was commented on in the case of *Dobbs and Hitchings* (1983) 5 Cr.App.R.(S.) 378, by Lord Lane C.J., who expressed the hope that Parliament would see fit to enable the court to suspend youth custody sentences in whole or in part, as the absence of this power often presented the court with a dilemma.

[2] In Northern Ireland the operational period may extend up to three years (Treatment of Offenders Act 1968, s. 18(1)).

consecutive (*George Wilkinson* [1970] 1 W.L.R. 1319). If when sentences are passed they are not stated to be consecutive, they will subsequently be treated as being concurrent (*Corry* [1973] Crim.L.R. 381). A suspended sentence cannot be made consecutive to an earlier suspended sentence which is not then being put into effect (*Blakeway* [1969] 1 W.L.R. 1233).

A suspended sentence will not take effect unless the offender, during the period of suspension, commits an imprisonable offence in Great Britain and, a court, having power to do so under section 23 of the Powers of Criminal Courts Act, orders the sentence to take effect (s. 22(1)).

When making an order suspending a sentence of imprisonment the court shall explain to the offender in ordinary language his liability to be sentenced for that offence if he commits a further imprisonable offence during the operational period (s. 22(4)).

A suspended sentence may not be passed unless it appears to the court that, in the absence of a power to suspend, a sentence of immediate imprisonment would have been appropriate (s. 22(2)). Time spent in custody on remand does not count towards a suspended sentence.

COMBINING A SUSPENDED SENTENCE WITH OTHER MEASURES

A suspended sentence cannot be combined with a probation order in respect of another offence of which the offender is convicted at the same time or for an offence which is dealt with by the court at that time (s. 22(3)).[3] It is wrong in principle either to pass a suspended sentence for one offence and impose a custodial sentence with immediate effect for another offence at the same time or to activate one suspended sentence while imposing another, as the main object of the suspended sentence is to avoid sentencing an offender to prison at all (*Sapiano* (1968) 52 Cr.App.R. 674; *Butters and Fitzgerald* (1971) 55 Cr.App.R. 515).[4] One exception to this principle, however, is the situation where a magistrates' court has imposed a suspended sentence for an offence committed during the operational period of a suspended sentence imposed by the Crown Court. In such a case, the Crown Court is not prevented from activating the suspended sentence (*Hamilton* [1985] Crim.L.R. 111). Equally it is wrong in principle to make a suspended sentence consecutive or concurrent to a sentence actually being served (*Flanders* [1969] 1 Q.B. 148; *Baker* (1971) 55 Cr.App.R. 182).

---

[3] This applies even when the court is sentencing an offender who has pleaded guilty to two indictments (*Wright* [1975] Crim.L.R. 728).
[4] See also *Jones* (1983) 5 Cr.App.R.(S.) 324.

Consecutive sentences passed on the same occasion may be suspended. By virtue of section 23(1) they constitute a single suspended sentence for the purposes of section 22 (*Gall* (1970) 54 Cr.App.R. 292).

A court may impose a fine when passing a suspended sentence for the same count, but the court should ensure that the fine is well within the offender's means (*King* [1970] 1 W.L.R. 1016; *Whybrew* (1979) 1 Cr.App.R.(S.) 121). The court may not, however, add a suspended sentence in a case where the principal sentence is a fine (*Barker* [1980] Crim.L.R. 600). The addition of a fine will be appropriate in two circumstances. First, as a means of depriving the offender of any profit he may have made. Secondly, it may be used where "the scales were very nicely balanced as to whether the deterrent sentence ought not to be a sentence of immediate imprisonment" (*Leigh* (1969) 54 Cr.App.R. 169). In this case it is regarded as a supplementary penalty adding a punitive element to the sentence. In *Genese* [1976] 1 W.L.R. 958 the correct approach in this second situation was outlined by the Court of Appeal:

> "If the court decides there is no other appropriate method of dealing with the offender than imprisonment, and imposes a prison sentence, the court can then, in the appropriate case, go on to consider that the sentence should be suspended .... [I]f the court does go on to consider that the sentence should be suspended ... the court can also consider whether an additional penalty by way of a fine is justified."[5]

In *Starie* (1979) 1 Cr.App.R.(S.) 172 the Court of Appeal stated that it is wrong in principle and bad sentencing practice to impose a community service order on the same occasion as a suspended sentence even though they relate to separate counts.

WHEN A SUSPENDED SENTENCE IS APPROPRIATE

Section 22(2) provides that a suspended sentence may not be passed unless it appears to the court that, in the absence of a power to suspend, a sentence of immediate imprisonment would have been appropriate. A suspended sentence should not be imposed if an immediate sentence of imprisonment would be inappropriate (*Whitehead* (1979) 1 Cr.App.R.(S.) 187).[6] Thus, if a fine would be appropriate but for the offender's lack of means, a suspended sentence should not be imposed but a conditional discharge will normally be appropriate (*Whitehead; Ball* [1982] Crim.L.R. 131).

---

[5] See also *Ankers* (1975) 61 Cr.App.R. 170 in relation to adding a prison sentence to a fine.

[6] See also *English* (1984) 6 Cr.App.R.(S.) 60 and *Watts* (1984) 6 Cr.App.R.(S.) 61.

The Court of Appeal in *O'Keefe* [1969] 2 Q.B. 29, laid down the procedure which a sentencer should follow in deciding upon a suspended sentence as appropriate for an offence:

> "The court must go through the process of eliminating other possible courses such as absolute discharge, conditional discharge, probation orders, fines and then say to itself: this is a case for imprisonment, and the final question, it being a case for imprisonment, is immediate imprisonment required, or can a suspended sentence be given?" (*per* Lord Parker C.J. at p. 32).[7]

The court should also determine the length of the term of imprisonment before considering whether to suspend; it is wrong to increase the length of the sentence because the court intends to suspend it (*Trowbridge* [1975] Crim.L.R. 295; see also *Webb* [1979] Crim.L.R. 466).

Consequences of a further conviction during the operational period
Where the offender is convicted of an imprisonable offence committed during the operational period of the suspended sentence, the Crown Court (before which he is convicted of that offence, or before which he is brought following a conviction by a magistrates' court where the suspended sentence was originally passed by the Crown Court), or a magistrates' court (where the sentence was passed by a magistrates' court), shall consider his case and deal with him by one of the following methods (s. 23(1) and 24(1)):

    (a) by ordering the suspended sentence to take effect with the original term unaltered;

    (b) by ordering the suspended sentence to take effect with the substitution of a lesser term for the original term;

    (c) by substituting a new operational period in the original order expiring not later than two years from the date of the variation;

    (d) by making no order with respect to the suspended sentence.

The court is obliged to make an order under paragraph (a) "unless the court is of opinion that it would be unjust to do so in view of all the circumstances, including the facts of the subsequent offence, and where it is of that opinion the court shall state its reasons" (s. 23(1)).[8]

---

[7] See also *Brewer* (1982) 4 Cr.App.R.(S.) 380. In *Stock* [1984] Crim.L.R. 764, the appellant, an animal welfare campaigner, committed a burglary in pursuance of the campaign. His previous good character and his motivation were accepted by the Court of Appeal as factors which should have led to the sentence of imprisonment imposed being suspended.

[8] Where a court deals with an offender under s. 23 in respect of a suspended sentence the court clerk shall notify the court clerk of the court which passed the sentence of the method adopted (s. 23(7)); and where the court makes no order with respect to a suspended sentence, the court clerk shall record that fact (s. 23(8)).

In order for a further offence to activate a suspended sentence during the operational period it must be an imprisonable offence. Where, however, the offence committed during the operational period is an offence punishable with imprisonment only when tried on indictment and the offender is convicted after a summary trial, this conviction will not render him liable to the activation of the suspended sentence (*Melbourne* (1980) 2 Cr.App.R.(S.) 116). Provided the offence was committed during the currency of the operational period, it does not matter that the conviction occurs after the expiration of the operational period.

If a further offence is dealt with by a court by an order for absolute or conditional discharge, or by a probation order, the suspended sentence cannot be put into effect, because under section 13(1) of the Powers of Criminal Courts Act the conviction is deemed not to be a conviction except for the purposes of the proceedings in which the order was made (*Tarry* [1970] 2 Q.B. 560). Similarly where the court dealing with a subsequent offence makes an order deferring sentence the suspended sentence cannot be activated during the period of deferment because ultimately the defendant may be dealt with by means of a discharge or probation, and therefore technically would not be convicted within section 23 (*Salmon* (1973) 57 Cr.App.R. 953). In *Tarry* it was suggested that where a magistrates' court is dealing with an offender who is subject to a suspended sentence imposed by the Crown Court, it should not make an order such as a probation order which would, as a matter of law, prevent the Crown Court from activating the suspended sentence, but should commit both matters to the Crown Court. In *Stewart* (1984) 6 Cr.App.R.(S.) 166, the Court of Appeal stated that while a community service order does not have the same effect as a probation order or discharge, a magistrates' court should not impose one where an offender is convicted before it of an offence while subject to a suspended sentence. Likewise if the magistrates' court is minded to impose a suspended sentence for the subsequent offence, the better course is to commit the offender to the Crown Court for sentencing (*Hamilton* [1985] Crim.L.R. 111).

It is to be noted that the effect of section 23 is that the suspended sentence does not automatically take effect as a sentence of imprisonment. The court has a discretion in dealing with the suspended sentence, ranging from imposing the full term of imprisonment to making no order at all. Nevertheless the suspended term of imprisonment must normally take effect with the original term unaltered (*Stevens* (1971) 55 Cr.App.R. 154), unless "the court is of opinion that it would be unjust to do so in view of all the circumstances which have arisen since the suspended sentence was passed, including the facts of the subsequent offence" (s. 23(1)).

Where the court is minded to do other than impose the original term it must state the reasons for so doing (s. 23(1)). In considering what circumstances would justify a course other than an immediate imposition of the full term of imprisonment, facts which are relevant include the offender's previous record and behaviour during the operational period up to the subsequent offence (*Griffiths* [1969] 1 W.L.R. 896), his personal circumstances (*Joshua* (1980) 2 Cr.App.R.(S.) 287), and his age (*Abrahams* (1980) 2 Cr.App.R.(S.) 10). The nature of the subsequent offence is also clearly relevant. In *Moylan* [1969] 3 W.L.R. 814, 817 Widgery L.J. stated:

> "We think it quite clear that the court may properly consider as unjust the activation of a suspended sentence where the new offence is a comparatively trivial offence and, particularly, where it is in a different category from that for which the suspended sentence was imposed. It is trite to say that every case depends on its own circumstances and so it does. But there must be many instances in practice where a relatively minor offence committed in drink can under the terms of the section give rise to the activation of a heavy suspended sentence, and we recognise that it is proper for the court considering the matter to regard this as unjust in an appropriate case. Equally we think that secion 23 in its terms indicates that the activation of a suspended sentence shall be the normal course on committing a further offence punishable with imprisonment."

Subsequent decisions of the court make clear that merely because the subsequent offence is of a different character, is not of itself sufficient reason for not bringing the sentence into effect (*Saunders* (1970) 54 Cr.App.R. 247).[9] It appears that the subsequent offence must be *both* trivial in nature and different in character to make a case for non-activation of the suspended sentence. In *Deck* [1970] Crim.L.R. 172, the defendant was under a suspended sentence of two years imprisonment for shopbreaking and larceny when he was convicted of driving while disqualified, for which he was sentenced to six months imprisonment. The Court of Appeal refused to say that the imposition of the suspended sentence was unjust, given the accused's record, and the fact that he had previous convictions for driving whilst disqualified.[10]

While it is not part of the function of a court considering the activation of a suspended sentence in any way to review its propriety, there are cases where justice cannot be done without

[9] See also *Stevens* (1971) 55 Cr.App.R. 154; *Vanston* [1972] Crim.L.R. 57; *Barton* [1974] Crim.L.R. 555.
[10] But *cf. Prince* [1982] Crim.L.R. 321; *O'Donnell* (1982) 4 Cr.App.R.(S.) 96.

fitting into the pattern of events leading to the further conviction the facts which led to the suspended sentence. In such cases it may be necessary for the court to inform itself of the circumstances in which the suspended sentence was passed, in order that proper assessment may be made of the overall position so as to determine the sentence which is to be passed and to make plain the grounds on which it is acting (*Munday* (1971) 56 Cr.App.R. 220).

Circumstances may not justify not activating the suspended sentence, but the court may, in an appropriate case, reduce the term of imprisonment when putting the sentence into effect, as where the subsequent offence is a trivial example of the type of offence for which the suspended sentence was imposed (*Preece* [1970] Crim.L.R. 296),[11] or where the subsequent offence is committed near the end of the operational period (*Branwhite* [1981] Crim.L.R. 193; *Windle* [1981] Crim.L.R. 351).

Where an offender who is subject to a suspended sentence appears before a court and is convicted of a subsequent offence and that court deals with the suspended sentence by making no order in relation to it but makes a community service order in respect of the later offence, there is no power in any subsequent court to deal again with the same breach of the suspended sentence notwithstanding that the C.S.O. is subsequently terminated and a sentence of imprisonment is imposed for the subsequent offence following the offender's failure to comply with the requirements of the order (*Folan* [1980] 1 W.L.R. 1; *R.* v. *Peterborough Justices, ex p. Casey* (1979) 1 Cr.App.R.(S.) 268; *Temperley* (1980) 2 Cr.App.R.(S.) 127).[12] In such a case the suspended sentence continues in force and if there is a further breach it may be activated. Where a court does decide to impose a C.S.O. or other non-custodial measure for the subsequent offence, this does not preclude it from activating the suspended sentence, but it will rarely be appropriate to do so. While the fact that the imposition of a C.S.O. does not of itself make the activation of the suspended sentence unjust, the consideration which led the court to impose a C.S.O. may also be grounds for

---

[11] See also *Fitzgerald* [1972] Crim.L.R. 583; *Cline* (1979) 1 Cr.App.R.(S.) 40; *Joshua* [1981] Crim.L.R. 61.

[12] It is not clear whether the same principle applies where the offender receives a conditional discharge or probation order in respect of the subsequent offence and contravenes either of these orders. As a conditional discharge or probation order does not constitute a conviction for the purposes of activating a suspended sentence (*Tarry* [1970] 2 Q.B. 561), it is arguable that a court dealing with the breach of a probation order or the commission of an offence during the currency of a conditional discharge or probation order may have power to deal with the suspended sentence under its power to deal with the offender for the offence for which the order was made in any manner in which the court could deal with him if it had just convicted him of that offence.

saying that activation of the suspended sentence would be unjust (see *Seymour* [1983] Crim.L.R. 410; *McElhorne* [1983] Crim.L.R. 487).

Where an offender is before the court for a fresh offence committed during the operational period of a suspended sentence the proper procedure is to sentence him first for the subsequent offence and then consider the suspended sentence. In *Ithell* [1969] 1 W.L.R. 272, the deputy chairman of Quarter Sessions had first dealt with the earlier suspended sentences of two years' imprisonment, ordering that they take effect, and then sentenced the defendants to 18 months' imprisonment to run consecutively, making a total of three and a half years. The Court of Appeal disapproved of the procedure: the sentencing court should decide the appropriate sentence for the current offence before activating the suspended sentence: the order in which these matters were to be done could have practical importance. Cases could easily arise where the type and duration of sentence imposed for the current offence would materially affect the courts' selection of the most suitable among the four courses open to it in relation to the suspended sentence (see also *Beacock* (1979) 1 Cr.App.R.(S.) 198). As it is wrong in principle to impose at the same time an immediate sentence of imprisonment in relation to one offence and a suspended sentence for another (*Sapiano* (1968) 52 Cr.App.R. 674), a court should not activate a suspended sentence at the same time as imposing a suspended sentence in relation to the new offence; nor should it extend the operational period of the suspended sentence while imposing a sentence of imprisonment for the new offence (*Goodlad* [1973] 1 W.L.R. 1102). Where the court imposes a prison sentence for the subsequent offence, the suspended sentence should be activated so as not to remain hanging over the offender's head on release from prison (*Baker* (1982) 4 Cr.App.R.(S) 231; *Crawley* [1985] Crim.L.R. 58). In addition, in fixing the sentences for the new offences, the court should not treat these as more serious and meriting more severe sentences because they were committed during the operational period of a suspended sentence, but should pass sentences appropriate to the offences themselves (*Davies* [1979] Crim.L.R. 62).

A court which orders that a suspended sentence shall take effect (with or without any variation of the original term) may order the sentence to take effect concurrently with, or consecutively to, another term of imprisonment passed on the offender by that or another court (s. 23(2)). Unless there are "some quite exceptional circumstances," a suspended sentence of imprisonment which has been activated should be consecutive and not concurrent to the sentence given for the subsequent offence (*Ithell* [1969] 1 W.L.R.

272; *May* (1979) 1 Cr.App.R.(S.) 124.[13] An example of an exceptional circumstance might occur where a very short suspended sentence is activated at the same time as a very long sentence for a subsequent offence (see *Christie* (1979) 1 Cr.App.R.(S.) 84). This is sometimes done to temper justice with mercy (*per* Lowry L.C.J., *McQuade* [1974] N.I.J.B.). Alternatively, where the operational period of the suspended sentence is almost expired, it may be activated concurrent to the sentence for the subsequent offence (*Kilroy* (1979) 1 Cr.App.R.(S.) 179; *Carr* (1979) 1 Cr.App.R.(S.) 53). However, when the court orders the sentence to run consecutively to that for the new offence, it may adjust the period either of the suspended sentence or the new sentence to ensure that the total sentence is not excessive in the circumstances (*Bocskei* (1970) 54 Cr.App.R. 519). The time for deciding whether a suspended sentence should be consecutive or concurrent is the time when the matter is before the court under section 23(1) and not at the time when the suspended sentence was first passed unless other suspended sentences were imposed at the same time. Accordingly, a suspended sentence cannot be made consecutive to an earlier suspended sentence which is not then being activated (*Blakeway* [1969] 1 W.L.R. 1233).

Courts empowered to deal with suspended sentences

An offender may be dealt with in respect of a suspended sentence by the Crown Court, or, where the sentence was passed by a magistrates' court, by any magistrates' court before which he appears or is brought (s. 24(1)). However, where the subsequent offence is tried summarily but the suspended sentence was imposed by the Crown Court, the magistrates' court may, if it thinks fit, commit the offender in custody or on bail to the Crown Court to be dealt with in respect of the whole matter, or, if it does not do so, it can deal with the offender for the immediate offence and give notice of the conviction to the clerk of the court which imposed the sentence so that the offender can be brought back before that court (s. 24(2)). If the magistrates opt for the second course of action they should not deal with the subsequent offence in a way which makes it impossible for the Crown Court to activate the suspended sentence, for example, by placing the offender on probation or discharging him absolutely or conditionally; their proper course of action in such a case should be to commit the offender to the Crown Court (see *Tarry* and *Stewart*, above).

---

[13] In the Northern Irish case of *McQuade* (unreported, February 1, 1974), the rationale behind this rule was stated to be that to do otherwise would rob the suspended sentence of its deterrent effect.

If it appears to the Crown Court (if the suspended sentence was passed by that court) or to a justice of the peace (acting for the area for which the magistrates' court acted if the suspended sentence was passed by a magistrates' court) that an offender has been convicted in Great Britain[14] of an offence punishable with imprisonment committed during the operational period of the suspended sentence and he has not been dealt with in respect of the suspended sentence, that court or justice may issue a summons or warrant for his arrest[15] requiring the offender to appear or be brought before the court by which the suspended sentence was passed (s. 25(1)(2)(5)).

Suspended sentence supervision orders

While it is not possible, on the one occasion, to impose a suspended sentence on an offender and put him on probation, a court may achieve a similar result by means of a suspended sentence supervision order in any case where it passes on an offender a suspended sentence for a term of more than six months for a single offence (s. 26(1)).[16] Under such an order the offender is placed under the supervision of a probation officer for a period specified in the order not exceeding the operational period of the suspended sentence (s. 26(1) and (3)).[17] The offender is required to keep in touch with the probation officer in accordance with such instructions as the officer may from time to time give him and he must notify the office of any change of address.[18]

On making such an order the court must forthwith give copies of the order to the probation officer assigned to the court and he must give a copy to the offender and the supervising officer (s. 26(5)). The court must explain in ordinary language the effects of the order to the offender (s. 26(11)).

[14] Where an offender is convicted by a court in Scotland of an offence punishable with imprisonment and the court is informed that the offence was committed during the operational period of a suspended sentence passed in England or Wales, the court must give written notice of the conviction to the appropriate officer of the court by which the suspended sentence was passed (s. 25(3)). There is no like provision for offences committed in Northern Ireland.

[15] Unless he is acting in consequence of a notice under s. 25(3), a justice of the peace shall not issue a summons except on information and shall not issue a warrant except on information in writing and on oath (s. 25(4)).

[16] Because of the six months minimum sentence it will be rare for a magistrates' court to have power to impose a suspended sentence supervision order. However the Home Secretary has power by order to reduce the minimum period or abolish it altogether (s. 26(2)).

[17] The order must specify the petty sessions area in which the offender resides or will reside (s. 26(3)).

[18] No additional requirements may be included in the order such as may be included in a probation order.

Where an offender is dealt with under section 23(1) for commission of a further offence during the operational period of the suspended sentence, and the court dealing with him either varies the operational period of the suspended sentence or makes no order with respect to the suspended sentence, the court may make a supervision order in respect of the offender:

(a) in place of any such order made when the suspended sentence was passed; or

(b) if the court which passed the sentence could have made such an order but did not do so; or

(c) if that court could not then have made such an order but would have had power to do so if subsection (1) had then had effect as it has effect at the time when the offender is dealt with under section 23.

(s. 26(10).)[19]

A supervision order ceases to have effect if before the end of the period specified in it:

(a) a court activates the suspended sentence under section 23; or

(b) the order is discharged or replaced.

(s. 26(8).)

An order may be discharged or replaced on the application of the supervising officer or the offender:

(a) if it was made by the Crown Court and included a direction reserving the power of discharging it to that court, by the Crown Court;

(b) in any other case by a magistrates' court acting for the petty sessions area for the time being specified in the order.

(s. 26(9).)

If at any time while the order is in force the offender breaches any of the requirements of section 26(4) he may be brought before the magistrates' court acting for the petty sessions area specified in the order and may be fined up to £400.

APPEALS

The normal appeal procedures apply with regard to the imposition of a suspended sentence. Any order made by a court under section 23 dealing with an offender for commission of an offence during the operational period, is to be treated as a sentence passed on the offender by that court for the offence for which the suspended sentence was passed (s. 23(9)), and, accordingly, may be appealed against in the normal way.

---

[19] *i.e.* where the Secretary of State has in the interim by order under s. 26(2) reduced or abolished the minimum sentence specified in s. 26(1).

THE PARTLY SUSPENDED SENTENCE

DESCRIPTION

The partly suspended sentence which was introduced on March 29, 1982, combines the features of a sentence of immediate imprisonment with those of a suspended sentence whereby the offender serves part of the total term imposed, the remainder being held in suspense with the possibility of activation if the offender is convicted of an imprisonable offence committed during the whole period of the sentence.

THE LAW

The power to pass a partly suspended sentence is contained in section 47 of the Criminal Law Act 1977 as amended by section 30 of the Criminal Justice Act 1982. A court passing a sentence of imprisonment of not less than three months and not more than two years may order part to be served immediately with the remainder held in suspense (s. 47(1)). As the power to partly suspend a sentence contained in section 47(1) only empowers a court which passes a sentence of imprisonment to suspend a part, a court activating a suspended sentence may not suspend part of the sentence being activated as that court is not "passing sentence" but rather is activating a sentence already passed (see *Gow* (1983) 5 Cr.App.R.(S) 250). The minimum period of the sentence to be served in prison is 28 days and at least one quarter of the whole term must be suspended (s. 47(2)). The offender will not be required to serve the suspended part unless it is restored following the offender's conviction of an imprisonable offence during the whole period of the original sentence (s. 47(2) and (3)). In passing a partly suspended sentence the court must explain to the offender in ordinary language, the consequences of conviction of an imprisonable offence before the expiration of the term of the sentence (s. 47(2)).

Section 67(2A) of the Criminal Justice Act 1967, as inserted by Schedule 14 of the Criminal Justice Act 1982, provides that time spent in custody awaiting trial is taken into account in the normal way as it counts towards the part of the sentence which the offender is ordered to serve. It also operates to reduce the whole period of the sentence for the purposes of section 47(3) but it does not reduce the

123

actual term ordered to be held in suspense under section 47(1).[1] The part to be served is also reduced by one third remission. The rules relating to release on licence also apply to the part of the sentence to be served in prison[2] (C.J.A. 1967, s. 60(1C)).

COMBINING A PARTLY SUSPENDED SENTENCE WITH OTHER MEASURES

If the court passes a partly suspended sentence it may not make a probation order in respect of another offence of which the offender is convicted by or before that court, or for which he is dealt with by that court (Sched. 9, para. 1). Following *Starie* (1979) 1 Cr.App.R.(S.) 172 it is likely that it will be improper practice to impose a partly suspended sentence at the same time as a C.S.O. Following *Sapiano* (1968) 52 Cr.App.R. 674, a partly suspended sentence should not be imposed at the same time as a fully suspended sentence. Provided the offender has the means to pay, there would seem to be no reason why a partly suspended sentence should not be combined with a fine or compensation order.

A court may sentence an offender to two or more consecutive sentences, each partly suspended (see Sched. 9, para. 3A(2)). The aggregate of such sentences must not exceed two years (P.C.C.A., s. 57(2); C.L.A., s. 47(8)). In such a case he will serve the prison terms first and then the suspended parts will be aggregated and he

---

[1] Time spent in custody does not count towards a suspended sentence. Thus it may, in some cases, be to the offender's advantage to receive a partly suspended sentence rather than a fully suspended sentence; the part he is ordered to serve may be reduced to nothing by the effect of the time served (and remission) and the remaining period of suspension will be shorter than in the case of a fully suspended sentence. For example, a sentence of 12 months is passed. In one case the court partly suspends it ordering three months to be served while in another it orders suspension of the whole period. In the former case if the offender has been in custody for two months and earned one third remission, he will be released immediately and will have nine months suspension still facing him. In the latter case, regardless of any period in custody awaiting trial, the offender will face 12 months suspension and consequently is at risk for a longer period.

[2] Where the whole term is more than 12 months and the part to be served is more than nine months an order for partial suspension may place the offender at a disadvantage compared with a sentence of the same length without any partial suspension. If an offender with a partly suspended sentence is released on licence he will be liable to imposition of the whole balance of the sentence up until the expiry of the whole term of the sentence, whereas an offender who receives a simple sentence of imprisonment will be liable to revocation of his licence only until such time as he would otherwise have been released had he been granted remission and the period of imprisonment he may be required to serve will be the remaining effective part of his sentence (see Commentary, *Farrand* [1984] Crim.L.R. 51 and Thomas, "The Partly Suspended Sentence" [1982] Crim.L.R. 288, at pp. 290–292).

will remain liable to the restoration of the balance of the sentences during this period (Sched. 9, para. 3A(2)). A court may also make a partly suspended sentence consecutive to an ordinary sentence of imprisonment (Sched. 9, para. 3A(1)) and again the aggregate must not exceed two years. This procedure, however, is unnecessarily complex and would seem to be suitable only where the offender is already serving a prison sentence. Where he is convicted of two or more offences at the same time the simplest procedure is to pass consecutive sentences and then order part of the total period to be served and the remainder held in suspense (see *McCarthy* (1983) 4 Cr.App.R.(S.) 364).

WHEN A PARTLY SUSPENDED SENTENCE IS APPROPRIATE

Section 47(1A) provides that a court shall not pass a partly suspended sentence unless the case appears to the court to be one in which a wholly suspended sentence would be inappropriate. In *Clarke* [1982] 1 W.L.R. 1090, the Court of Appeal took the opportunity of laying down guidelines on the imposition of partly suspended sentences. It is considered appropriate to quote at length from the judgment of Lord Lane C.J.:

"Before imposing a partly suspended sentence the Court should ask itself the following question: First of all, is this a case where a custodial sentence is really necessary? If it is not, it should pass a non-custodial sentence. But if it is necessary then the Court should ask itself secondly this: can we make a community service order as an equivalent to imprisonment, or can we suspend the whole sentence? That problem requires very careful consideration. . . . If it is possible to make a community service order or to suspend the whole of the sentence, then of course that should be done. If not, then the third point arises: what is the shortest sentence the Court can properly impose? In many cases, of which an obvious example is the case of the first offender for whom a short term of imprisonment is a sufficient shock, without any suspension, that would be enough. Sometimes 14 or 28 days may suffice, which is shorter than the shortest term which is at present available under section 47, which of course is one–quarter of six months, that is, one-and-a-half months.

In that case that should be the order of the Court, without any partial suspension at all. The imposition of a very short term will also make possible the ordering of a fine or a compensation order in addition, when such a course is appropriate.

If imprisonment is necessary, and if a very short sentence is not enough, and if it is not appropriate to suspend the sentence altogether, then partial suspension should be considered. Great care must be taken to ensure that the power is not used in a way which may serve to increase the length of sentence. . . .

In general the type of case that we have in mind is where the gravity of the offence is such that at least six months' imprisonment is merited, but when there are mitigating circumstances which point towards a measure of leniency not sufficient to warrant total suspension. Examples are always dangerous, but we venture very tentatively to suggest a few: first of all, some serious "one off' acts of violence which are usually met with immediate terms of imprisonment: some cases of burglary which at present warrant 18 months' or two years' imprisonment, where the offender is suitably qualified in terms of his record: some cases of fraud on public departments or some credit card frauds, where a short immediate sentence would be insufficient; some cases of handling involving medium-range sums of money; some thefts involving breach of trust; some cases of stealing from employers. All these are examples of cases where it may be possible to suspend part of the sentence without harm to the public and with benefit to the prisoner.

We would like to echo the words of the Advisory Council on the Penal System in paragraph 282 of their 1968 report on the review of maximum penalties: "We view the partially suspended sentence as a legitimate means of exploiting one of the few reliable pieces of criminological knowledge—that many offenders sent to prison for the first time do not subsequently reoffend. We see it not as a means of administering a "short, sharp shock," nor as a substitute for a wholly suspended sentence, but as especially applicable to serious first offenders or first-time prisoners who are bound to have to serve some time in prison, but who may well be effectively deterred by eventually serving only a small part of even the minimum sentence appropriate to the offence. This, in our view, must be its principal role.' We would like to add another type of offender: prisoners whose last term of imprisonment was some considerable time ago. We think that the power can be used on occasions where something more than a short sentence of immediate imprisonment is required to mark public disapproval and as a deterrent to others, but where the circumstances of the particular offender are such that some short term of immediate imprisonment, coupled with the threat involved in the suspension of the remainder, is enough to punish him for what he has done and to deter him in the future."

Restoring the balance of the sentence

If the offender is convicted of an offence punishable with imprisonment committed during the whole term of the original sentence, a competent court *may* restore the part of the sentence held in suspense and order the offender to serve it (s. 47(3)).[3] If the court is of opinion that (in view of all the circumstances including the facts of the subsequent offence) it would be unjust fully to restore the part of the sentence held in suspense, it shall either restore a lesser part or declare, giving reasons, its decision to make no order (s. 47(4)). If a court orders only part of the balance to be restored under section 47(4) no further order may be made in respect of any remaining part of the partly suspended sentence should there be a further conviction for an offence committed during the whole term of the sentence (s. 47(4A).[4] Where a court restores the balance or a part thereof it may direct that term to be served either immediately or consecutively to another term of imprisonment passed on the offender by that or another court (s. 47(5)).

Provided the offence was committed during the whole term of the sentence, it does not matter that the conviction occurs subsequent to the expiration of the whole term. The competent court's power to restore the balance of the sentence derives from there being a conviction; if the offence is dealt with by a discharge, probation order or sentence is deferred or the offence was only taken into consideration in dealing with the offender for some other offence, the court cannot restore the suspended part of the sentence (see p. 4 above). The competent courts are the Crown Court and, where the sentence was passed by a magistrates' court, any magistrates' court before which the offender appears or is brought (Sched. 9, para. 2(1)). Where an offender is convicted by a magistrates' court of an imprisonable offence committed during the whole period of a partly suspended sentence passed by the Crown Court the court may commit him to the Crown Court (para. 2(2)).

If it appears to the Crown Court (if the original sentence was passed by that Court) or to a justice of the peace (acting for the area for which the magistrates' court acted if the sentence was passed by

---

[3] Where an offender is before a court with a view to the exercise by that court of its powers under s. 47(3), the court clerk shall: (a) if the court decided not to exercise the powers, record that fact; and (b) whether or not it exercised them, notify the clerk of the court which passed the original sentence as to the manner in which the offender was dealt with (para. 5).

[4] It should be noted that the power to restore the balance of a partly suspended sentence is expressed in permissive terms whereas in relation to a fully suspended sentence activation of the sentence in full is mandatory unless it would be unjust. Thus in the case of partly suspended sentences, the court would seem to have an unfettered discretion.

a magistrates' court) that an offender has been convicted in Great Britain[5] of an offence punishable with imprisonment committed during the whole period of the partly suspended sentence and that he has not been dealt with in respect of the part of the sentence held in suspense, the court or justice may issue a summons or warrant for his arrest[6] requiring the offender to appear or be brought before the court by which the original sentence was passed (para. 3(1) and (5)).

APPEALS

The normal rights of appeal apply. Any order made by a court to restore the balance or a part thereof of a partly suspended sentence is to be treated as a sentence passed on the offender by that court for the original offence (para. 6) and, accordingly may be appealed against in the normal way.

---

[5] Where an offender is convicted by a court in Scotland of an offence punishable with imprisonment and that court is informed that the offence was committed during the whole period of a partly suspended sentence passed in England and Wales, it must give written notice of the conviction to the appropriate officer of the court in England and Wales by which the original sentence was passed (para. 3(3)). There is no like provision for offences committed in Northern Ireland.

[6] Unless he is acting in consequence of a notice under para. 3(3), a justice of the peace shall not issue a summons except on information and shall not issue a warrant except on information in writing and on oath.

CLASSIFICATION OF OFFENDERS UNDER 21 YEARS

Following the Criminal Justice Act 1982, the law may now be said to distinguish for sentencing purposes;
  (a) *adult offenders*: that is offenders aged 21 years or more;
  (b) *young offenders*: defined as offenders aged 14 years or more but under 21 years;
  (c) *young persons*: defined in the Children and Young Persons Acts as aged 14 years or more but under 17 years.
  (d) *children*: defined in the Children and Young Persons Acts as aged 10 years or more, but under 14 years.
Categories (b) and (c) overlap, but the category *young persons* remains important to distinguish for general criminal proceedings as well as sentencing, because it is this group along with children who come before the juvenile court, and in the case of both groups, the court is required with respect to all dispositions custodial and non-custodial to give primacy to the welfare of the person. (C.Y.P.A. 1933, s. 44.) Within the general category of young offender, 14 years to 21 years, the availability of certain sentences or orders depends on the offender reaching a particular age within that class. The major distinction between (a) and (b), above is the abolition of the sentence of imprisonment for offenders under 21 years. This was achieved by the Criminal Justice Act 1982, s. 1.

For purposes of this section, the sentencing powers of the courts will be distinguished in terms of: (a) young offenders; (b) young persons; (c) children.

YOUNG OFFENDERS

The Criminal Justice Act 1982, Part I, introduced four custodial measures for young offenders; a detention centre order, default detention, youth custody and custody for life. By virtue of this Act, no person under 21 years may be sentenced or committed to prison (s. 1(1)). Sentences of Borstal training have also been abolished (s. 1(3)).

The intention of the 1982 Act is to encourage greater use of non-custodial measures for young offenders and this is to be achieved by restricting the circumstances in which custodial sentences are available to the courts. At the same time, the Act goes some way towards implementing the recommendations of the Advisory

Council on the Penal System for a more flexible scheme of custodial treatment where such is necessary for young people.[1]

On the choice between non-custodial and custodial measures the Court must be first of opinion that no non-custodial method of dealing with the offender is appropriate by reason of:

(a) the unwillingness or inability on the part of the offender to respond to non-custodial measures; or

(b) the danger to the public; or

(c) the grave nature of the offence.

(s. 1(4).)

The interpretation of these requirements to date has been uneven. In *Moffett* (1984) 6 Cr.App.R.(S)90, a young offender who had served custodial sentences previously had a 12-month youth custody order (see below) varied to one of probation as the evidence did not show that he would not respond to a non-custodial sentence (the other two grounds did not apply). However, in *Dunning* [1984] Crim.L.R. 635, *Hooper* [1984] Crim.L.R. 637 and *Forrest and Gray* [1984] Crim.L.R. 764 young offenders were sentenced to custodial sentences in circumstances where none of the requirements in the Act seemed to apply. The Court of Appeal made no reference to this and in both cases upheld the imposition of a custodial sentence.[2] This failure by the Court of Appeal to apply consistently C.J.A. 1982, s. 1(4) means that the application of the statutory criteria is becoming more confused. These criteria are the only acceptable reasons for imposing a custodial sentence but the Court of Appeal on occasions appears to pay scant attention to them. In *Forrest and Gray* the only basis upon which a custodial sentence could possibly have been justified was the third criterion that the offence was so serious that a non-custodial sentence could not be justified. However, the court failed to give any explanation of how such a conclusion could be supportable on the facts of the case. By contrast, in *McDermott* [1985] Crim.L.R. 245, a differently constituted court quashed a sentence of 12 months' youth custody and substituted a community service order where the trial judge had failed to consider alternatives to custody in accordance with the statutory criteria. As it was not clear that the offence was so serious that a non-custodial sentence could not be justified, the judge had clearly failed to apply the statutory criteria.

[1] Advisory Council on the Penal System, *Young Adult Offenders*, and see the Green Paper, *Youth Custody and Supervision—a non Sentence*, 1978 (Cmnd. 7406), the White Paper, *Young Offenders*, 1980 (Cmnd. 8045). For an account of the effect of these various proposals on the 1982 Act's provisions for young offenders see C. Emmins, *A Guide to the Criminal Justice Act 1982*, Pt. Two (1982, Financial Training Publications).

[2] In *Hooper* the order was varied due to a change in the offender's circumstances.

The Act requires the sentencing judge to state the ground he is relying on to justify a custodial sentence and sets out the procedure by which the determination is to be made. A social inquiry report is usually, but not always required (s. 2) and there is a requirement that the defendant be legally represented unless he or she is ineligible or unwilling (s. 3). Taking these and other requirements detailed below, it may be said that there is something like a presumption in favour of non-custodial treatment, but it is too early to say whether the new provisions will lead to a reduction in custody sentences for the young offender.

1. *Detention Centre Order*

THE LAW

Detention centre orders are now governed by section 4 of the Criminal Justice Act 1982.[3] The sentence is available for *male* offenders only between the age of 14 and 21 years, for offences which would be imprisonable in the case of an adult offender. The minimum term of detention which may be directed is 21 days (subject to one exception) and the maximum term is four months (subject to one exception) (s. 4).[4] The exception to the minimum term of detention can arise where following release from a detention centre, the offender fails to comply with the compulsory supervision requirements of the sentence. Failure to comply is an offence and he may be sentenced to any term of detention up to 30 days (s. 15(ii)). The exception to the maximum term of four months, arises where the maximum term of imprisonment and therefore of detention is less than four months (s. 4(2)). A detention centre order may not be made where the court considers it unsuitable by reason of the offender's mental or physical condition (s. 4(5)). An offender who has or is serving a sentence of: (a) imprisonment; (b) detention under section 53 of the Children and Young Persons Act; (c) Borstal training; (d) youth custody; (e) custody for life, cannot be sentenced to detention in a detention centre, unless there are special circumstances justifying this course of action (s. 4(5)(*a*)(*b*)).

Sentencing procedure

When considering the imposition of a detention centre order, the court must first eliminate all non-custodial methods as inappropriate for the case (C.J.A. 1982, s. 1). In order to determine this the

[3] Previously C.J.A. 1961, s. 4.
[4] The Secretary of State may by order subject to affirmative resolution vary maximum lengths of detention or other custodial sentences (C.J.A. 1982, s. 14).

court must obtain and consider information about the circumstances of the offence, and must take into account any information before the court relevant to character and physical and mental condition of the offender (s. 2). No doubt a court will obtain much of the required information from the proceedings themselves, but the 1982 Act, imposes a requirement in every case, unless the court is of the opinion that it is unnecessary, to obtain a social inquiry report in order to determine whether there might not be an appropriate non-custodial measure (s. 2(2)(3)). Should a magistrates' court be of the opinion that it is unnecessary to obtain a social inquiry report, and it does order detention in a detention centre, then it must state its reason in open court for not seeking a report, record the reason in the warrant of commitment and cause it to be entered in the court register (s. 2(4)(6)(7)). No such requirements are imposed on the Crown Court. On imposing a detention centre order, a magistrates' court is further required to state in open court the reason why a non-custodial sentence is inappropriate by reference to one of the grounds in section 1 (or presumably a combination), namely that it would appear to the court that the offender is unable or unwilling to respond to non-custodial penalties, or that a detention centre order is necessary in the interests of the public or that because of the seriousness of the offence, a non-custodial sentence cannot be justified. Failure by any court to advert to the need for a social inquiry report will not invalidate the sentence (s. 2(8)), but the Act is silent on the effect of a failure to fulfil the various requirements to state reasons or to record them imposed on magistrates' courts. It is submitted that since these are expressed as mandatory, failure will invalidate sentence.[5]

Legal representation

Before a magistrates' court or a Crown Court makes a detention centre order, it must comply with the provisions governing legal representation. These are, that where the defendant is unrepresented he must be informed of his right to apply for legal aid, and be given the opportunity to do so (s. 3(1)). If an application is refused because the defendant does not appear eligible, or because he fails to apply or refuses having been informed of the right, the court may proceed to sentence.

The similar provision in section 3 of the Powers of Criminal Courts Act 1973, has been held to be mandatory and a failure to comply will render the sentence a nullity; (*McGinlay and Ballantyne*

---

[5] But see *McGinlay and Ballantyne* (1975) 62 Cr.App.R. 156 in the section "Legal Representation," below.

(1975) 62 Cr.App.R. 156). However in that case it was stated that such non-compliance by the sentencing court does not effect the power of the appellate court to make any order or sentence which they consider appropriate which the court below has power to pass.

Remission, release and supervision

A term of detention in a detention centre attracts remission for good conduct and industry, up to one third of the total of the sentence reduced by any period in custody pre trial or before sentence (C.J.A. 1967, s. 67 as added to by C.J.A. 1982, s. 10).

Assuming full remission, the maximum period of a detention centre order, which is four months, should result in actual detention of about 11 weeks. Remission is not available for a detention centre order of less than five days (a possible term for default detention), and remission may not in any event reduce the terms of a detention centre order to less than five days (Detention Centre Rules 1983, r. 6).

Supervision following release was for a period of 12 months under previous legislation, but will now be for three months (C.J.A. 1982, s. 15(1)). Supervision is the responsibility of the probation service or a social service department social worker (s. 15(1)). The requirements of supervision are laid down by the Secretary of State and failure to comply with these is a summary offence, punishable by a maximum fine of £400, or by a sentence of detention or youth custody to a maximum of 30 days (s. 15(10)(11).[6]

COMBINING DETENTION WITH OTHER MEASURES (INCLUDING FURTHER DETENTION ORDERS)

Consecutive orders of detention are permissible provided the aggregate does not exceed four months (C.J.A. 1982, s. 5(1)(2)). If a consecutive sentence is passed which does exceed four months detention, then in the case of an offender who is 15 years or over, the sentence is to be treated as a term of youth custody (see below). In any case where an offender who is 15 years or over is before a court for sentence and he is serving a term of detention at the date of sentence, then, if the court considers it appropriate to impose a custodial sentence, of such duration as would exceed four months taking into account the unexpired term of detention being served at the detention centre, the court may impose a youth custody

---

[6] No liability to supervision arises following release from a detention centre for the offence of failing to obey the supervision requirements under s. 15(11). However, the prior liability to supervision will continue until the end of the three months period, which may or may not lapse before the offender is released for the second time (C.J.A. 1982, s. 15(13)).

sentence (s. 5(5)). The effect of this is that the detention centre order is merged into the youth custody sentence (s. 5(6)). Apart from this special case when a detention centre order is converted into a youth custody sentence, it is not possible to make a youth custody sentence or other custodial measure consecutive to a detention centre order. There is no restriction on a court imposing a fine, or making an ancillary order (*e.g.* disqualification) when making a detention centre order.

WHEN A DETENTION CENTRE ORDER IS APPROPRIATE

The intention behind the new detention centre order is apparently to reflect the "short, sharp shock" philosophy associated with detention centres when first introduced in 1961. This is emphasised by the reduction of the maximum length of the detention centre order from six to four months, and the reduction of the minimum sentence to 21 days. The criteria which the court must be satisfied on when imposing a detention centre order underlines that it is intended as a short period of custodial discipline and as punishment for the young offender who in the ordinary case has not previously been dealt with by a custodial sentence. The shock effect of this sentence is likely to be diminished if the offender has either been in a detention centre before or subject to another custodial measure previously, and it is submitted that it continues to be inappropriate to impose a second sentence of detention when the offender has already served a term of detention (*Brian Moore* [1968] 1 W.L.R. 397). Detention centre orders are not available for female young offenders, who may be sentenced to a youth custody sentence of four months or less instead (s. 4(4)).

APPEAL

The detention centre order is a sentence which may be appealed in the ordinary way. Where an appeal court is considering an appeal from the imposition of a detention centre order and the trial court had not considered it necessary or had failed to obtain a social inquiry report, the appeal court shall obtain a report and consider it in deciding whether to substitute a different sentence unless it in turn considers it unnecessary (C.J.A. 1982, s. 2(8)).

2. *Default Detention*

THE LAW

Section 9 of the Criminal Justice Act 1982 introduces a new sentence for the category of young offenders between the ages of 17 and 20 years who default in payment of a fine or other sum or are in contempt of court or guilty of a kindred offence. Where a court would have had power to commit such person to prison, it will now have power to order detention or to fix a term of detention under this section in the event of default. The section gives no name to this sentence which is called here default detention. No specific requirements are made as to duration of a term of default detention. However, the provisions of section 31(2) of the Powers of Criminal Courts Act as substituted by section 69(1) of the Criminal Justice Act 1982, fixing a variable maximum of detention based on the scale of the fine applies (see "Requirements on imposing a fine," pp. 63–64 above). The term of detention may be served in such institution as the authorities determine. The sentence is available for male an*. female defendants.

Sentencing procedure

Before any court orders detention under section 9, it must be of opinion that no other method of dealing with him is appropriate (s. 1(5)). Since no other custodial option is available, this means that the court must eliminate all non-custodial methods before making a default detention order. A social inquiry report is not required, but the court must obtain and consider information about the circumstances including the person's physical and mental condition before determining sentence. Where a magistrates' court orders a term of default detention, it is required to state in open court the reasoning a non-custodial option is inappropriate in the case and the reason is to be recorded in the warrant of committment and in the court register (s. 1(5)(7)).

Legal representation

The Act's restrictions on imposing custodial sentences on persons under 21 years not legally represented, do not apply to default detention under section 9 (s. 3(1)).

3. *Youth Custody Sentence*

DESCRIPTION

The youth custody sentence was created by the Criminal Justice Act 1982, s. 6. It replaces Borstal and imprisonment for young offenders. As originally proposed by the Advisory Council, it was to be the only custodial sentence for young offenders, *i.e.* it was to substitute for detention centres as well as Borstal and imprisonment. The courts would determine the length of sentence and the authorities the appropriate treatment and institution.[7] The Act considerably modifies these proposals but the notion of the youth custody sentence as the generic sentence is reflected to some extent in the possibilities of merging or converting other sentences into youth custody sentences. The basic purpose of the sentence is to provide training in contrast to the detention centres where the emphasis is on short periods of custodial discipline.

THE LAW

The sentence is available for *male* and *female* offenders. However, only *males not less than* 15 years but *under* 21 years, and only females *not less than* 17 years *but under 21* years may be sentenced to youth custody. There is, therefore, no custodial sentence for female young offenders under 17 years except under section 53 of the Children and Young Persons Act 1933 (discussed below) and default detention under section 9. *Male* offenders aged 14 years and over may be sentenced to a detention centre order.

Youth custody (in contrast to Borstal) is a determinate sentence. A court may in the usual case pass a youth custody sentence only if it considers that a term of custody in *excess* of four months is appropriate. However, in the case of a young offender unsuitable for a detention order, and in the case of female offenders (17 to 21 years), the term of a youth custody sentence may be reduced to a minimum of 21 days at the discretion of the court (C.J.A. 1982, s. 7(6)). A youth custody sentence may in one instance be less than 21 days, that is on conviction following release from a youth custody sentence for breach of conditions of supervision (s. 15(11)). The sentence may not exceed the maximum term of imprisonment for the offence (s. 7(1)). The *maximum* term of youth custody for a male offender under 17 years is 12 months (s. 7(8)).[8] If in a single or aggregate sentence such an offender is awarded a longer sentence, so much of the sentence as exceeds 12 months is to be treated as remitted (s. 7(8)(*b*)). Subject to the maximum of 12 months in the case of offenders under 17 years, a court is able to pass consecutive terms of youth custody, as it would had the sentence been one of imprisonment. For older offenders, it may also order sentences of imprisonment to run consecutive to a youth custody sentence and where the person is already serving a custodial sentence, a youth custody sentence may be ordered to run consecutive to it (*Oliver* (1983) 5 Cr.App.R.(S) 477. The youth custody order expands the

---

[7] Emmins, *op. cit.* note 1 above.

[8] The Secretary of State has power to increase the maximum period of 12 months for offenders under 17, note 4 above.

role of the court in the treatment of young offenders. Any male young offender sentenced to between four and 18 months youth custody will serve it in a training establishment (s. 12). The court can differentiate between offenders by imposing sentences which vary within this range. A youth custody sentence served in a training establishment is equivalent to Borstal but it is of a different status. The case of *Coleman* ((1976) 64 Cr.App.R. 124) highlighted the special status of Borstal. An offender could be sentenced to Borstal training for a minor offence (in *Coleman*, it was breaking a pane of glass) so that the time spent in custody was disproportionate to the offence. This could be done if it was in the best interests of the offender. A youth custody sentence served in a training establishment clearly shares the same quality of training that provided the basis of the decision in *Coleman*, however, the principles that guide the imposition of a youth custody sentence are the same as guide the imposition of imprisonment. The sentence must fit the crime (*Hart and Hart* (1983) 5 Cr.App.R.(S) 385).

Generally, the principles used in determining the length of sentence would seem to be the same as those which govern length of imprisonment with the age of the offender considered as a mitigating factor. This does not preclude the imposition of the maximum sentence in an appropriate case. The principle of reflecting credit for a plea of guilty applies to youth custody sentences, so that as a general rule, a young person who pleads guilty may not be given a 12 month sentence (*Warrior* [1984] Crim.L.R. 188). In *Dobbs and Hitchings* (1983) 5 Cr.App.R.(S.) 378, the Court of Appeal commented on the lack of a power to partly suspend a sentence of youth custody. In that case the court reduced the sentence to the length that would have been the unsuspended part of a partly suspended sentence. In *Trew* [1985] Crim.L.R. 168, this approach was also adopted.

A youth custody sentence may be served in a remand centre, a youth custody centre or a prison (Prisons Act 1952, s. 43 as substituted by C.J.A. 1982, s. 11). Youth custody centres are training establishments such as Borstals or young offenders centres which have been redesignated. Upon being sentenced, an offender initially goes to an allocation unit and a decision is taken by the authorities as to where he should serve his sentence. He may be detained in a prison or a remand centre for a temporary purpose (C.J.A. 1982, s. 12(4)).

The administrative authorities do not have a complete discretion as to where the young offender should serve his sentence. A male young offender sentenced from four to 18 months must be detained in a youth custody centre (s. 12(1)). The Secretary of State has powers, however, to direct that an inmate of a youth custody centre be transferred to prison, either because he has reached 21 years or being 18 years, he has been reported by the Board of Visitors as disruptive and a bad influence (s. 13).

A male young offender who is given a youth custody sentence of less than four months because detention in a detention centre would be unsuitable due to his mental condition might serve his sentence in a youth custody centre or a remand centre (s. 12(3)).

Sentencing procedure

The requirements set out above for detention centre orders apply equally to the youth custody sentence, with the additional requirement that the court must be of opinion that the appropriate term of a custodial sentence is in excess of four months (C.J.A., s. 6).

Legal representation

The provisions are the same as with detention centre orders.

Remission, release and supervision

The effective term of youth custody is to be computed with reduction for any period of pre-trial or pre-sentence detention (C.J.A. 1967, s. 67 as added to by C.J.A. 1982, s. 10). A young offender under a youth custody sentence will be entitled to the same remission as if sentenced to imprisonment. He is entitled to apply to the Parole Board after 12 months or one-third of the sentence whichever is the greater (C.J.A. 1967, s. 60 as amended by C.J.A. 1982, Sched. 14). Varying periods of compulsory supervision are required following release, under the direction of a probation officer or a social worker. Where an offender is released on licence under section 60 of the Criminal Justice Act 1967 it will be a condition of the licence that he come under supervision until the date had he not been released on licence, he would have earned release by remission. However, if the offender is still under 22 years at that point, supervision continues until the expiry of the sentence (*i.e.* the date of release if no remission had been granted), his twenty-second birthday or the anniversary of his release whichever is the earliest (s. 15(4)(8)). Where the young offender is refused parole but granted remission supervision lasts until the expiry of the sentence, subject to the proviso that if the expiry date of the sentence is less than three months from the release date the supervision will be for three months, and if more than 12 months, it will end after 12 months (s. 15(2)(8)(9)). Breach of a supervision condition where the offender is on licence will involve a return to custody to complete sentence. Breach of a supervision condition required under section 15 of the Criminal Justice Act 1982 for other offenders is a summary offence and may be dealt with by a fine of up to £400 or a youth custody sentence or detention order for up to 30 days (s. 15(10),(11),(12)).[9]

WHEN YOUTH CUSTODY IS APPROPRIATE

Youth custody is, as with a detention centre order, a last resort sentence. The courts must be satisfied that a non-custodial sentence cannot be imposed in the case before passing the sentence (C.J.A. 1982, s. 6). In general terms, therefore, youth custody can be appropriate only where the grounds laid out in section 1 of the Act apply; that the offender is unable or unwilling to respond to any non-custodial measures, or that there is an issue of protection of the public or that the gravity of the offence rules out a non-custodial measure. Training is the basis of the youth custody regime once imposed, and insofar as the sentencer will know that the young offender sentenced to any term from four to 18 months will serve it in a training centre, the court's role in sentencing has to that extent been extended (C.J.A. 1982, s. 12).

APPEAL

Full appeal rights apply in the case of a youth custody sentence as in the case of a sentence of imprisonment. An appeal court, considering an appeal from the imposition of a youth custody sentence, should order a social inquiry report if none was obtained by the court which imposed the sentence, unless it considers it unnecessary to do so. If contemplating a different sentence to youth custody, the appeal court should consider the social inquiry report, if any, before changing the sentence (C.J.A. 1982 s. 2(8)(9)).

4. *Custody for Life*

THE LAW

As a consequence of the abolition of imprisonment for young offenders, the sentence of custody for life is available where in the case of an adult the court must impose a sentence of life imprisonment, or where in the case of grave offences a discretionary life sentence is a sentence provided by law. The sentence of custody for life is created by section 8 of the Criminal Justice Act 1982.

Where an offender, male or female, who is under 21 years and not less than 18 years is convicted of murder, he or she must be sentenced to custody for life (s. 8(1)). Where a young offender, male

---

[9] For liability to supervision following sentence of youth custody for breach of supervision requirements under an early sentence see note 5 above.

or female, between the ages of 17 and 21 years commits an offence punishable by life imprisonment, he or she, may be sentenced to custody for life (s. 8(2)).

The discretionary custody for life sentence is a restricted sentence under the Criminal Justice Act, 1982 and is, therefore, a last resort sentence, where the court has ruled out a non-custodial sentence on the grounds set out in section 1 of the Act.

Young offenders between the ages of 14 to 17 years are not eligible for a sentence of custody for life, but instead are liable to be detained at Her Majesty's pleasure under the Children and Young Persons Act 1933, s. 53(1) (see "Young Persons" below).

A young offender sentenced to custody for life may at the direction of the Secretary of State serve the sentence in prison or, where the offender is a female or a male under 22 years of age, in a youth custody centre (C.J.A. 1982, s. 12).

Sentencing procedure

When considering a discretionary sentence of custody for life (C.J.A. 1982, s. 8(2)), the court must fulfil the sentencing procedures as laid down in the Act before the imposition of sentence. These are identical to these set out about in the case of a detention order and youth custody.

Legal representation

The requirements as to legal representation are the same as detention centre order and a youth custody sentence, above.

Release and supervision

The release of a young offender on licence serving a sentence of custody for life is a matter for the Secretary of State. Release must be recommended by the Parole Board and as in the case of adults subject to life imprisonment, the Home Secretary must consult with the Lord Chief Justice and the trial judge if possible (C.J.A. 1967, s. 61(ii), C.J.A. 1982, Sched. 14, para. 20). When released on licence, the licence will remain in force for the rest of the offender's life. Supervision can be required as a condition of the release on licence. (See "Release on Licence," pp. 100–108 above).

WHEN A DISCRETIONARY CUSTODY FOR LIFE SENTENCE IS APPROPRIATE

Given the 1982 Act's aim to encourage the courts to use non-custodial sentences wherever possible, and the availability of youth custody sentences, a sentence of custody for life where this is discretionary could only be appropriate in the most serious cases.

APPEAL

A sentence of custody for life which may only be imposed by a Crown Court may be appealed in the ordinary way under the Criminal Appeal Act 1968.

YOUNG PERSONS

The term "young person" refers to persons aged 14 years and under 17 years (C.Y.P.A. 1969, s. 70). The custodial measures which can be used in the sentencing of young persons who will normally come before the juvenile court are governed largely by the Criminal Justice Act 1982. Detention under section 9 (default detention) is not available but youth custody orders and detention centre orders are, provided the young person has reached the age of 15 years. A detention centre order may not be made in the case of a female. Before imposing these sentences, the court must form an opinion that non-custodial measures are inappropriate. This opinion is formed on the same grounds and by the same procedure as for all young offenders and is set out in section 1(2) of the Criminal Justice Act 1982.

The court has a further general duty imposed by the Children and Young Persons Act 1933, s. 44 (as amended by C.Y.P.A. 1969, Sched. 6). This duty is to consider the welfare of the young person and to take proper steps to remove him from undesirable surroundings and to make proper provision for his education and training.

Detention centre order and youth custody sentences have already been outlined under "Young Offenders," above. The remaining custodial options for young persons are detention under the Children and Young Persons Act 1933, s. 53(1) or (2).

Detention during Her Majesty's Pleasure under section 53(1) of the Children and Young Persons Act 1933

This is the young person's equivalent of the detention of a young offender (18 to 21 years) in custody for life under section 8(1) of the Criminal Justice Act 1982. It must be imposed following a conviction of murder and cannot be imposed at any other time. For the purpose of a conviction for murder only "young persons" can be taken to extend to the offender who is 17 years old, since section 53(1) applies to all persons under 18 years of age at the time of the offence. The young person may be detained wherever the Home Secretary directs, and may be released on licence at any time by the Home Secretary following a recommendation from the Parole Board and after consultation with the Lord Chief Justice and the trial judge if he is available (C.J.A. 1967, s. 61(1); C.J.A. 1982, Sched. 14, para. 20).

Detention under section 53(2) of the Children and Young Persons Act 1933

Where a child or young person is convicted on indictment of an offence which would merit 14 years or more in the case of an adult, and the court considers that no other alternative method is open, it may sentence the offender to be detained in accordance with the direction of the Secretary of State, for such period as it determines, not exceeding the maximum sentence of imprisonment for the offence (s. 53(2)). For the purposes of this section, a "young person" is a person aged 14 and under 17 years of age.

As first enacted, section 53(2) dealt only with homicide offences other than murder and only with offenders under 15 years. At this time, the minimum age for both Borstal and imprisonment was 15 years and section 53 was enacted to give powers of detention for persons under 15 years who were convicted of grave crimes. When the Criminal Justice Act 1961 raised the minimum age for imprisonment to 17 years, section 53(2) was modified to deal with offenders under 17 years. It was further expanded to deal with all offences which carried a minimum sentence of 14 years' imprisonment. It, therefore, became an alternative to Borstal for 15 and 16 year olds.[10]

Since the coming into force of the Criminal Justice Act 1982, section 53(2) detention provides an alternative to the 12-month youth custody maximum sentence for 15 and 16 year olds under that Act (s. 7(8)).

There is no minimum or maximum term for section 53(2) detention. The length of detention is at the discretion of the Secretary of State. The detention will be served wherever the Secretary of State directs. This includes prisons, youth custody centres and remand centres, but could also include a secure community home.[11] It should be noted that section 53(1) provides the only method by which 14-year-olds may be detained for more than four months other than detention at pleasure under section 53(1).

Sentencing procedure

Despite the fact that a youth custody sentence is less severe than section 53(2) detention, there are more legislative requirements associated with the former. Although section 3 of the Criminal

---

[10] See Commentary to *Oakes* [1984] Crim.L.R. 186, 187–188.
[11] Emmins, *op. cit.* note 1 above, p. 15.

Justice Act, 1982 (legal representation) applies to detention under section 53(2), the provision of subsections 1(4) and (5) of the Criminal Justice Act and the procedure for implementing them by way of social inquiry reports do not apply. However, the court is required to be of opinion that no other method of dealing with the case is appropriate. This would seem to suggest (as the case of *Butler* [1985] Crim.L.R. 56 confirms) that the correct approach is first of all to consider whether 12 months' youth custody is sufficient. In so doing the court will necessarily consider the criteria in C.J.A. 1982 s. 1(4) for a custodial sentence. The court should only pass on to consider section 53(2) where it finds one of those criteria satisfied but considers 12 months youth custody as inadequate. Then it must consider the appropriate term under section 53(2). In *Massheder* (1983) 5 Cr.App.R.(S.) 442, the Court of Appeal took it for granted that a social inquiry report was required, and that an adequate reason had to be given before a custodial sentence could be imposed. This view is supported by an earlier Court of Appeal decision (Barton [1977] Crim.L.R. 435), which stated that even if no statutory provision existed requiring that a social inquiry report be obtained before a young offender is sentenced, it would still be wise to have a report before passing a custodial sentence.

Remission, release and supervision

There is no automatic remission but Widgery L.J. indicated in *Fuat, Storey and Duignan* (1973) 57 Cr.App.R. 840 that an offender can be released at any time and the administrative authorities should not apply a one-third rule before allowing parole. Release on licence is governed by the Criminal Justice Act 1967, s. 61 and the Home Secretary may only act on the recommendation of the Parole Board and after consulting the Lord Chief Justice and the trial judge if possible (see "Release on Licence", pp. 100–108 above). Supervision can be made a condition of release on licence.

WHEN SECTION 53(2) DETENTION IS APPROPRIATE

The appropriate circumstances for use of section 53(2) detention and how the sentence should relate to the scheme of custodial sentences for young offenders under the Criminal Justice Act 1982 remain unclear. The case of *Ward* (1983) 5 Cr.App.R.(S.) 372 provides an illustration of the use of section 53(2). A group of youths aged between 16 and 18 years attacked and robbed a bus driver. The case was heard before the implementation of the Criminal Justice Act 1982 and the offender over 17 was given a sentence of three years' imprisonment, while the juveniles were sentenced to three years' detention under section 53(2). The young persons appealed on the grounds that the availability of automatic remission for the sentence of imprisonment worked an injustice against them. The Court of Appeal did not accept this reasoning but did reduce their detention under section 53(2) to 18 months to differentiate between them and the older offender who had been the ringleader. The differences between release procedures for section 53(2) and the young offender's sentence of imprisonment (which would take effect as youth custody) did not mean that the juveniles' sentence should be varied to one of youth custody. The appropriate sentence was 18 months and as the maximum youth custody sentence could be imposed for offenders under 17 was 12 months, detention under section 53(2) was correct.

The Court of Appeal has stated that section 53(2) is to be used as a last resort (*Mulkerrins* [1981] Crim.L.R. 512). This conforms with the approach towards custodial sentences generally for young offenders in Part I of the Criminal Justice Act 1982. It is clear therefore that section 53(2) cannot be used as a simple alternative to youth custody.

In *Oakes* (1983) 5 Cr.App.R.(S) 389, the Court of Appeal took the view that the 12-month maximum for youth custody reflected a legislative policy that young persons should only be detained for more than 12 months in the most exceptional of circumstances. The Court of Appeal felt that burglary could not come under section 53(2) and that although a 12-month sentence was inadequate to meet the justice of the case, this was all that was allowed by statute and it was not legitimate to use section 53(2) to avoid the provisions of the Criminal Justice Act 1982. However, on very similar facts, although involving robbery and burglary, a Court of Appeal which did not have a report of *Oakes* available to it, held that the circumstances need not be exceptional but merely provide proper grounds for taking the extreme step of imposing a substantial custodial sentence on an offender under 17 (*Nightingale* [1984] Crim.L.R. 373).

Nightingale was followed in *Storey* (1984) 6 Cr.App.R.(S.) 65 and both cases support the view that section 53(2) may still be imposed if one of the two traditional grounds, general deterrence, or the protection of the public, apply. The *Nightingale* approach was again preferred by the Court of Appeal in *Butler* [1985] Crim.L.R. 56. Detention under section 53(2) can be ordered if a sentence of general deterrence is appropriate (*Bosomworth* (1973) 57 Cr.App.R. 708; *Llewllyn* [1978] Crim.L.R. 105; *Stringer* (1980) 2 Cr.App.R.(S.) 138). This was the case in *Storey*, above. Three 15 and 16 year olds were convicted of arson. They had set fire to a school and caused £370,000 worth of damage. It was felt it should be made plain to all schoolboys that arson is a serious offence. They were given five years detention reduced to three years on appeal. The case demonstrates how a sentence of general deterrence should be calculated. The sentence will not be that applicable to an adult, rather that sentence must be calculated and then adjusted to allow for the young person's relative grasp of time. The sentence was reduced so that it would not seem so long to the young person that the far end of it was out of sight. This indicates the ground of general deterrence will only rarely provide the basis of a long sentence.

Long sentences are rare but perhaps less rare when based on the second ground. In *Storey, Fuat and Duignan* [1973] 1 W.L.R. 1045, Widgery L.J. stated that the safety and protection of the public must be to the forefront of the sentencing decision. In this case, young persons committed a vicious and unprovoked attack in which mental illness or diminished responsibility played no part. The judge considered that this justified sentences of 20 and 10 years' detention. He felt the analagous sentence for adults would be life imprisonment. The offender could be released at any time, once they had matured sufficiently so that the likelihood of any repeat of the attack was lessened. However, were the sentences too short, they might be released while an element of risk to the public still existed. A persistent young offender involved in serious crime may also be sentenced to detention under section 53(2) (*May* (1979) 1 Cr.App.R.(S.) 9).

APPEAL

Under the Criminal Appeal Act, s. 9, a sentence of section 53(2) detention which may be imposed only by a Crown Court may be appealed as with any other sentence.

CHILDREN

The only forms of custodial measures which apply to children (over 10 and under 14 years) are detention at Her Majesty's pleasure under section 53(1) or detention for a period determined by the court under section 53(2) of the Children and Young Persons Act 1933. No criminal jurisdiction may be exercised in the case of children under 10 years; the law conclusively presumes that no child under 10 years can be guilty of an offence.[12]

---

[12] C.Y.P.A. 1933, s. 50 as amended by C.Y.P.A. 1963, s. 16(1). The C.Y.P.A. 1969, s. 4 made provision for the progressive raising of the age of criminal responsibility by ministerial order up to 14 years, but this has not been implemented. In the case of children over 10 years, there is a rebuttable presumption that they have not reached the age of discretion and are incapable of committing a crime by reason of lack of mens rea. This presumption can be rebutted (*R.* v. *B, R.* v. *A.* [1979] 1 W.L.R. 1185, C.A. but the nearer a child is to 10 years, the greater the evidence in rebuttal must be (*B.* v. *R.* (1958) 44 Cr.App.R. 1).

Detention under section 53(1)(2) of the Children and Young Person's Act 1933

Detention under subsection (1) or (2) of section 53 is governed by the same principles as those which governed its application to young persons, above. Section 53(1) requires that a sentence of indefinite detention at Her Majesty's pleasure be imposed following a conviction on the charge of murder. Section 53(2) detention remains an option of last resort and the consideration of the age of the offender in calculating the length of sentence applies to a greater extent in the case of children. The youth of the child may lead the court to choose a non custodial order. In *Bryson* (1973) 58 Cr.App.R. 464 a 14-year-old boy was sentenced to be detained for life under section 53(2). This was favoured over a care order as the latter would expire when the boy was 19 and the court preferred an indefinite order. In the case of a younger child, a care order until age 19 might seem sufficiently lengthy.

PART III
ANCILLARY ORDERS

INTRODUCTION

In addition to the imposition of the non-custodial and custodial sentences outlined in Parts I and II above, courts have important powers to impose additional sanctions upon conviction. In this Part these are considered under the heading of Ancillary Orders. The main types of order are:

(1) compensation orders;
(2) restitution orders;
(3) criminal bankruptcy orders;
(4) forfeiture orders;
(5) disqualifications;
(6) recommendations for deportation;
(7) orders for costs.

While the above orders must generally be made in addition to and not in substitution for, a sentence they are regarded as "sentences" for the purposes of appeals.

COMPENSATION ORDERS

DESCRIPTION

The Powers of Criminal Courts Act, s. 35, contains the provisions governing compensation arising from a criminal offence. A court convicting an offender of an offence may order him to pay compensation in respect of any personal injury, loss or damage resulting from the offence or from any other offence which is taken into consideration by the court in determining sentence. The policy behind compensation orders was stated by Scarman L.J. in *Inwood* (1975) 60 Cr.App.R. 70, where he said that the orders were introduced "as a convenient and rapid means of avoiding the expense of resorting to civil litigation when the criminal clearly has the means which would enable the compensation to be paid."

THE LAW

Section 35(1) (as substituted by C.J.A. 1982, s. 67) provides:

> "Subject to the provisions of this Part of this Act and to section 40 of the Magistrates' Court Act 1980 . . . , a court by or before which a person is convicted of an offence, instead of or in addition to dealing with him in any other way, may, on application or otherwise, make an order . . . requiring him to pay compensation for any personal injury, loss or damage resulting from that offence or any offence which is taken into consideration by the court in determining sentence."

The power to make compensation orders applies to both the Crown Court and magistrates' courts. There is no limit to the amount of compensation that the Crown Court may order. The maximum amount of compensation which a magistrates' court may order is £2,000 in respect of any offence of which the court has convicted an offender (M.C.A., s. 40(1), as increased by S.I. 1984 No. 447). If the compensation is ordered in relation to offences taken into consideration but with which the offender has not been formally charged, the total amount of compensation ordered may not exceed the maximum amount that could be ordered for all the offences for which he has been formally charged and convicted (s. 40(1)). For example, D is charged and convicted of two offences and asks the court to take another offence into consideration. The court orders compensation of £1,200 in relation to each of the two offences of which he was convicted. The maximum amount of

150

compensation the court may order in relation to the offence D has asked to be taken into consideration is £1,600.

Under the new subsection (1) of section 35 of the Powers of Criminal Courts Act a court may make a compensation order not merely in addition to but also instead of dealing with the offender in any other way.[1] Accordingly, a compensation order is a sentence in its own right and not merely an ancillary order and in suitable circumstances a court may use a compensation order as the only sentence to impose on an offender.

Compensation may be ordered for "personal injury, loss or damage resulting from [the] offence." It is not necessary for the appellant to be liable civilly for the loss (although in most cases he will be) as such a requirement would involve reading into the statute the word "actionable" before the words "personal injury, loss or damage" in section 35(1) (*Chappel* [1984] Crim.L.R. 574. The court need only consider whether personal injury, loss or damage has resulted from the offence. Thus, where the director of a company which had ceased trading was criminally liable personally, a compensation order was made for loss sustained by the Customs and Excise due to him recklessly causing to be delivered a return of VAT which understated the value of supplies made by the company, even though civilly it was the company who was liable. In assessing compensation for "loss" the court may include a sum by way of interest in the order (*Schofield* [1978] 2 All E.R. 705). The phrase gives the court a wide discretion to order compensation. It will cover, for example, cases of damage to clothing during an assault without there necessarily being a charge of criminal damage. And cases of financial loss following a fraud offence. Provided it is clearly related to a particular sum owing to a particular person and relating to a particular offence, whether one alleged in the indictment or taken into consideration on sentence, a compensation order may be made (see *Oddy* [1974] 1 W.L.R. 1212 where a global sum of compensation which could not be so related, was quashed). However, for the purposes of compensation the test is not whether a particular loss results solely from the offence charged, but whether it can be said fairly to have resulted from the offence (*Rowlston* v. *Kenny* (1982) 4 Cr.App.R.(S.) 85). The defendant pleaded guilty to obtaining benefit by a false representation which had been made in the original claim form and which had resulted in one payment, and then repeated each week in a separate form. The magistrates' court refused to award compensation for the total amount defrauded as the charge, being based on the original misrepresentation, related to

[1] Formerly a compensation order could only be made in addition to dealing with the offender in any other way.

one instance only. It was held on an application by way of case stated, that the magistrates were empowered to make a compensation order for the whole amount where loss could fairly be said to result from the offence.

The personal injury, loss or damage must have resulted from the offence. However, in *Thomson Holidays Ltd.* [1974] Q.B. 592 Lawton L.J. delivering the judgment of the Court of Appeal stated:

> "Parliament, we are sure, never intended to introduce into the criminal law the concepts of causation which apply to the assessment of damages under the law of contract and tort.... [T]he reference to offences taken into consideration shows that the court making a compensation order may not be appraised of the detailed facts of such offences. It must do what it can to make a just order on such information as it has. Whenever the making of an order for compensation is appropriate the court must ask itself whether loss or damage can fairly be said to have resulted to anyone from the offence for which the accused has been convicted or has been taken into consideration."

The appellants were convicted of an offence under section 14(1)(*b*) of the Trade Descriptions Act 1968 following a complaint by Mr. and Mrs. B. who booked a holiday at a hotel described in the appellant's brochure. One of the grounds of the appeal was that compensation (£50) should not have been ordered as Mr. and Mrs. B. had not suffered any loss or damage as a result of the offence. The Court of Appeal held that on the evidence the failure to provide Mr. and Mrs. B. with the amenities which they expected to find available did result from the offence of recklessly making a false statement in the course of their trade or business.

Accordingly, where the handler of stolen goods sells them to an innocent purchaser a compensation order in favour of the innocent purchaser is appropriate upon the handler's conviction (*Howell (A.)* (1978) 66 Cr.App.R. 179). However, where the defendant is convicted of possession of a controlled drug a compensation order is not appropriate where the tablet is given to another who thereafter becomes ill as the "injury" cannot be said to have resulted from the offence of simple possession (*Berkeley* v. *Orchard* [1975] Crim.L.R. 225). An order would probably have been appropriate if the defendant had been convicted of supplying a controlled drug rather than possession.

In relation to offences under the Theft Act 1968 (including taking a conveyance without the owner's consent or other lawful authority contrary to s. 12(1)), any damage to the property occurring while it is out of the owner's possession is treated, for the purposes of compensation, as having resulted from the offence regardless of how or by whom the damage is caused (P.C.C.A., s. 35(2)). There is no power to make a compensation order where a stolen article has been recovered and restored to the owner there being no evidence that the article has suffered any damage or that it is now of any less value to the owner (*Sharkey* [1976] Crim.L.R. 388; *Cadamarteris* [1977] Crim.L.R. 236; *Hier* (1976) 62 Cr.App.R. 233).

Compensation may not be ordered in respect of loss suffered by the dependants of a person as a result of his death (s. 35(2)). Similarly, no compensation may be ordered in respect of "injury, loss or damage due to an accident arising out of the presence of a motor vehicle on a road or other public place," except such damage as is treated by subsection (2) as resulting from an offence under the Theft Act. Thus, in *Quigley* v. *Stokes* [1977] 1 W.L.R. 343 the appellant successfully appealed against two amounts of compensation in respect of two cars he damaged when he was involved in an accident driving a third vehicle which he had taken without the owner's consent. The Divisional Court held that the only damage due to the presence of a motor vehicle in a road for which compensation could be ordered was the damage to the car which was the subject matter of the offence under section 12 of the Theft Act 1968.

Where a child or young person is convicted of an offence or where care proceedings are brought under section 1(1)(f) of the Children and Young Persons Act 1969 against a child or young person on the ground that he is guilty of an offence and the court makes an order for compensation, it is under a duty to order that the compensation be paid by the parent or guardian of the child or young person unless the court is satisfied:

(i) that the parent or guardian cannot be found; or
(ii) that it would be unreasonable to make an order for payment having regard to the circumstances of the case.

(C.Y.P.A. 1933, s. 55(1) as substituted by C.J.A. 1982, s. 26 and C.Y.P.A. 1969, s. 3(6) as substituted by C.J.A. 1982, s. 27.) An order must not be made under either provision without giving the parent or guardian an opportunity of being heard, unless, the parent or guardian having been required to attend, has failed to do so (C.Y.P.A. 1933, s. 55(2) and C.Y.P.A. 1969, s. 3(6A)). For the purposes of section 55 a local authority is not a "parent or guardian" of a child in its care (*Re Leeds City Council* (1982) 4 Cr.App.R.(S.) 26).

Where the court makes a compensation order it may allow time for payment of the sum or direct payment by instalments (P.C.C.A., s. 34 and M.C.A., s. 75(1)).

COMBINING COMPENSATION WITH OTHER MEASURES

A compensation order may be made either instead of or in addition to dealing with the offender in any other way (P.C.C.A., s. 35(1) as substituted by C.J.A., s. 67). It is expressly provided that a compensation order may be imposed with a probation order or discharge (P.C.C.A., s. 12(4)), and a community service order (P.C.C.A., s. 14(8)), but it may not be imposed at the same time as a criminal bankruptcy order (P.C.C.A., s. 39(1)). While it is not wrong in law or in principle to combine a compensation order with a suspended sentence, careful consideration should be given to the case before doing so as the suspended sentence may be activated which could bring to an end the offender's capacity to pay (see *Whenman* [1977] Crim.L.R. 430 and *McGee* [1978] Crim.L.R. 370).

Section 35(4A) of the Powers of Criminal Courts Act (as inserted by C.J.A. 1982, s. 67) provides

> "Where the court considers—
> > (*a*) that it would be appropriate both to impose a fine and to make a compensation order; but
> > (*b*) that the offender has insufficient means to pay both an appropriate fine and appropriate compensation,
> the court shall give preference to compensation (though it may impose a fine as well)."

WHEN A COMPENSATION ORDER IS APPROPRIATE

The courts have enunciated several principles in relation to making compensation orders. These principles do not always rest easily alongside each other and have, on occasions, been ignored by courts in particular cases. The best that can be done is to state the principles and cases which appear to support them.

In the case of *Miller* (1979) 68 Cr.App.R. 56, the Court of Appeal stated seven principles which could be deduced from the cases; there are several more which may be added to these.

(1) *A compensation order is not an alternative to a sentence* (*Miller*, *Lovett* (1870) 11 Cox C.C. 602; *Inwood* (1974) 60 Cr.App.R. 70).

Section 35(1) of the Powers of Criminal Courts Act now provides that a compensation order may be made instead of dealing with the offender in any other way. In appropriate cases a court need not pass any other sentence on an offender. However, it is submitted that the words of Scarman L.J. in *Inwood* (at p. 73) are still applicable

> "Compensation orders were not introduced into our law to enable the convicted to buy themselves out of the penalties for crime. . . . [T]hey were introduced . . . as a convenient and rapid

means of avoiding the expense of resort to civil litigation when the criminal clearly has means which would enable the compensation to be paid."

(See also *Stapleton and Lawrie* [1977] Crim.L.R. 366[2] and *Copely* (1979) 1 Cr.App.R.(S.) 55).

(2) *An order should only be made where the legal position is clear* (*Miller*).

In *Kneeshaw* [1975] Q.B. 57, the appellant pleaded guilty to burglary. Items listed in the particulars of the offence included four rings. The defendant, however, in the course of mitigation, denied that the rings had been stolen (all the other property except the rings had been recovered). The victim of the burglary made no application for compensation but the court made an order. On appeal, compensation in respect of the rings was set aside, the Court of Appeal stating that where in the course of proceedings the accused denies that particular items have been stolen, the court should not consider making a compensation order unless an application is made and the applicant is prepared to adduce evidence that the items in question have been stolen. Even then the court, in the exercise of its discretion, should hesitate to embark on an investigation of complicated issues of fact.

(3) *The power to order compensation provides a quick and simple machinery which should only be used for dealing with claims in straightforward cases* (*Daly* [1974] 2 W.L.R. 133; *Donovan* [1982] R.T.R. 126).

In *Donovan* the appellant pleaded guilty to taking a conveyance without the owner's consent contrary to section 12 of the Theft Act 1968. The appellant had hired the car from a car rental company for two days but he kept it until the company recovered it some four and a half months later. The court made a compensation order for £1,388.05p on the basis of loss of use. The Court of Appeal quashed the order on the grounds that compensation orders were appropriate only in simple straightforward cases where the amount of compensation could be readily and easily ascertained, which was open to argument in the present case.

Where two or more defendants are convicted of a joint offence the court should not make a joint and several order for compensation, in view of the complications likely to arise from the administration of such an order, if substantial justice can be achieved by orders made severally (*Grundy and Moorhouse* [1974] 1 W.L.R. 139).

---

[2] In this case the Court of Appeal made it clear that it is wrong to pass lower sentences on co-defendants who are able to pay compensation than upon other co-defendants who are not.

(4) *"Compensation . . . shall be of such amount as the court considers appropriate having regard to any evidence and to any representations that are made by or on behalf of the accused or the prosecutor"* (P.C.C.A., s. 35(1A) inserted by C.J.A. 1982, s. 67).

Prior to this provision being enacted the principle laid down in the cases was that an order should not be made unless the sum claimed by the victim had either been agreed or proven (*Vivian* [1979] 1 W.L.R. 291; *Amey* [1983] 1 W.L.R. 346). In *Swann* (1984) 6 Cr.App.R.(S) 22 the Court of Appeal stated that this sub-section was designed simply to ameliorate the strict require-ments laid down in the cases in respect of the burden of proof required before compensation orders are made. The effect of subsection (1A) was to reduce slightly the obligation which was laid down in *Vivian*.

> "Presumably this means that the sentencer may use his own knowledge to a limited extent to supplement a deficiency in the evidence of the amount of a loss, but it seems clear that there must be some evidence of the nature of a loss before a compensation order can be made: an intelligent guess unsup-ported by evidence will not be sufficient." (Commentary to *Swann* [1984] Crim.L.R. 300.)

(5) *In considering whether or not to make a compensation order the question whether or not the offender has profited from the offence is not relevant. The proper question for consideration is what loss has the victim sustained* (*Ford* [1977] Crim.L.R. 114; *Maynard* [1983] Crim.L.R. 821.

(6) *The order for compensation must be precise: it must be related to an offence of which the offender has been convicted or to an offence which he has asked to have taken into consideration, and the total amount and the instalment amount must be specified in the order* (*Miller*).

In *Oddy* [1974] 1 W.L.R. 1212, one of the grounds for discharging an order for £2,000 compensation was that it was a global sum not related to any specific offence or to any specific loss, as the appellant had been convicted on four counts of obtaining property by deception and had asked for 28 other offences to be taken into consideration.

However, a compensation order in a single sum representing the total of the amounts involved may be made where the offender is convicted of a series of offences in relation to the same victim (*e.g.* a series of thefts) (*Warton* [1976] Crim.L.R. 520).

(7) *Loss or damage having been established, the court in determining whether to make a compensation order against any*

person and in determining the amount to be paid under such an order, must have regard to that person's means so far as they appear or are known to the court (P.C.C.A., s. 35(4); *Miller*). *The fact that an offender has no means or limited means does not mean that no order should be made against him* (*Bradburn* (1973) 57 Cr.App.R. 948).

In *Bradburn* Widgery L.C.J. stated:

> "We think that as long as a man has his normal physical health and is, therefore, capable of earning something it is perfectly proper to make a compensation order against him although the amount may well be restricted by reason of the probability that his earnings will be comparatively small. It is not right to restrict compensation orders to cases where the defendant can easily pay."

However, it is no use making a compensation order if there is no realistic possibility of it being complied with (*Webb and Davis* (1979) 1 Cr.App.R.(S.) 16; see also *Mortimer* [1977] Crim.L.R. 624). In *McCullough* [1982] Crim.L.R. 461, the appellant aged 40 was convicted of obtaining £2,500 sickness and invalidity benefit by deception. He was sentenced to nine months' imprisonment, and, although he had no savings, the judge imposed a compensation order for £2,500 stating that he would have to repay the taxpayer (*i.e.* the D.H.S.S.) even though it took him the 40 years he had left. The Court of Appeal quashed the order stating that it was wrong to sentence a man to imprisonment, depriving him of the opportunity of repaying, and then to contemplate that he should go on paying for the rest of his life. ([1982] 4 Cr.App.R. 98.)

(8) *The promises of a relative or friend to pay or help to pay compensation should be disregarded when considering the offender's means* (*Inwood*; *Hunt* [1983] Crim.L.R. 270).

(9) *While an order may be coupled with an immediate custodial sentence, it must not be oppressive. The court should bear in mind that a discharged prisoner is often short of money, and he must not be tempted to commit further offences to provide the cash to satisfy an order* (*Miller*; *Wylie* [1975] R.T.R. 94; *McCullough*; *Morgan* (1982) 4 Cr.App.R.(S.) 358).

In *Oddy* the court also said that the order imposed on the appellant was inappropriate since it was unlikely that on his release from prison he would be able to obtain employment that would enable him to earn sufficient money to comply with the order and as a result he would be tempted to think up new and dishonest ways of obtaining money quickly. However, in *Workman* (1979) 1 Cr.App.R.(S.) 335, the Court of Appeal upheld an order for £2,118 compensation to be paid in instalments of £10 pw after the appellant's release from a six-month sentence, although it recognised that the order "might put upon her so heavy a burden as to tempt her to commit other offences in order to meet the obligation under it." The court found justification for its approach in the fact that the appellant had used the money she stole to buy expensive household goods and some had been used to help purchase the house where she would continue to live after being released from prison.

(10) *It is rarely appropriate to combine a compensation order with a custodial sentence to take immediate effect* (*Wilkinson* [1980] 1 W.L.R. 396; *Shenton* (1979) 1 Cr.App.R.(S.) 81) *unless there is evidence that the offender has the proceeds of his crime or has assets out of which the order can be paid* (*Morgan*).

(11) *It is generally wrong in principle to make an order which would inevitably mean the sale of the offender's house* (*Harrison* (1980) 2 Cr.App.R.(S.) 313; *Heath* [1985] Crim.L.R. 247), *but it is legitimate to expect household items bought with the proceeds of the crime to be sold to pay compensation* (*Workman* (1979) 1 Cr.App.R.(S.) 335).

(12) *An order may be made for payment by instalments, the first of which is to be paid within a specified period of the offender's release from custody* (*Bradburn* (1973) 57 Cr.App.R. 948).

(13) *The order must be realistic, (that is, it should not be made unless the offender will be able to pay off the amount of compensation within a reasonable time, usually taken to be two to three years). An order for payment by instalments over a long period is to be avoided* (*Miller*).

In *Miller* an order for £6,100 which the appellant was able to pay off only at £5 per week was quashed. In *Daly* an order for £1,200 to be paid over six years was reduced to £600 to be paid over three years (see also *McCullough* and *Making* [1982] Crim.L.R. 613; *Brown, The Times*, October 10, 1984).

In *Bradburn* the Court of Appeal stated:

"... in general ... a compensation order which requires as long as four years for its fulfilment ... is being stretched out to what will generally be an unreasonably long period. It is generally much better that these orders should be sharp in their effect rather than protracted."

(14) *There may be good moral reasons for making an order, including an order for payment by instalments, to remind the defendant of the evil he has done* (*Miller; Bradburn*).

"This ... may apply particularly in the case where a non-custodial penalty is imposed and the compensation which is appropriate is a sum which is not too great." (*Per* Pain J. in *Miller* (1979) 68 Cr.App.R. 56, at p. 58.)

(15) *Where several claimants for compensation establish claims against a convicted person and he has insufficient funds to meet each claim in full, the court should normally make orders which apportion the compensation on a pro rata basis, but it may depart from that basis where there are strong grounds for doing so.*

For example where there are several small claims and one large claim and a pro rata apportionment would lead to the small claimants being compensated to a wholly inadequate degree, the court may select some of the claimants and order that compensation be paid to them to the exclusion of the others (*Amey* [1983] 1 W.L.R. 346).

(16) *Where two or more persons are jointly convicted and one claimant for compensation establishes a claim against them with regard to one item, the court should generally make an order requiring each of them to pay the amount awarded in equal proportions. The court should not draw a distinction between the two convicted persons unless it is shown that one of them was more responsible than the other or that their ability to pay is markedly different* (*Amey*).

APPEALS

There is the same right of appeal against a compensation order as against any other sentence imposed by a court.

Where the order is made on indictment it is suspended automatically until 28 days from the date of conviction, and where notice of appeal or of application for leave to appeal is given within 28 days from the date of conviction, it remains suspended until the determination of the appeal (P.C.C.A., s. 36(1) and C.A.A. 1968, s. 30(1)).[3]

A compensation order made by a magistrates' court is suspended until the expiration of the period prescribed for giving notice of appeal (P.C.C.A., s. 36(2)) which currently is 21 days from the day on which the decision appealed against was given or the offender sentenced where the court has adjourned the trial after conviction (r. 7(3) of the Crown Court Rules, S.I. 1982 No. 1109). Where notice of appeal is given within this period, the order will be suspended until determination of the appeal (P.C.C.A., s. 36(2)(*b*)).

---

[3] The order will be suspended for a further 14 days from the decision of the Court of Appeal to allow time for an application for leave to appeal to the House of Lords to be made, and if such an application is made, it will be suspended while that appeal is pending (P.C.C.A., s. 36(1) and C.A.A., s. 42(1)).

If the conviction in respect of which the compensation order was made is quashed on appeal, the order will not take effect. On appeal, the appeal court may vary or quash the compensation order.

Where a compensation order is made in respect of an offence which the offender asks to be taken into consideration on his conviction of another offence, he may appeal against the order (P.C.C.A., s. 36(3)(b)). Similarly, in such a case, if the original conviction (or if more than one offence was involved the conviction of all the offences) is quashed on appeal, the compensation order made in respect of the offence which the offender asked to be taken into consideration will cease to have effect (P.C.C.A., s. 36(3)(a)).

RESTITUTION ORDERS

DESCRIPTION

A restitution order is loosely designed to restore to a person entitled to them, goods which have been "stolen" from him where a person is convicted of any offence with reference to the theft or to restore to him the proceeds of the goods or a sum of money, not exceeding their value, out of monies found in the offender's possession on apprehension.

THE LAW

The law on restitution orders is contained in section 28 of the Theft Act 1968 (as extended by C.J.A. 1972, s. 6 and amended by C.L.A. 1977, Sched. 12).

The power to order restitution (which is available to both the Crown Court and magistrates' courts) may be exercised where:

"goods have been stolen, and either a person is convicted of any offence with reference to the theft (whether or not stealing is the gist of his offence), or a person is convicted of any other offence but such an offence as aforesaid is taken into consideration in determining his sentence . . . " (s. 28(1)).

The words "stolen" and "theft" refer, as well as to theft (which includes robbery and burglary), to offences of obtaining property by deception, blackmail and handling of goods stolen or obtained by deception or blackmail. The provision may also include conspiracy to steal or assisting offenders contrary to section 4(1) of the Criminal Law Act 1967 (see *Archbold*, §5–297).

On convicting[1] the offender the court may make any of a number of orders. However

"The court shall not exercise [its] powers . . . unless . . . the relevant facts sufficiently appear from evidence given at the trial or the available documents, together with admissions made by or on behalf of any person in connection with any proposed exercise of the powers; and for this purpose "the available documents' means any written statements or admissions which were made for use, and would have been

---

[1] The court may make a restitution order even though the passing of sentence is in other respects deferred (T.A., s. 28(1) as amended by C.L.A., Sched. 12).

admissible, as evidence at the trial, the depositions taken at any committal proceedings and any written statements or admissions used as evidence in those proceedings" (s. 28(4)).[2]

(a) Order for restoration of the stolen goods

Under section 28(1)(*a*) the court may order *anyone having possession or control* of stolen goods to restore them to anyone entitled to recover them from him. The person in "possession or control" need not be the offender but could be an innocent purchaser of the goods and an order may be made provided the original owner is able to establish a right to recover the goods from him. If there is any doubt as to title to the property, the criminal court is not the correct forum for deciding the issue; the court will only make an order in a clear case (*Stamp* v. *United Dominions Trust Ltd.* [1967] 1 Q.B. 418).

(b) Order relating to goods representing stolen goods

Section 28(1)(*b*) provides:

"on the application of a person entitled to recover from the person convicted any other goods directly or indirectly representing the first mentioned goods (as being the proceeds of any disposal or realisation of the whole or part of them or of goods so representing them), the court may order those other goods to be delivered or transferred to the applicant."

An application must be made by the person claiming the right to recover the identifiable proceeds of the stolen property. The application may only be made to recover goods from the person convicted as opposed to a third party. The applicant must be able to show a clear right under the civil law to follow the stolen goods into the goods which he claims to represent them. Only where the case is clear will the court make an order.

(c) Order relating to money in the possession of the convicted person

Section 28(1)(*c*) provides:

"the court may order that a sum not exceeding the value of the ["stolen'] goods shall be paid, out of any money of the person convicted which was taken out of his possession on his apprehension, to any person who, if the goods were in the possession of the person convicted, would be entitled to recover them from him."

---

[2] For the purposes of this subsection a trial comes to a conclusion when sentence is passed (*Church* (1971) 55 Cr.App.R. 65).

Such an order may be made without any application being made in that behalf or on the application of any person appearing to the court to be interested in the property concerned (C.J.A. 1972, s. 6(2)).

The requirement that the money must have been "taken out of his possession on his apprehension" does not mean that it actually must have been found on his person at the time of his arrest. In *Ferguson* [1970] 1 W.L.R. 1246, £2,000 which was taken from the offender's safe deposit box 11 days after his arrest, was found to have been in his possession at the time of his apprehension. There is no requirement to show that the money was stolen in the relevant offence or that it is the proceeds of that offence; all that is necessary, is that it be shown that the money belongs to the offender (*Lewis* [1975] Crim.L.R. 353). In *Lewis* £5,445 was taken from the offender's home on his arrest. He was convicted of a robbery committed by four men in which £8,000 was stolen. He claimed that his share was £2,000. A restitution order in the sum of £5,445 was made and upheld by the Court of Appeal on the basis that civil liability to pay the proceeds of the robbery being joint and several as to those who took part in it, there was no reason why the order should not relate to the whole sum in his possession even if he had only received £2,000 from the robbery.

Where the goods which are the subject of the charge are recovered, it is an incorrect exercise of discretion to make a restitution order under section 28(1)(c) as a means of making the offender pay compensation in respect of other stolen goods, not the subject of any conviction of him (*Parker* [1970] 1 W.L.R. 1003).

Where the offender is no longer in possession of the stolen goods, but the court would have power to make an order under section 28(1)(b), as he is in possession of some assets representing them, and under section 28(1)(c), as money belonging to him seized at the time of his arrest, section 28(2) provides that the court may make orders under both provisions provided that the person in whose favour the orders are made does not thereby recover more than the value of those goods.

(d) Order for compensation for a bona fide purchaser or lender

An order under section 28(1)(a) may be made against "anyone having possession or control of the goods." In some cases this may be someone who has, in good faith, bought the goods from the convicted person or who has, in good faith, lent money to the convicted person on the security of the goods. In such a case the court may, under section 28(3), order the payment of compensation to the purchaser or lender out of the convicted person's money taken out of his possession on his apprehension. The compensation is not to exceed the amount paid for the goods or the amount owed in respect of the loan. An order under section 28(3) may be made without application being made in that behalf or on the application of any person appearing to the court to be interested in the property concerned (C.J.A. 1972, s. 6(2)).

COMBINING RESTITUTION ORDERS WITH OTHER MEASURES

The making of a restitution order is dependent only upon conviction of the offender. Accordingly, an order may be made in combination with any other sentence the court may choose to impose. An order may be made at the time of conviction even though the sentence is in other respects deferred (s. 28(1)). From the wording of section 35(2) of the Powers of Criminal Courts Act it would appear that a compensation order and a restitution order may be made in respect of the same goods if the goods are recovered in a damaged condition.

WHEN A RESTITUTION ORDER IS APPROPRIATE

The making of restitution orders is confined to theft and its related offences. Thus this type of order is available in a more limited range of cases than compensation orders. However, the court making a restitution order is not required to investigate or consider the offender's means, which could render a restitution order permissible where a compensation order is not. Provided the case is clear the court may make a restitution order.

APPEALS

There is a right of appeal against an order made under section 28 as against any other sentence (M.C.A., s. 108 and C.A.A. 1968, s. 50(1)).

Where the order was made on a conviction on indictment it is suspended automatically for 28 days from the date of conviction and where notice of appeal or of application for leave to appeal is given within 28 days from the date of conviction, it remains suspended until the determination of the appeal (C.A.A. 1968, s. 30(1)). However, an order will not be suspended where the trial court directs to the contrary "in any case in which, in the court's opinion, the title to the property is not in dispute" (C.A.A. 1968, s. 30(1)).[3] The Court of Appeal may by order annul or vary any

---

[3] The order will be suspended for a further 14 days from the decision of the Court of Appeal to allow time for an application for leave to appeal to the House of Lords to be made, and if such an application is made it will be suspended while that appeal is pending (C.A.A. 1968, s. 42(1)).

order made by the court of trial for the restitution of property to any person, although the conviction is not quashed (C.A.A. 1968, s. 30(4)).

A restitution order made by a magistrates' court is suspended until the expiration of the period prescribed for giving notice of appeal (C.J.A. 1972, s. 6(5)(*a*)) which currently is 21 days from the day on which the decision appealed against was given or the offender sentenced where the court has adjourned the trial after conviction (r. 7(3) of the C.C.R., S.I. 1982 No. 1109). Where notice of appeal is given within this period, the order will be suspended until determination of the appeal (C.J.A. 1972, s. 6(5)(*b*)). However, an order will not be suspended where the court directs to the contrary, "being of opinion that the title to the goods to be restored or, as the case may be, delivered or transferred under the order is not in dispute" (C.J.A. 1972, s. 6(5)).

Where a restitution order is made in respect of an offence which the offender asks to be taken into consideration on his conviction of another offence, he may appeal against the order (C.J.A. 1972, s. 6(4)). Similarly, in such a case, if the original conviction (or if more than one offence was involved, the convictions of all the offences) is quashed on appeal, the restitution order made in respect of the offence which the offender asked to be taken into consideration will cease to have effect (C.J.A. 1972, s. 6(4)(*a*)).

CRIMINAL BANKRUPTCY ORDERS

DESCRIPTION

The criminal bankruptcy order is designed to make it harder for a major offender against property to keep the proceeds of his offence. It builds on the normal bankruptcy system so that the offender is deemed to have committed an act of bankruptcy on the date on which the order is made.

THE LAW

The Crown Court may make a criminal bankruptcy order where a person is convicted before it and as a result of that or those offence(s), together with any taken into consideration, loss or damage (not attributable to personal injury), to a total exceeding £15,000, has been suffered by one or more persons whose identity is known to the court (P.C.C.A., s. 39(1)). There is no requirement that the loss should be a necessary ingredient of the offence (*Mayer* [1984] Crim.L.R. 633). The order may be made against two or more offenders in respect of the same loss or damage (s. 39(4)).

Where the offender has been engaged in a systematic course of dishonesty and only sample counts are charged in the indictment, the other alleged offences cannot be deemed to have been taken into consideration for the purpose of arriving at an aggregate sum in excess of £15,000; the offender must have admitted the offences and agreed to them being taken into consideration (*D.P.P.* v. *Anderson* [1978] A.C. 964, H.L.).

The order must specify:

(a) the amount of the loss or damage appearing to the court to have resulted from the offence or each offence;

(b) the person or persons to have suffered that loss or damage;

(c) the amount of loss or damage suffered by each victim[1];

(d) the date or the earliest date on which the offence or, if more than one, the earliest of the offences was committed.[2]

---

[1] The loss should be apportioned between the offences but failure to do so may be corrected outside the 28 days allowed by S.C.A., s. 47(2) for variation of sentence (*Saville* [1981] Q.B. 12).

[2] Where an offence is a continuing offence it is proper to select the commencement date of the offence for the purposes of P.C.C.A., s. 39(3)(*d*) (*Raeburn* (1982) 74 Cr.App.R. 21).

In *De Poix* [1978] Crim.L.R. 634 a criminal bankruptcy order was held to be a nullity where the offender had been convicted of two counts of handling stolen property, part only of the proceeds of a robbery and a burglary, as, although the victims of the robbery and burglary had suffered loss in aggregate in excess of £15,000, there was no evidence before the court that this loss was as a result of De Poix's offences.

It is not necessary that the trial judge should be able to specify each of the matters specified above at the end of the trial. The primary duty of the trial judge is to decide, first, whether he has jurisdiction to make the order, and second, if so, whether or not to make the order (*Downing* (1980) 71 Cr.App.R. 316). Provided the order is made in open court, there can be "no objection whatever to that order being perfected afterwards, either by the learned judge himself, or by somebody in the office, or counsel for the prosecution, anyone who can most readily work out and set down on a piece of paper the particulars required by section 39(3)" (*per* Ormrod L.J. at p. 320).

A criminal bankruptcy order is administered by the "Official Petitioner" who is the Director of Public Prosecutions (P.C.C.A., s. 40(1)). The offender is treated as a debtor who has committed an act of bankruptcy on the date on which the order is made (P.C.C.A., Sched. 2, para. 1).

COMBINING A CRIMINAL BANKRUPTCY ORDER WITH OTHER MEASURES

Section 39(1) of the Powers of Criminal Courts Act specifically provides that a court which convicts an offender may make a criminal bankruptcy order against him in addition to dealing with him in any other way, but it may not make such an order if it makes a compensation order against him. Section 14(8) specifically provides that a criminal bankruptcy order may be combined with a community service order.

There is nothing wrong in principle in making a criminal bankruptcy order at the same time as fining an offender, although care must be taken to see that there are assets which would allow the accused to pay his fine. The combination of a fine and a criminal bankruptcy order, however, will be rare (*Michel, Berry and Eade* [1985] Crim.L.R. 162). If there is reason to believe that there are other assets which may not be the subject of the criminal bankruptcy order, in the sense that they are abroad, there is nothing wrong in principle in making the order (*Hill* (1982) 4 Cr.App.R.(S) 319).

APPEALS

There is no right of appeal against the making of a criminal bankruptcy order (P.C.C.A., s. 40(1)). However, where an offender successfully appeals against his conviction the court must rescind the order unless he was convicted in the same proceedings of another offence of which he remains convicted and a criminal bankruptcy order could have been made without reference to loss or damage caused by the other offence (P.C.C.A., s. 40(2)). In such a case the court must amend the order by striking out so much of it as relates to loss or damage caused by the other offence (s. 40(2)).

An application for leave to appeal against the making of a criminal bankruptcy order may be made where it is contended that the order was a nullity (*Anderson*).

FORFEITURE

ORDER DEPRIVING OFFENDER OF PROPERTY USED, OR INTENDED FOR USE, FOR PURPOSES OF CRIME

DESCRIPTION

Courts are empowered to deprive convicted persons of their property where it has been used, or intended for use, for purposes of crime. Such an order (here referred to as a "deprivation order") operates to deprive the offender of his rights, if any, in the property to which the order relates, and the property is required to be taken into police possession if it is not already in their possession.

THE LAW

A deprivation order under section 43 of the Powers of Criminal Courts Act may be made where a person is convicted of an offence punishable on indictment with imprisonment for two years or more. On conviction the court may make a deprivation order when it is satisfied that any property which was in his possession or under his control at the time of his apprehension has been used, or was intended by him to be used "for the purpose of committing, or facilitating the commission of, any offence." "Facilitating the commission of an offence" includes "the taking of any steps after it has been committed for the purpose of disposing of any property to which it relates or of avoiding apprehension or detection" (s. 43(2)).

In *Lucas* [1976] Crim.L.R. 79, an order for forfeiture of the offender's car was quashed on appeal as the car had not been used for the purpose of committing or facilitating the commission of the offence. The appellant and others met a girl and offered her a lift in the car. She consented to certain familiarities and the appellant drove the car to wasteland where she was indecently assaulted. The use of the car was independent of the commission of the offence and it had not been proved that any offence had been intended when the journey started.[1] By contrast in *Attarde and Waterfield* [1975] Crim.L.R. 729, an order depriving the appellant of his car was upheld where he had used equipment, which included a petrol pump which could be operated from the dashboard of his car, to steal petrol from other vehicles. Similarly, in *Lidster* [1976] Crim.L.R. 80, the Court of Appeal, observing that the intention of

---

[1] See also *Riley* (1983) 5 Cr.App.R.(S) 335, below, at p. 177.

the section was to provide an additional penalty, upheld an order depriving the appellant of his car which had been used to transport stolen goods.[2] The car was an integral part of the offence as "the reason why the thieves had come to [the appellant] was because he had a motor car suitable for transferring the goods." The additional penalty of depriving the offender of his car used to convey the appellant and his co-accused from the scene of a robbery, was considered too severe in *Miele* (Note) [1976] R.T.R. 238, as the robbery had been committed on the spur of the moment.

The property,[3] to be the subject of an order, must have been in the possession or control of the offender at the time of his apprehension. In *Hinde* (1977) 64 Cr.App.R. 213, the appellant's car containing stolen goods was seized by the police at the scene of a burglary but the appellant escaped. He was arrested four days later. An order depriving him of the car was quashed as it had not been in his possession or control at the time of his apprehension (see also *Thompson* (1977) 66 Cr.App.R. 130). If the offender is not apprehended, as for example where proceedings are commenced by summons pursuant to a complaint, a deprivation order cannot be made (*Bramble* (1984) 6 Cr.App.R.(S.) 80).

An order under section 43 is an additional penalty and must be used as such; it cannot be used as security for the payment of a fine or compensation. In *R.* v. *Kingston-Upon-Hull JJ., ex p. Hartung* (1981) 72 Cr.App.R. 26, on an application for judicial review by way of certiorari, the Divisional Court quashed an order as the magistrate who made it was using it as security for the payment of a fine and compensation imposed at the same time. The magistrate had ordered the forfeiture and sale of the applicant's van used in the commission of various thefts, the proceeds to be used for the payment of the fine and order of compensation, the balance being repaid to the applicant. In *Thiebeault* (1983) 76 Cr.App.R. 201, the Court of Appeal reiterated the point that section 43 is not a compensation section. In making an order the court does not have power to order the sale of the property seized and to direct the distribution of the proceeds. Rather an order under section 43 operates simply "to deprive the offender of his rights, if any, in the property to which it relates, and the property shall (if not already in their possession) be taken into the possession of the police" (s. 43(3)).

In deciding whether to make an order under section 43, the sentencer may act on his own initiative, or the prosecution may

---

[2] *Cf. Buddo* (1982) 4 Cr.App.R.(S.) 268.
[3] "Property" for the purposes of s. 43 means personal property (*Khan* [1982] 1 W.L.R. 1405).

apply for such an order (see *Pemberton* [1983] Crim.L.R. 121). Such an order may not be made without supporting evidence. If the conditions in section 43(1) are not established by evidence adduced to prove guilt or are not admitted, then the prosecution must be prepared to call such evidence (*Pemberton*).

COMBINING A DEPRIVATION ORDER WITH OTHER MEASURES

As an order under section 43 is an additional penalty (*Lidster; R. v. Kingston-Upon-Hull JJ.*), it may be used only in combination with other measures of a punitive nature. This point was emphasised in *Hunt* [1978] Crim.L.R. 697 where the Court of Appeal held that as an order under section 43 was an additional penalty, it could not be combined with an absolute discharge which can be made only where the court is of "opinion . . . that it is inexpedient to inflict punishment" (P.C.C.A., s. 7(1)). Likewise a section 43 order cannot be combined with a conditional discharge (*Savage* [1983] Crim.L.R. 687). By the same token a section 43 order cannot be combined with a probation order which may be made "instead of sentencing" the offender (P.C.C.A., s. 2(1)).

WHEN AN ORDER UNDER SECTION 43 IS APPROPRIATE

An order under section 43 is appropriate only where use of the property of which the offender is to be deprived was (or would have been) an integral part of the offence of which he is convicted, and such an order does not constitute too severe a punishment in the circumstances (see *Miele*). In *Tavernor* (Note) [1976] R.T.R. 242, an order depriving the appellant of a car used to transport drugs in a burglary was quashed as it was too severe a penalty since the car had been bought out of compensation moneys for physical injuries and the appellant required the use of the car as a means of transport because of those injuries (see also *Buddo* (1982) 4 Cr.App.R.(S.) 268).

Orders for deprivation of property are appropriate only in simple cases. In *Troth* (1980) 71 Cr.App.R. 1, the Court of Appeal quashed an order made in relation to a lorry of which the appellant was co-owner and which was partnership property. The court stated:

> "Just as in cases where compensation orders are made this Court has repeatedly said that orders ought not to be made unless they are simple orders and there are no complicating factors, we consider that forfeiture orders ought not to be made except in simple, uncomplicated cases. If a person has an interest in an object which is not free from encumbrances then difficulties are likely to arise."

Where several offenders are equally responsibe for an offence, it is wrong to make a deprivation order solely in respect of one of them (*Ottey* (1984) 6 Cr.App.R.(S.) 163).

APPEALS

An appeal lies against an order under section 43 in the same way as against any other order or sentence of the court. If an appeal against conviction is successful an order made on conviction will be quashed.

FORFEITURE UNDER OTHER STATUTES

Certain statutes contain their own forfeiture provisions relating to offences committed under those Acts or to property regulated under those or related Acts.

(a) *Misuse of Drugs Act 1971*

THE LAW

Section 27(1) provides:

"... the court by or before which a person is convicted of an offence under this Act may order anything shown to the satisfaction of the court to relate to the offence, to be forfeited and either destroyed or dealt with in such other manner as the court may order."

The power to make a forfeiture order under the section is strictly limited to convictions of offences under the Act. In *Cuthbertson* [1981] A.C. 470, the House of Lords quashed forfeiture orders as the defendants had been convicted of conspiracy at common law to contravene the provisions of section 4 of the 1971 Act and not an offence expressly created by the Act.

Any personal property which relates to the offence may be made the subject of an order; this includes money (*Beard* [1974] 1 W.L.R. 1549) and tangible things capable of being physically destroyed, but does not cover choses in action or other intangibles (*Cuthbertson*). There is no jurisdiction to forfeit tangible things situate abroad (*Cuthbertson*).

The property forfeited must relate to the offence of which the offender is convicted. In *Morgan* [1977] Crim.L.R. 488, the appellant was convicted of possession of cannabis and cocaine with intent to supply. The court made a forfeiture order in relation to scales and money (£393) found in his possession at the time of his arrest. The Court of Appeal quashed the order in relation to the money as, although it was probably part of his working capital for trading in drugs, there was no evidence that it related to the offence of which he had been convicted. In *Ribeyre* (1982) 4 Cr.App.R.(S.) 165, a forfeiture order in relation to £700 which the appellant had admitted was the proceeds of drugs sales, was quashed as the money had not been shown to be related to the offences of which the appellant had been convicted.[4]

COMBINATION WITH OTHER MEASURES

A forfeiture order is a sentence (*Customs and Excise Commissioners* v. *Menocal* [1980] A.C. 598). The principle in *Hunt* will apply and it will be inappropriate to combine such an order with a probation order or an absolute or conditional discharge.

WHEN AN ORDER IS APPROPRIATE

An order may be made in relation to any property which relates to the offence. In the absence of authority it is assumed that the principles in *Miele* (Note) [1976] R.T.R. 238; *Tavernor* (Note) [1976] R.T.R. 242; and *Troth* (1980) 71 Cr.App.R. 1 above apply.

APPEALS

Appeal lies against a forfeiture order under the Act in the same way as against any other order or sentence of the court.

(b) *Firearms Act 1968*

THE LAW

Under section 52(1) of the Firearms Act 1968, a court, in the following circumstances, may make an order for the forfeiture or disposal of any firearm[5] or ammunition found in a persons possession where he:

(a) is convicted of an offence under the Act[6];
(b) is convicted of a crime for which he is sentenced to imprisonment or detention in a detention centre;
(c) has been ordered to enter into a recognisance to keep the peace or to be of good behaviour, a condition of which is that he shall not possess, use or carry a firearm; or

---

[4] Nor could an order under P.C.C.A., s. 43 be made as it had not been demonstrated that the money was intended to be used in connection with any future offences.
[5] This includes an imitation firearm which is readily convertible into a firearm to which s. 1 of the 1968 Act applies (Firearms Act 1982, s. 1).
[6] With the exception of an offence under s. 22(3) or offences under ss. 22(4)(5), 23(1) and 24(4) which specifically relate to air weapons.

(d) he is subject to a probation order containing a requirement that he shall not possess, use or carry a firearm.

In addition to an order for forfeiture or disposal, the court may cancel any firearm certificate or shotgun certificate held by the person concerned.

Where a person is convicted of an offence under section 6(3) or section 49(3), the court before which he is convicted may, if the offender is the owner of the firearms or ammunition, make such order as to the forfeiture of the firearms or ammunition as it thinks fit (Sched. 6, Pt. II, para. 2).

APPEALS

An appeal lies against the above orders in the same way as against any other order or sentence of the court.

(c) *Prevention of Crime Act 1953*

Where any person is convicted under section 1(1) of having in any public place any offensive weapon without lawful authority or reasonable excuse, the court may make an order for the forfeiture or disposal of any weapon in respect of which the offence was committed (s. 1(2)).

(d) *Obscene Publications Act 1964*

Where articles are seized under section 3 of the Obscene Publications Act 1959, and a person is convicted under section 2 of the Obscene Publications Act 1959 of having them for publication for gain, the court on his conviction shall order the forfeiture of those articles (s. 1(4)).

An order under this subsection shall not take effect

"... until the expiration of the ordinary time within which an appeal in the matter of the proceedings in which the order was made may be instituted, or where such an appeal is duly instituted, until the appeal is finally decided or abandoned; and for this purpose—

(*a*) an application for a case to be stated or for leave to appeal shall be treated as the institution of an appeal; and

(*b*) where a decision on appeal is subject to further appeal, the appeal shall not be deemed to be finally decided until the expiration of the ordinary time within which a further appeal may be instituted or, where a further appeal is duly instituted, until the further appeal is finally decided or abandoned."

(s. 1(4).)

(e) *Incitement of Disaffection Act 1934*

Section 3(4) provides that where any person is convicted of an offence under the Act, the court dealing with the case may order any documents connected with the offence to be destroyed or dealt with in such other manner as may be specified in the order. Such destruction may not take place until the expiration of the period within which an appeal may be lodged, and if an appeal is lodged, until after the appeal has been heard and decided.

The relevant offences are those of "maliciously and advisedly" endeavouring to seduce any member of Her Majesty's forces from his duty or allegiance to Her Majesty (s. 1); or, with intent to commit or to aid, abet, counsel or procure such an offence, having in one's possession or under one's control any document of such a nature that the dissemination of copies of it among members of the forces would constitute such an offence (s. 2(1)).

(f) *Forgery and Counterfeiting Act 1981*

Where a person is convicted of an offence under Part II of the Act, the court by or before which he is convicted, may order anything relating to the offence to be forfeited and either destroyed or dealt with in such other manner as the court may order (s. 24(3)). The court may not order anything to be so forfeited where a person claiming to be the owner of or otherwise interested in it, applies to be heard by the Court, unless an opportunity has been given to him to show cause why the order should not be made (s. 24(4)).

(g) *The Immigration Act 1971*

Under section 25(1) it is an offence to be knowingly concerned in making or carrying out arrangements for securing or facilitating the entry into the United Kingdom of anyone whom he knows or has reasonable cause for believing to be an illegal entrant. Where at the time of the offence the person is:

(a) the owner or one of the owners of a ship, aircraft or vehicle used or intended to be used in carrying out the arrangements in respect of which the offence is committed; or

(b) a director or manager of a company which is the owner or one of the owners of any such ship, aircraft or vehicle; or

(c) captain of any such ship or aircraft;

then the court before which he is convicted on indictment may order forfeiture of the ship, aircraft or vehicle (s. 25(6)).

The court may not make a forfeiture order where a person

claiming to be the owner of the ship, aircraft or vehicle or otherwise interested in it applies to be heard by the court, unless an opportunity has been given to him to show cause why the order should not be made (s. 25(8)). Restrictions are placed on the ships and aircraft in respect of which an order may be made (s. 25(7)).

(h) *The Prevention of Terrorism Act 1984*

Where a court convicts a person of:
  (a) belonging to or professing to belong to a proscribed organisation; or
  (b) soliciting, or inviting financial or other support for a proscribed organisation, or knowingly making or receiving any contribution in money or otherwise to the resources of a proscribed organisation; or
  (c) arranging or assisting in the arrangement or management of, or addressing a meeting knowing that the meeting is to support or to further the activities of a proscribed organisation, or is to be addressed by a person belonging or professing to belong to a proscribed organisation,
it may order the forfeiture of any money or other property which, at the time of the offence, was in his possession or under his control for the use or benefit of the proscribed organisation (s. 1(10)).

Where a person:
  (a) solicits or invites any other person to give or lend or otherwise make available, whether for consideration or not, any money or other property; or
  (b) receives or accepts from any other person, whether for consideration or not, any money or other property,
intending that the money or other property shall be applied or used for, or in connection with, the commission, preparation or instigation of acts of terrorism to which this section applies, he shall be guilty of an offence (s. 10(1)) and a court by or before which he is convicted may order the forfeiture of any money or other property:
  (a) which, at the time of the offence, he had in his possession or under his control; and
  (b) which, at that time, he intended should be applied or used for or in connection with the commission, preparation or instigation of acts of terrorism to which this section applies.
(s. 10(4).)

DISQUALIFICATIONS, PROHIBITIONS, INCAPACITIES AND OTHER MISCELLANEOUS ORDERS

There are various types of disqualification, prohibition, incapacity, etc., which may ensue from a conviction for a criminal offence. The major forms of these orders will be examined separately.

1. *Orders Relating to Driving Licences*

(1) DISQUALIFICATION IN RELATION TO ROAD TRAFFIC OFFENCES

These orders will be considered in Part IV.

(2) DRIVING DISQUALIFICATION WHERE VEHICLE IS USED FOR THE PURPOSES OF CRIME

DESCRIPTION

An order for disqualification from holding or obtaining a driving licence may be made where a motor vehicle was used by the person convicted, or by anyone else, for the purpose of committing or facilitating the commission of the offence in question.

THE LAW

Section 44(1) of the Powers of Criminal Courts Act provides that such an order may be made by the Crown Court where a person is convicted before it of an offence punishable on indictment with imprisonment for a term of two years or more, or has been committed to it for sentence under section 38 of the Magistrates' Courts Act 1980 following a conviction by a magistrates' court of such an offence. It is not necessary for the motor vehicle to have been used in the course of committing the crime in question provided it has been used for the purpose of committing or facilitating the commission of the offence. Under section 43(2) of the Powers of Criminal Courts Act "facilitating the commission of an offence" is defined as including "the taking of any steps after it has been committed for the purpose of disposing of any property to which it relates or of avoiding apprehension or detection." In *Riley* (1983) 5 Cr.App.R.(S) 335 a disqualification was quashed where the accused had been convicted of conspiracy to steal. The agreement to steal had been made prior to his use of a motor vehicle to inspect a possible target. Thus, as the element of conspiracy which was criminal was the agreement, the use of the vehicle in furtherance of an agreement which had already been made did not amount to "facilitating the commission of the offence in question."[1]

The offender does not have to be the person who was driving the vehicle; it is sufficient that a motor vehicle was used in the course of committing, or facilitating the commission of, the offence (see *Matthews* [1975] R.T.R 32).

The court may disqualify the offender for such period as it thinks fit.

A person against whom an order of disqualification has been made will be required to produce to the court any licence held by him and if he does not produce the licence as required, he shall be guilty of an offence under section 101(4) of the Road Traffic Act 1972 (P.C.C.A., s. 44(3)(*a*)). A person against whom an order of disqualification is made may apply under section 95 of the Road Traffic Act for the disqualification to be removed. In such a case if the court orders the removal of the disqualification, subsection (4) of that section requiring particulars of the order to be endorsed on the licence, shall not apply but the court shall send notice of the order to the Secretary of State (s. 44(3)(*b*)).

COMBINING AN ORDER OF DISQUALIFICATION WITH OTHER MEASURES

Section 13(3) of the Powers of Criminal Courts Act prohibits the combination of a disqualification with a discharge or probation order. Section 102(1) of the Road Traffic Act specifically provides for disqualification from driving under section 93 or 101 of the Road Traffic Act to be combined with a probation order. However, no provision is made for disqualifications under section 44 of the Powers of Criminal Courts Act so these may not be combined with a discharge or probation order.

WHEN AN ORDER OF DISQUALIFICATION IS APPROPRIATE

An order may be made only where the offence of which the

---

[1] In *Brown (Edward)* [1975] Crim.L.R. 293 the appellant's disqualification for 2½ years was upheld where he drove a vehicle containing stolen goods from a warehouse. An order under P.C.C.A., s. 43 depriving him of the car was also upheld. In *Thomas (Derek)* [1975] Crim.L.R. 296 the offender was disqualified for five years where he drove a thief to the scene of the crime where the latter stole jewellery worth £20,000. In *Ackers* [1977] R.T.R. 66 the appellant was disqualified for 12 months for using his heavy goods vehicle licence to hire a van and lorry to enable him to dispose of stolen tyres.

offender is convicted is punishable on indictment with two years or more imprisonment. Whether an order will be made in any case is essentially a matter for the discretion of the court. However, in *Wright (D.S.)* (1979) 1 Cr.App.R.(S.) 82, the court stated that it was wrong in principle to impose a period of disqualification which would still be operational after the offender's release from prison if the disqualification would prevent him from obtaining employment on his release as where he depended on his ability to drive a motor vehicle to earn his living. This principle was followed in *Kent and Tanser* (1983) 5 Cr.App.R.(S) 16 where the period of disqualification was reduced to such a period that it would end on the date on which the appellant would first be eligible for release on licence. In such a case the disqualification is wholly symbolic and there would seem to be little point in imposing a disqualification in such circumstances.

APPEAL

There is the same right of appeal against an order of disqualification as against any other order or sentence. It would seem that the court making the order may suspend it pending appeal under section 94(2) of the Road Traffic Act.

2. *Disqualification Order under the Companies Act 1985, s. 296*

Section 296 of the Companies Act 1985, provides that where a person is convicted of an indictable offence (whether on indictment or summarily) in connection with the promotion, formation, management or liquidation of a company or with the receivership or management of the property of a company, the court by or before which he is convicted may make a disqualification order against him. A disqualification order is an order that the person against whom the order is made shall not, without leave of the court, be a liquidator or director or receiver or manager of the property of a company or in any way, whether directly or indirectly, be concerned or take part in the promotion, formation or management of a company for such period as may be specified in the order (s. 295(1)). The maximum periods for which orders may be made are five years where made by a court of summary jurisdiction and 15 years where made by the Crown Court. The "leave" to act referred to in section 295(1) may be granted only by a court having jurisdiction to wind up the company in regard to which leave is sought.

Where an order of disqualification is made under section 296 the order should be expressed to run from the date of conviction and not from the date of release from any custodial sentence (*Bradley* [1961] 1 W.L.R. 398).

3. *Disqualification following conviction for Treason*

Under section 2 of the Forfeiture Act 1870 (as amended by C.L.A. 1967, s. 10(2) and Sched. 3) a person convicted of treason will forfeit any military or naval office, any civil office under the Crown or other public employment, or any place, office or emolument in any university, together with certain pensions. Such forfeiture will continue unless the offender receives a free pardon from the Queen, within two months after such conviction, or before the filling up of such office, employment or place if given at a later period. Such an offender becomes and continues (until he has suffered the punishment to which he was sentenced or receives a pardon from the Queen) incapable of holding any military or naval office, or any civil office under the Crown or other public employment, or of being elected, or sitting or voting as a member of either House of Parliament, or of exercising any right of suffrage or other parliamentary or municipal franchise.

4. *Disqualification for Election and Holding Office as a Member of a Local Authority*

Under section 80 of the Local Government Act 1972 a person is disqualified for being elected or being a member of a local authority if he has within five years before the day of election, or since his election, been convicted in the United Kingdom, the Channel Islands or the Isle of Man of any offence and has had passed on him a sentence of imprisonment (whether suspended or not) for a period of not less than three months.

5. *Incapacities on Conviction of Corrupt or Illegal Practices Under the Representation of the People Act 1949*

Under section 151(*a*) where a person is convicted on indictment of a corrupt practice he shall for five years from the date of conviction be incapable of being registered as an elector or voting at a parliamentary election to public office, or being elected or sitting in the House of Commons or holding any public or judicial office. If he has already been elected to the House of Commons or already holds such office he shall vacate the seat or office from the date of conviction.

Under section 151(*b*) where a person is convicted of an illegal practice he shall, for five years from the date of conviction, be incapable of being registered as an elector or voting at any parliamentary election or at any election to a public office in accordance with the provisions of paragraphs (*a*) and (*b*) of section 140(4).

6. *Order Divesting Person of Authority Following Conviction for Incest*

Section 38(1) of the Sexual Offences Act 1956 (as substituted by Guardianship of Infants Act 1973, Sched. 1) provides that on convicting a person of incest with a girl under the age of 18 under section 10 of the Act, or incest with a boy under the age of 18 under section 11, or attempting to commit such an offence, a court may by order divest that person of all authority over the girl or boy. If the person is the guardian of the girl or boy the order may remove that person from the guardianship (s. 38(2)). The order may also appoint a person to be the guardian of the girl or boy during his or her minority or any less period.

7. *The Licensed Premises (Exclusion of Certain Persons) Act 1980*

Under section 1(1) a court by or before which a person is convicted of an offence committed on licensed premises, if satisfied that in committing that offence he resorted to violence or offered or threatened to resort to violence, may make an "exclusion order" prohibiting him from entering those premises or any other specified premises, without the express consent of the licensee of the premises or his servant or agent. An exclusion order may be made in addition to any sentence for the offence or in addition to a probation order or absolute or conditional discharge (s. 1(2)). The order may be made for any period not less than three months or more than two years (s. 1(3)).

Entering any premises in breach of an exclusion order is an offence punishable on summary conviction with a fine of up to £200 and/or imprisonment for up to one month (s. 2(1)), but there is no power to extend the order, although the court may, if it thinks fit, terminate the exclusion order or vary it by deleting the name of any specified premises (s. 2(2)).

8. *Prohibition of Possession of Firearms by Persons Previously Convicted of Crime*

Section 21(1) of the Firearms Act 1968 (as amended) prohibits a person who has been sentenced to custody for life or imprisonment for a term of three years or more or to youth custody for such a term, from having a firearm or ammunition in his possession at any time. The same prohibition applies for a term of five years from the date of release where a person has been sentenced to borstal training, to imprisonment for a term of three months or more but less than three years, or to youth custody for such a term, or to detention in a detention centre for three months or more (s. 21(2)). A person subject to a licence granted by the Home Secretary under section 53 of the Children and Young Persons Act 1933 (in respect of a child or young person detained for grave crime), or subject to a recognisance to keep the peace or to be of good behaviour, a condition of which is that he shall not possess, use or carry a firearm, or is subject to a probation order containing such a requirement, may not at any time during the currency of such licence, recognisance or order, have a firearm or ammunition in his possession (s. 21(3)).

Under section 21(1) the term of three years imprisonment may be made up of separate shorter sentences or the implementation of a suspended sentence ordered to run consecutively (*Tomlinson* (1980) 71 Cr.App.R. 279). Section 21(2) does not apply to a person who has received a suspended sentence (*Fordham* [1970] 1 Q.B. 77).

RECOMMENDATIONS FOR DEPORTATION

DESCRIPTION

Under the Immigration Act 1971 the Secretary of State may order the deportation from the United Kingdom of persons who are not British citizens. In certain circumstances a court convicting a person of a criminal offence may make a recommendation to the Secretary of State to deport that person.

THE LAW

Under section 3(6) of the Immigration Act 1971 a person of 17 or over at the time of his conviction, who is not a British citizen may be recommended for deportation where he is convicted of an offence punishable with imprisonment in the case of a person over 21. The Secretary of State has a discretion whether or not to make a deportation order on the basis of such a recommendation (s. 5). A Commonwealth citizen or a citizen of the Irish Republic shall not, on conviction of an offence, be recommended for deportation if *at the time of the conviction* he had for the last five years been ordinarily resident in the United Kingdom and Islands (s. 7(1)). Periods of six months or more spent in prison or detention do not count towards this five years (s. 7(3)). Whether continuity of residence has been broken by periods spent abroad is a question of fact for the sentencer to decide (*Hussain* (1972) 56 Cr.App.R. 165), but temporary absence, such as for holidays, will be ignored (*Edgehill* [1963] 1 Q.B. 593; *Hussain*).

Whenever any question arises under the Act as to whether or not a person is a British citizen (*i.e.* a person with the right of abode in the United Kingdom), or is entitled to any exemption under the Act, the onus is on the person asserting it to prove that he is (s. 3(8)). However, section 6(2) provides that a court shall not recommend a person for deportation unless he has been given at least seven days written notice stating "that a person is not liable for deportation if he is a British citizen, describing the persons who are British citizens and stating (so far as material) the effect of section 3(8) and section 7." The court may adjourn after conviction either to allow the notice to be served or, if the notice has been served, to allow the seven days to elapse. Where a court is considering making a recommendation for deportation, the defence should be given the opportunity of making submissions to the court on this matter (*Antypas* (1973) 57 Cr.App.R. 207; *R.* v. *Secretary of State for the*

Home Department, ex p. Mario Santillo [1981] 1 Q.B. 778; *Nazari* (1980) 2 Cr.App.R.(S.) 84). No court should make a recommendation for deportation without full inquiry into all the circumstances; it should not be done as an afterthought and the court should state the reasons for its decision (*Nazari*).

COMBINING A RECOMMENDATION FOR DEPORTATION WITH OTHER MEASURES

A recommendation for deportation is an ancillary measure which is additional to the sentence imposed for the offence. Although there is no statutory limitation on the types of measures with which it may be combined, it would not appear to be suitable to combine a recommendation for deportation with any measure other than a fine or imprisonment (even up to life imprisonment: s. 6(4)), or with any other ancillary orders such as orders for compensation or restitution. However, it has been held in one case that a recommendation may be combined with a conditional discharge (*Akan* [1973] Q.B. 491).

WHEN A RECOMMENDATION FOR DEPORTATION IS APPROPRIATE

It should be noted that it is the Home Secretary who makes the final decision whether a person recommended for deportation should be deported. Guidance is emerging through recent cases on the issues which a court should consider before making a recommendation for deportation. The most important case is *Nazari* (1980) 2 Cr.App.R.(S.) 84, at p. 91, where the Court of Appeal laid down specific guidelines:

(1) The court must consider whether the accused's continued presence in the United Kingdom is to the country's detriment (see *Caird* (1970) 54 Cr.App.R. 499). Offenders who have committed serious crimes or who have long records are suitable for recommendation, but a minor offence such as shoplifting by a visitor would not normally merit a recommendation, unless it were part of a series of offences committed on different occasions or carried out as part of a planned raid by a member of a gang.

This principle is closely related to the principles contained in Articles 3 and 9 of the Council Directive 64/221/EEC considered by the European Court (see *Bouchereau* [1978] Q.B. 732; *R.* v. *Secretary of State for Home Affairs, ex p. Santillo* [1980] 2 C.M.L.R. 308) and the Court of Appeal in *R.* v. *Secretary of State for the Home Department, ex p. Santillo*. The effect of this is that where an offender is an EEC national a court should not make a recommendation for deportation solely on the ground that the offender has a criminal record, but a recommendation may be made if the court considers that the previous criminal record of the offender, together with his most recent offence, renders it likely that he will offend again. Where a court makes a recommendation against an offender, it should give its reasons for its decision, and indicate the extent to which the current and previous convictions of the offender have been taken into account, and the evidence which they are thought to give of the likely nature of the offender's personal conduct in the future.

In the most recent case of *Kraus* [1982] Crim.L.R. 468, the Court of Appeal upheld a recommendation for the deportation of the appellant, a citizen of West Germany who had been convicted of stealing two sums, totalling over £2,000, from his employer. It was argued that the appellant did not constitute a threat to the fundamental interests of society, as required by the decision in *Bouchereau*, as his only offence was against property, and there was no evidence that he was likely to commit any offence against public policy in the future. The appellant's offences, however, were committed as a result of blackmail related to his membership of the Nazi party in Germany, which was an illegal organisation. The court held that there was a reasonable apprehension that the appellant would be subject to further acts of blackmail, and there was no guarantee that he had surrendered his beliefs. His presence in the United Kingdom was accordingly "a genuine and sufficiently serious threat to the requirements of public policy affecting one of the fundamental interests of society."

The Court of Appeal also appears to have applied these considerations in cases where offenders have not been covered by the EEC Treaty. Deportation will be recommended, it appears, where the offender has committed a serious offence and appears likely to offend again (see *David* (1980) 2 Cr.App.R.(S.) 362; *Ariquat* (1981) 3 Cr.App.R.(S.) 83; *Tshuma* (1981) 3 Cr.App.R.(S.) 97).

(2) The court is not concerned with the political systems which operate in other countries, and it would be undesirable for any other court to express views about regimes which exist outside the United Kingdom. It is for the Home Secretary to decide in each case whether an offender's return to his country of origin would have consequences which would make his compulsory return unduly harsh (see also *Caird* (1970) 54 Cr.App.R. 499; *Antypas* (1973) 57 Cr.App.R. 207; but *cf. Thoseby and Krawczyk* (1979) 1 Cr.App.R.(S.) 280).

(3) In deciding whether to recommend deportation, the court should consider the effect of the recommendation on others who are innocent and are not before the court, such as members of the offender's family.

Personal hardship encountered by the offender if deported may be considered (*Walters* [1978] Crim.L.R. 175).

(4) Where there is evidence of mental instability connected with, or resulting in the commission of a serious criminal offence that in itself is a good reason for recommending deportation.

(5) Where the offender is an illegal immigrant a recommendation should normally be made.

APPEALS

A recommendation for deportation is a sentence for the purpose of any enactment providing an appeal against sentence (I.A., s. 6(5)(*a*)). Accordingly an appeal may be made against a recommendation. As long as the appeal or further appeal is pending against the recommendation or conviction on which it was made, a deportation order may not be made by the Home Secretary (I.A., s. 6(6)).

COSTS

DESCRIPTION

The Costs in Criminal Cases Act 1973 governs the award of costs to or against the parties to criminal proceedings. An order may be made either for the payment of costs out of central funds or for the payment of the costs of the successful party by the unsuccessful party. This section will only consider orders made against convicted defendants to pay the costs of the prosecution.

THE LAW

On conviction following a summary trial a magistrates' court may order payment by the defendant to the prosecutor of such costs as it thinks just and reasonable (C.C.C.A. 1973, s. 2(2)). There are two limitations to this power:

(1) where under the conviction the court orders payment of any sum as a fine, penalty, forfeiture or compensation, and the sum so ordered does not exceed 25p, no order for costs may be made unless in any particular case the court thinks fit to make one; and

(2) where the offender is under 17 years old, the amount of costs ordered to be paid by him personally shall not exceed the amount of any fine which he has been ordered to pay personally.[1]

(C.C.C.A., s. 2(2).)

If the court makes an order for costs it must specify the amount of costs to be paid (s. 2(3)).

On conviction following a trial on indictment before the Crown Court, the court may order the defendant to pay the whole or any part of the costs incurred in or about the prosecution and conviction, including any proceedings before the examining justices (C.C.C.A., s. 4(1)). Where the Crown Court orders the defendant to pay the costs of the prosecution, if it does fix a sum, the amount to be paid will be ascertained as soon as practicable by the appropriate officer of the Crown Court (s. 4(2)).

---

[1] Under C.Y.P.A. 1933, s. 55 (as substituted by C.J.A. 1982, s. 26) where a child or young person is convicted or found guilty of any offence and a fine or costs is imposed, the court must order the fine or costs to be paid by the parent or guardian unless satisfied that the parent or guardian cannot be found or that it would be unreasonable to make an order for payment, having regard to the circumstances of the case.

Whether a convicted defendant will be ordered to pay costs is in the discretion of the court. The Crown Court, in deciding whether to order a convicted defendant to pay costs, is entitled to take all the circumstances of the case into account, including the strength of the case against him and his knowledge of its strength at the time he pleaded not guilty (*Yoxall* (1973) 57 Cr.App.R. 263). It is not an automatic consequence of conviction that a defendant will be ordered to pay the costs of the prosecution; rather it is a means of marking the manner in which a case has been conducted, for example, by fighting a hopeless case or contesting a case where the truth must have been known to the defendant (*Singh* [1982] Crim.L.R. 315). The fact that the accused pleaded guilty does not automatically mean that an order for costs is inappropriate; a guilty plea is a factor to be taken into account, although the weight to be given by the court to a guilty plea must depend on the nature of the case and the stage of the proceedings at which the plea is offered (*Maher* [1983] Q.B. 784). It is wrong to approach the question of costs on the basis that a defendant must pay costs if he is convicted following election for trial by jury although this is a factor to which the judge should have regard when exercising his discretion as to costs if he regards such election as an extravagant and unreasonable one in all the circumstances (*Dawood* [1974] Crim.L.R. 486). Thus costs should not be used as a means of punishing the defendant for having elected for trial by jury; but if it is an appropriate case in which to order the defendant to pay costs, it is inevitable that the amount of those costs will be greater where he has elected to go to the Crown Court (*Hayden* [1975] 1 W.L.R. 852; *Bushell* (1980) 2 Cr.App.R.(S.) 77).

As with other financial orders, when ordering a defendant to pay costs the court should have regard to his means (*Whalley* (1972) 56 Cr.App.R. 304; *Mountain and Kilminster* (1978) 68 Cr.App.R. 41). It is normally desirable for the court when making an order for costs to either fix a sum or to direct that the final assessment should not exceed a particular sum (*Hier* (1976) 62 Cr.App.R. 233; *Newlove* (1978) 66 Cr.App.R. 1); in this way the order may be related to the defendant's means and any other financial penalty imposed (see *Rowe* [1975] R.T.R. 309).[2] Where an offender is sentenced to a substantial custodial sentence he should not be ordered to pay costs unless he has private capital as on his release from prison his earnings will be necessary for his rehabilitation (*Judd* (1970) 55 Cr.App.R. 14; *Gaston* [1971] 1 W.L.R. 85; *Maher* [1983] Q.B. 784).

In *Maher* the defendant Sinclair was convicted of murder,

---

[2] But in *Mountain and Kilminster* (1978) 68 Cr.App.R. 41, the court stated that while this is a convenient practice it does not necessarily have to be followed in all cases.

conspiracy to import heroin and conspiracy to supply heroin, and ordered to pay costs amounting to £1 million. On appeal it was held that a costs order under section 4(1)(*a*) could only be made in respect of items which in the first instance fell to be borne by the prosecution, and which the Crown Court could order as costs to be paid out of central funds. Such items as jury expenses, overtime pay of police officers investigating the case, judge's lodgings and security arrangements at court were not chargeable to the prosecution and so could not be made the subject of orders against the defendants. However, payment of counsel's fees, the Director of Public Prosecution's costs and witness expenses could properly be so ordered. The order was accordingly reduced to £175,000.

In cases where it seems likely that in the event of a conviction the court may be minded to make an order for costs, it is desirable that the prosecution should be in a position to give an estimate of the costs of the prosecution, and that the estimate given should be one that will not be an overestimate (*Maher*).

Both the Court of Appeal when it dismisses an appeal or an application for leave to appeal, and the Crown Court when it dismisses an appeal from a sentence imposed by, or a conviction by, a magistrates' court, may order the applicant or appellant to pay the whole or any part of the costs of the appeal or application in the case of the Court of Appeal (C.C.C.A., s. 9(1)), or such costs as it thinks just and reasonable in the case of the Crown Court (S.C.A., s. 48(2)(*c*)). Where the Court of Appeal or the House of Lords dismiss the defendant's application for leave to appeal to the House of Lords under Part II of the Criminal Appeal Act 1968, the Court or House may, if it thinks fit, order him to pay the whole or any part of the costs of the application (C.C.C.A., s. 11(1)).

APPEALS

An appeal may be made against an order to pay costs or its amount made by the Crown Court (C.A.A. 1968, s. 50(1); *Hayden*). There is no right of appeal against an order of costs imposed by a magistrates' court (M.C.A. 1980, s. 108(3)).

PART IV
SENTENCING THE ROAD TRAFFIC OFFENDER

DISQUALIFICATION

A disqualification operates to disqualify the offender from holding or obtaining a driving licence or a provisional licence for such period as is specified in the order. There is no power to limit the disqualification to the driving of a motor vehicle of the same class or description as the vehicle in relation to which the offence was committed.[1] Under section 93(7) of the Road Traffic Act 1972 the court before which a person is convicted of any offence involving obligatory or discretionary disqualification may, whether or not it orders his disqualification generally, order him to be disqualified until he has passed a driving test.

OPERATION AND DURATION OF DISQUALIFICATION

A period of disqualification commences as soon as it is ordered (*Taylor* v. *Kenyon* [1952] 2 All E.R. 726),[2] and there is no power to order a disqualification to operate consecutively to another disqualification whether or not both were passed at the same time (*Higgins* [1964] 3 All E.R. 714n.).[3] In addition a period of disqualification may not be ordered to commence at the end of a sentence of imprisonment (*Meese* [1973] 1 W.L.R. 675); but when imposed at the same time as a sentence of imprisonment, the period of disqualification should normally be long enough to ensure that it will not have expired on the offender's release from prison (*Phillips* [1955] 1 W.L.R. 1103; but *cf. Pashley* [1973] R.T.R. 149). Unless the minimum period disqualification is limited by statute, disqualification can be for such period as the court thinks fit. The period of disqualification must be certain and definite, but disqualification for life is certain and definite (*Wallace* [1955] N.I. 137; *Tunde-Olarinde* [1967] 1 W.L.R. 241). Such a period of disqualification should only be given in very unusual circumstances (*North* [1971] R.T.R. 366), and the Court of Appeal tends to discourage disqualification for life or long periods (see *Ward* [1971] Crim.L.R. 665; *Lee* [1971] Crim.L.R. 177; *Peat* [1985] Crim.L.R. 110).

An order of disqualification operates to revoke a driving licence (R.T.A., s. 98(1)); consequently, before an offender may drive again

---

[1] There is such a power in Northern Ireland under art. 194(1) of the Road Traffic (NI) Order 1981.

[2] See also *Graham* [1955] Crim.L.R. 319; *Phillips* [1955] 1 W.L.R. 1103.

[3] See also *Jones* v. *Powell* [1965] 2 Q.B. 216; *Johnston* (1972) 56 Cr.App.R. 859.

after the expiration of the period of disqualification, he must apply for a new driving licence.

Disqualification runs from the moment it is pronounced. In determining the date upon which a period of disqualification ends section 94(4) provides that any time after the conviction during which the disqualification was suspended or the offender was not disqualified is to be disregarded. Thus if the case is adjourned before sentence is passed, disqualification will run from the date on which it was pronounced. If the operation of the disqualification is suspended pending an appeal, the disqualification will commence when the suspension ends (assuming that the disqualification is upheld on appeal).

Disqualifications run concurrently whether they are ordered on the same occasion or a different occasion (*Higgins* [1964] 3 All E.R. 714n.; *Williamson* v. *MacMillan* [1962] S.L.T. 63).

DISCRETIONARY DISQUALIFICATION

Part I of Schedule 4 to the Road Traffic Act 1972 lays down the penalties for offences and stipulates those offences which carry obligatory disqualification and those for which disqualification is discretionary. The discretionary power of disqualification under section 93(2) of the Road Traffic Act arises in relation to all offences for which endorsement is obligatory but which do not involve obligatory disqualification under section 93(1). Whether or not to order disqualification, and the duration of such disqualification if ordered, is entirely a matter for the discretion of the court. Disqualification may be ordered where the court makes a probation order or an order for absolute or conditional discharge (R.T.A., s. 102). Where an offender pleads guilty in writing under section 12 of the Magistrates' Courts Act 1980 he may not be disqualified in his absence unless he has been given the opportunity of attending at an adjourned hearing (M.C.A., s. 11(4)). If the offender has been duly notified and warned of the intention to disqualify and fails to attend he may be disqualified in his absence. Where the defendant fails to appear on being summoned and is found guilty in his absence he may not be disqualified at that first hearing but the case should be adjourned. If the justices do disqualify in such a case the Divisional Court will quash the order (*R.* v. *Bishop's Stortford JJ., ex p. Shields* (1968) 113 S.J. 124).

In considering whether to exercise their discretion to disqualify a court should pay heed to the guidance given in the Court of Appeal in *Cooper* [1983] R.T.R. 183 by Skinner J.:

> "Disqualification, as a general rule, should be reserved for cases involving bad driving, for persistent motoring offences, or

for cases involving the use of the vehicle for the purpose of crime. In any event, except where bad driving is involved, courts ought to think very carefully before imposing a disqualification which might deprive a man of his livelihood . . . " (at p. 185).

Where a person aids, abets, counsels, or procures or incites an offence involving obligatory or discretionary disqualification the court has a discretion whether or not to disqualify him (s. 93(6)).

OBLIGATORY DISQUALIFICATION

Where an offender is convicted of an offence involving obligatory disqualification he must be disqualified for not less than 12 months unless the court for "special reasons" thinks a shorter period or no disqualification is appropriate (s. 93(1)). Where within 10 years of a conviction of one of the following offences, a person commits an offence of driving or attempted driving when unfit or with more than 80mg of alcohol, or refusing to give a blood or urine specimen, he will be disqualified under section 93(1) for three years (s. 93(4)).

A court cannot disqualify a defendant in his absence unless the case has been adjourned and he has been notified of the intention to disqualify (*R. v. Bishop's Stortford JJ., ex p. Shields*, above). However, on an application for certiorari the court may not quash a disqualification in such circumstances if there is no indication of the possibility of any special reasons existing for not disqualifying or for disqualifying for a shorter period (*R. v. Macclesfield JJ., ex p. Jones* [1983] R.T.R. 143, D.C.).

For "special reasons" for not disqualifying, see below.

APPEALS

Where a disqualification is imposed by a magistrates' court the offender may appeal against the order in the same manner as against a conviction (R.T.A., s. 94(1)). The magistrates' court may, if it thinks fit suspend the disqualification pending the appeal (s. 94(2)) or the Crown Court may do so (s. 94A(2)). Where the offender applies to have a case stated or applies to the High Court for an order of certiorari or for leave to make such an application, the High Court may, if it thinks fit, suspend the disqualification (s. 94A(4)(5)).

Where an order of disqualification is imposed by the Crown Court, there is an appeal, with the leave of the Court of Appeal, Criminal Division, to that court (C.A.A. 1968, ss. 9, 10(3), 11(1) and 50(1)). The Crown Court may, if it thinks fit, suspend the disqualification pending an appeal against the order (R.T.A.,

s. 94(2)). Alternatively, the Court of Appeal may, if it thinks fit, suspend the disqualification (R.T.A., s. 94A(2)) and its power to do so may be exercised by a single judge (C.A.A. 1968, s. 31(2A)), and where he refuses an application, the applicant is entitled to have the application determined by the Court of Appeal (C.A.A. 1968, s. 31(3)).

Where a person ordered to be disqualified has appealed or applied for leave to appeal to the House of Lords whether from a decision of the Divisional Court of the Queen's Bench Division, or from a decision of the Court of Appeal, the Divisional Court or, as the case may require, the Court of Appeal, may, if it thinks fit, suspend the disqualification (s. 94(3)). The power of the Court of Appeal to suspend the disqualification may be exercised by a single judge, but where he refuses such an application, the applicant is entitled to have the application determined by the Court of Appeal (C.A.A. 1968, s. 44(2)).

APPLICATION FOR REMOVAL OF DISQUALIFICATION

Where a person is disqualified (whether that disqualification was obligatory or discretionary), he may apply to the court which made the order to remove the disqualification (R.T.A., s. 95(1)). An application cannot be made before the expiration of certain periods from the date on which the order was made. These periods depend on the length of the order and are as follows:

  (a) two years, if the disqualification is for less than four years;
  (b) one-half of the period of the disqualification, if it is for less than 10 years but not less than four years;
  (c) five years in any other case.

Where the period of disqualification imposed is two years or less the disqualified person cannot apply for removal of the disqualification.

On an application for removal, the court will have "regard to the character of the person disqualified and his conduct subsequent to the order, the nature of the offence, and any other circumstances of the case" (s. 95(1)), and may either refuse the application or remove the disqualification from such date as may be specified in the order. While the discretion to remove the disqualification may be exercised in favour of the applicant whether or not the disqualification was mandatory, a court may, if it thinks fit, regard a mandatory disqualification as one which it is somewhat less ready to remove than a discretionary disqualification (*Damer* v. *Davison* [1976] R.T.R 44).

If an application is refused a new application may be made after the expiration of three months from the date of the refusal (s. 95(3)).

Where in pursuance of section 93(5) of the Road Traffic Act

under the old "totting up" procedure, a person was subjected to an additional period of disqualification consecutive to any other period, the periods will be treated as one continuous period of disqualification for the purposes of an application under section 95 (Transport Act 1981, s. 20). In such a case it would seem that the application should be made to the court which imposed the most recent order of disqualification.

ORDER OF DISQUALIFICATION PENDING PASSING A DRIVING TEST

Where a driver is convicted of an offence involving discretionary or obligatory disqualification, the court may order him to be disqualified until he passes a driving test whether or not it also orders his disqualification (R.T.A., s. 93(7)). Where such an order is made on its own, the offender may drive as soon as he obtains a provisional licence (s. 98(3)). If he is also disqualified from driving he cannot take out a provisional licence until the expiration of the period of ordinary disqualification. A disqualification under section 98(3) expires as soon as evidence of passing the test is produced to the licensing authority.

Section 93(7) is not a punitive provision but is designed to provide protection for the public from incompetent drivers (*Donnelly* [1975] 1 W.L.R. 390; *Banks* [1978] R.T.R. 535; *Peat* [1985] Crim.L.R. 110). The power should only be exercised where, because of the offender's age, infirmity, inexperience or the circumstances of the offence, there is reason to suspect that he may not be a competent driver. Sometimes the Court of Appeal in reducing a period of disqualification may make an order under section 93(7) (see *Guilfoyle* [1973] R.T.R. 272; *Heslop* [1978] R.T.R. 441; *Raynor* [1982] R.T.R. 286). In *Guilfoyle,* the Court stated that the longer the period of disqualification the more important it is that the offender should be ordered to undergo a driving test before he again obtains a full licence. An order under section 93(7) cannot be removed under section 95 of the Road Traffic Act, but it should be noted that there is no power to impose such an order when an application under section 95 to remove an order of disqualification is being considered (*Bentham* [1982] R.T.R. 357).

ENDORSEMENT OF LICENCES

Endorsement of an offender's licence is obligatory in three circumstances:

(1) where he is convicted of an offence specified in Schedule 4, Part I to the Road Traffic Act (*i.e.* those offences for which disqualification is obligatory or discretionary);

(2) where he is convicted of manslaughter (Sched. 4, Pt. II);

(3) where he is convicted of an offence specified in Schedule 4, Part III.

In such a case the court must order that the following be endorsed on any licence held by him:

(a) particulars of the conviction;

(b) particulars of any disqualification ordered; or

(c) if the court does not order him to be disqualified, particulars of the offence, including the date of its commission and the appropriate number of penalty points.[1]

The endorsement may be produced as prima facie evidence of the matters endorsed (R.T.A., s. 101(1) as amended by Transport Act 1981, Sched. 9). If the court does not order disqualification it need not order endorsement if for "special reasons" it thinks fit not to do so (R.T.A., s. 101(2) as amended). If the court does not order endorsement it must state in open court the grounds for so doing and, if it is a magistrates' court, it must cause those grounds to be entered in the register of proceedings (R.T.A., s. 105(1)).

Where a person is prosecuted for an offence involving obligatory endorsement he must either deliver his licence to the court or send it by registered post or recorded delivery service to arrive at the court not later than the day of the hearing, or produce it at the hearing (R.T.A., s. 101(11)). If he is convicted the court will require the licence to be produced before ordering endorsement (s. 101(4)). Where the licence is produced the court, in determining sentence, may take into account particulars of any previous conviction or disqualification, or any penalty points endorsed on the licence (R.T.A., s. 101(4A), as amended by Transport Act 1981, Sched. 9).

An endorsement normally remains effective for the following periods:

---

[1] If the court does not order disqualification it is bound to endorse the licence with penalty points, but if it does disqualify it need not endorse penalty points (*R.* v. *Kent (Peter)* [1983] 1 W.L.R. 793).

(1) if an order is made for his disqualification, until four years have elapsed since the conviction;

(2) if no order for disqualification is made, until either four years have elapsed since the commission of the offence or such an order is made.

(R.T.A., s. 101(7A) as inserted by Transport Act 1981, Sched. 9.)

However, where the conviction is for reckless driving or causing death thereby, the endorsement remains effective for four years from the date of conviction and if it was for an offence under section 5(1) or section 6(1)(a) or section 8(7) involving drink or drugs it remains effective for 11 years after the conviction (s. 101(7A)).

A person whose licence has been endorsed becomes entitled to a licence free from endorsement if, after the period applicable has passed, he applies for a new licence pursuant to section 88(1) of the Road Traffic Act, surrenders any subsisting licence, pays the prescribed fee and satisfies any other requirements under section 88(a) (R.T.A., s. 101(7)).

An aider or abettor who aids or abets an endorseable offence must have his licence endorsed (M.C.A., s. 44).

APPEAL

There is no right of appeal against an order of endorsement as endorsement is obligatory pursuant to a conviction of certain offences. Thus endorsement is excluded from the definition of "sentence" in section 108(3) of the Magistrates' Courts Act 1980, while under sections 9 and 50 of the Criminal Appeal Act 1968 it amounts to a sentence fixed by law against which there can be no appeal.

PENALTY POINTS

The penalty points system which came into operation on November 1, 1982 is contained in section 19 of Schedule 7 to the Transport Act 1981. Under this system points are endorsed on an offender's licence according to the offence for which he has been convicted. Once 12 points have been accumulated within a prescribed period the offender is liable to disqualification; this replaces the old "totting up" disqualification procedure under section 93(3)(5) (now repealed).

ENDORSEMENT

Where a person is convicted of an endorseable offence and the court does not order his disqualification he will have the penalty points allocated to the offence by Schedule 7 endorsed on his licence unless the court for "special reasons" thinks fit not to endorse his licence. Schedule 7 sets out a fixed number of points for most offences except for four where the court fixes the number of points to be endorsed within a prescribed range (careless or inconsiderate driving: 2–5; failing to stop after an accident: 5–9; failing to give particulars or report an accident: 4–9; and using, etc., a motor vehicle without insurance: 4–8).

Where a person is convicted of two or more offences committed on the same occasion the number of penalty points to be endorsed "shall be the number or highest number that would be endorsed on a conviction of one of the offences" (Transport Act 1981, s. 19(1)). Thus, if all the offences have the same number of points the court must impose the number of points for any one of those offences. Where the points for the offences differ, the court must impose the points for the offence which incurs the highest number of points. Where one of the offences has variable points the court should first consider the number of points appropriate to this offence and if this is the highest of the offences of which the offender is convicted, this number should be endorsed.

DISQUALIFICATION

Where an offender is convicted of an offence involving obligatory or discretionary disqualification and he has 12 or more points which are required to be taken into account, he will be disqualified for a minimum period of six months (s. 19(2)(4)). This disqualification will be concurrent with any other period of disqualification (see

Sandwell, [1984] R.T.R. 45. The minimum of six months applies where he has no previous disqualification to be taken into account. The minimum is increased to one year if he has one such disqualification and two years if more than one is to be taken into account (s. 19(4)). A previous disqualification is taken into account if it was imposed within the three years immediately preceding the commission of the latest offence in respect of which penalty points are taken into account (s. 19(4)).

The points required to be taken into account in determining the total number of points accumulated are laid down in section 19(3). First, the court takes into account the number of points that are imposed for the present conviction or which would be imposed if he was not then being disqualified. For example, if the offender already has eight reckonable points and is then convicted of an offence which carries obligatory disqualification, the four points which such an offence carries, while not being endorsed on his licence, will be taken into account and lead to the court considering a penalty points disqualification. Secondly, the court takes into account any points ordered to be endorsed on a previous occasion except that:

  (i)   no points are to be taken into account if since that occasion and before conviction, the offender has been disqualified; and

  (ii) points will not be added together where any of the offences in respect of which points were endorsed was committed more than three years before another.

"WIPING THE SLATE CLEAN"

As soon as a disqualification is ordered the points imposed prior to it can no longer be taken into account in reckoning points for future possible disqualification (see s. 19(3)(*b*)).

MITIGATING CIRCUMSTANCES

Were 12 or more points are taken into account a court must disqualify the offender unless it is satisfied, having regard to all the circumstances, that there are grounds for mitigating the normal consequences of conviction and thinks fit to order him to be disqualified for a shorter period or not to order him to be disqualified (s. 19(2)). Certain circumstances may not be taken into account:

  (a)   any circumstances that are alleged to make the offence or any of the offences not a serious one;

  (b)   hardship, other than exceptional hardship; or

  (c)   any circumstances which, within the three years immediately preceding the conviction have been taken into account under

section 19(2) of the Transport Act or section 93(3) of the
Road Traffic Act in ordering the offender to be disqualified
for a shorter period or not ordering him to be disqualified
(s. 19(6)).

SPECIAL REASONS

A court may, for "special reasons" refrain from disqualifying an offender in respect of an offence for which disqualification is obligatory or refrain from endorsing in respect of an endorseable offence.

The phrase "special reasons" has not been defined by statute but it was defined by Andrews L.C.J. in the Northern Irish case of *R. (Magill)* v. *Crossan* [1939] N.I. 106.

> "A 'special reason' . . . is one which is special to the facts of the particular case, that is, special to the facts which constitute the offence. It is, in other words, a mitigating or extenuating circumstance, not amounting in law to a defence to the charge, yet directly connected with the commission of the offence, and one which the Court ought properly to take into consideration when imposing punishment. A circumstance peculiar to the offender as distinguished from the offence is not a 'special reason' within the exception."

This passage received approval from Lord Goddard in *Whittall* v. *Kirby* [1947] K.B. 194. The special reason must be found outside the facts which constitute the mischief of the offence itself (*Nicholson* v. *Brown* [1974] R.T.R. 177). A blood-alcohol level marginally above the prescribed limit does not amount to a special reason (*Delaroy-Hall* v. *Tadman* [1969] 2 Q.B. 208). Nor are special reasons to be found in the fact that the defendant is of good character, has a good driving record, or that he, his family or employees, will suffer personal financial or other hardship, however severe (*Whittall* v. *Kirby* [1947] K.B. 194). The fact that a licence is important or vital to the offender's employment is not a special reason (*Gordon* v. *Smith* [1971] Crim.L.R. 173; *Holroyd* v. *Berry* [1973] R.T.R. 145).

Special reasons have been found to exist in the following circumstances in relation to disqualification: the exaggerated effect of a small quantity of drink on a defendant suffering, unknown to himself, from diabetes (*Wickins* (1958) 42 Cr.App.R. 236); a laced drink (*Shippam* [1971] Crim.L.R. 434; *Williams* v. *Neale* [1971] R.T.R. 149); an emergency arising after consuming drink (*Brown* v. *Dyerson* [1969] 1 Q.B. 45), but the defendant must first explore other reasonable alternatives (*Baines* [1970] Crim.L.R. 590; *Evans* v. *Bray* [1977] R.T.R. 24). Where the defendant is charged with refusing to supply a laboratory specimen (or undergo a medical examination), if the reason for so doing does not amount to a reasonable excuse, there cannot exist a special reason (*Scobie* v. *Graham* [1970] Crim.L.R. 589; *Hockin* v. *Weston* [1971] 115 S.J. 675).[1] However, circumstances arising after the commission of the offence have been held to amount to special reasons. In *Anderson* [1972] Crim.L.R. 245, special reasons were found to exist where the defendant, after being told that he would not be prosecuted, destroyed the sample of blood which he had been given for analysis. The Court of Appeal held that he had been deprived of a possible defence, particularly bearing in mind that the prosecution analysis was 81mg (but see *Doyle* v. *Leroux* [1981] R.T.R. 438).

Where the defendant alleges that there are special grounds for mitigating the sentence he must substantiate that allegation with admissible evidence on oath (*Jones* v. *English* [1951] 2 All E.R. 853; *Flewitt* v. *Horvath* [1972] R.T.R. 123), unless the prosecution make a formal admission of the facts relied on (*Brown* v. *Dyerson*). The defendant must prove the facts on which his plea of special reasons is based on a balance of probabilities (*Puglsey* v. *Hunter* [1973] 1 W.L.R. 578). If the court finds special reasons to exist it must specify those reasons in the order.

---

[1] See also *Horgan* [1976] Crim.L.R. 319; *Brown* v. *Ridge* [1979] R.T.R. 136.

PART V
MENTALLY DISORDERED OFFENDERS

MENTALLY DISORDERED OFFENDERS

It is a commonplace observation that not all offenders suffer from mental disorder but that some mentally disordered persons do commit offences. The courts have a range of alternatives in dealing with an accused or a convicted person who is or is believed to be mentally disordered. These measures are not designed to punish but to ensure appropriate treatment, and where necessary, to protect society.[1]

The method most frequently availed of in sentencing mentally disordered offenders is a probation or supervision order with a condition requiring psychiatric treatment.[2] These modes of disposal are considered also in Part I (pp. 19–34 and 71–78, above). The approach of the courts to mentally disordered offenders including persons with personality difficulties or disorders who for one reason or another have not been sentenced under the Mental Health Act is considered in Part VI (pp. 269–270, below).

A considerable (but currently declining) number of mentally abnormal offenders are dealt with under the powers contained in the Mental Health Act 1983 and these will be examined here.[3] The 1983 Act consolidates the Mental Health Act 1959, which is the foundation of the modern approach to the treatment of all mentally disordered persons, and the Mental Health (Amendment) Act 1982, which incorporated many amendments to the 1959 Act following the Reports of the Aarvold and Butler Committees.[4] The Mental Health Act 1983, s. 1(2) provides that "mental disorder" for the purposes of the Act "means mental illness, arrested or incomplete development of mind, psychopathic disorder and any other disorder

---

[1] The best legal accounts of the system of care for the mentally disordered apart from official reports mentioned in note 4 are L. Gostin, *A Human Condition: the law relating to mentally abnormal offenders: Observations, Analysis and Proposals for Reforms*, Vol. 1, *Mind* (1977, London); B. Hoggett, *Mental Health Law*, (2nd ed., 1984, London, Sweet & Maxwell). The annotations to the Mental Health Act 1983, by Richard M. Jones in *Current Law Statutes Annotated* (1983) are also a valuable reference source.

[2] Hoggett, *op. cit.* p. 165.

[3] In 1970 1,317 hospital orders were made and 759 in 1979, Hoggett, *op. cit.* pp. 175–176.

[4] "Report on the Review of Procedures for the Discharge and Supervision of Psychiatric Patients subject to Special Restrictions" (Aarvold Report), Cmnd. 5191 (H.M.S.O., 1973); "Interim Report of the Committee on Mentally Abnormal Offenders" (Butler Committee), Cmnd. 5698 (H.M.S.O., 1974); "Report of the Committee on Mentally Abnormal Offenders" (Butler Committee), Cmnd. 6244 (H.M.S.O., 1978). See also "Reform of Mental Health Legislation," Cmnd. 8405, a Government white paper of November 1981.

or disability of mind." Section 1 gives definitions for each of the specified conditions but provides that a person may not be dealt with under the Act as suffering from mental disorder "by reason only of promiscuity or other immoral conduct, sexual deviancy or dependence on alcohol or drugs" (s. 1(3)).

HOSPITAL ORDERS

The purpose of a hospital order is to enable the mentally disordered offender to be admitted to and compulsorily detained in hospital for as long as is necessary in his own and the public interest. The powers of the court are contained in section 37 of the 1983 Act. The order is available following conviction for any imprisonable offence in the Crown Court and a magistrates' court, other than an offence the sentence for which is fixed by law (in practice, murder). A magistrates' court may, however, proceed to make a hospital order in respect of a person suffering from either "mental illness" or "severe mental impairment" (but not "psychopathic disorder" or "mental impairment") without first convicting him if satisfied that the accused did the act or made the omission charged (s. 37(1)).[5] Before making a hospital order a number of conditions must be fulfilled:

(1) the court must consider the written or oral evidence of two registered medical practitioners, which satisfies it that the offender is suffering from one of the forms of mental disorder: mental illness, psychopathic disorder, severe mental impairment, or mental impairment;

(2) one of the two doctors must be approved by the Secretary of State (in practice, the district health authority) as having special experience in the diagnosis or treatment of mental disorder, and both must agree on the form of mental disorder which the person is said to be suffering from (M.H.A., ss. 37(2)(a), (7), 54);

(3) in addition, the court must be satisfied that the mental disorder is of a nature or degree which makes it appropriate for the person to be detained in a hospital for medical treatment;

(4) where the forms of mental disorder evidenced is a psychopathic disorder or mental impairment, the court must also be satisfied that any such treatment is likely to alleviate or prevent a deterioration of the patient's condition (s. 37(2)(i));

(5) the court must be of opinion having regard to all circum-

[5] *Lincolnshire (Kesteven) Justices, ex p. O'Connor* [1983] 1 W.L.R. 335, the power was described as unusual and appropriate occasions for its use "very rare," *per* Lord Lane, at p. 338.

stances connected with the offence and the offender and
having considered other methods of dealing with the case,
that a hospital order is the most suitable method (s. 37(2)(*b*));

(6) the court has further to be satisfied on the written or oral
evidence of the registered medical practitioner who would be
in charge of treatment in the hospital, or someone representing the managers of the hospital that a bed is available in the
hospital for him within 28 days from the making of the order
(s. 37(4)).

In *Blackwood* (1974) 59 Cr.App.R. 170, the Court of Appeal
stated that a court should only exceptionally consider making a
hospital order without the defendant being legally represented. The
major difficulty with these conditions concerns (6), above. A source
of frustration for the courts has been the lack of available secure
suitable hospital accommodation, and the unwillingness of hospital
managements and sometimes nursing staff to receive convicted
patients.[6]

The Health Authorities are not obliged under the Act to supply
beds, but must, on request from a court contemplating a hospital
order, provide information as to the availability of beds in its region
for the admission of the person under a hospital order (s. 39(1)).[7]

It should also be noticed that (4) above (s. 37(2)(i)(*a*)) introduces
a "treatability" test, which should ensure that dangerous offenders
would normally be sent to prison and not to hospitals where little
can be done for them and which are not secure. It will also reduce
the risk of offenders who are not severely mentally handicapped
being made the subject of hospital orders.[8]

INTERIM HOSPITAL ORDERS[9]

Section 38 of the Mental Health Act enables a court (including a
juvenile court) to order detention of an offender in a hospital for an
initial maximum period of 12 weeks renewable for further periods
of not more than 28 days at a time to a maximum of six months. The
order known as an interim hospital order derives from a recommendation of the Butler Committee which, "gained the impression that
many doctors found it difficult to decide whether to recommend

---

[6] See the comments of Lawton L.J. in *Harding (Bernard), The Times* June 15, 1983,
where he noted that obstruction of a hospital order once made may constitute
contempt of court.
[7] In contrast to the position in Northern Ireland, although practice is in effect the
same, Mental Health Act (Northern Ireland) 1961, s. 51.
[8] Hoggett, *op. cit.* p. 168.
[9] This order became available from October 10, 1984 on the coming into force of
M.H.A., s. 38, Mental Health Act Commencement Order, S.I. 1984 No. 1357.

that a hospital order should be made where they have been able to examine the patient only briefly in a prison hospital under the pressure of impending court proceedings, since it was often impossible to know how he would react subsequently to the psychiatric hospital regime."[10] Before making an interim order, the court must be satisfied on broadly the same conditions that apply to the full order, that the offender appears to be suffering from a mental disorder, and that a hospital is willing to take him (s. 38(1)(4)). The section, however, requires that one of the registered medical practitioners who gives evidence must be employed at the hospital where the person is to be detained. The Court may, at the termination of an interim order, make a hospital order or dispose of the case in some other way. Where the court proposes to make a hospital order, the offender who is subject to an interim hospital order must be in court or if not, be represented by counsel or solicitor (s. 38(2)). A similar provision applies where a renewal of the interim hospital order is being considered by the court (s. 38(6)).

EFFECT OF HOSPITAL ORDER

An admission to a hospital by means of a hospital order has the same effect for most purposes as a compulsory civil commitment under Part II of the Act, except that the nearest relative cannot discharge the patient and the hospital order patient cannot apply to a Mental Health Review Tribunal within the first six months of detention (M.H.A., Sched. 1, paras. 2, 9).

DURATION

The order lapses after six months and must be renewed if the patient is to be further detained (M.H.A., s. 20, Sched. 1).

COMBINING A HOSPITAL ORDER WITH OTHER SENTENCES

Section 37(8) of the Mental Health Act provides that when a hospital order is made, the court shall not pass a sentence of imprisonment or order for detention or impose a fine or make a probation order in respect of the offence, or care or supervision order in the case of a child or young person. However, the section also provides that the court may make any it has power to make. Thus, any ancillary order (Part III above) including a compensation order or disqualifications may be made.

---

[10] Hoggett, *op. cit.* p. 183 and pp. 299–306.

GUARDIANSHIP ORDERS

A guardianship order may be made under section 37 of the Mental Health Act on the same conditions as a hospital order, except;

   (i)   that there is no condition that a mental disorder diagnosed as psychopathy or mental impairment must be treatable, and

   (ii) in the case of an offender over 16 years, the mental disorder must be "of a nature or degree which warrants his reception into guardianship."

   (s. 37(2)(a)(ii).)

The patient is placed under the guardianship of the local social services authority or an individual approved by them, willing to receive him into guardianship (s. 37(1), (6)).

The powers of a guardian are set out in section 8(1) of the Mental Health Act, and in summary are: to determine place of residence; to require attendance for treatment, occupation, education or training; and to require access to the patient in any place of residence for a doctor, social workers or other specified person.

Little use is made of guardianship orders by the courts, because this measure along with other community based treatments are undeveloped. However, a leading authority on mental health has argued that lawyers should consider pressing for this order in appropriate cases, as it may often be in the interests of the client or patient, and preferable to a hospital order.[11]

EFFECT OF GUARDIANSHIP ORDER

The effects of a guardianship order, including duration are the same as those relating to the hospital order.

COMBINING A GUARDIANSHIP ORDER WITH OTHER SENTENCES

The position is as set out above in the case of a hospital order.

RESTRICTION ORDERS

In making a hospital order but not a guardianship order, a court may if it thinks it necessary for the protection of the public from *serious harm*, having regard to the nature of the offence, the antecedents of the offender and the risk of his committing further offences if set at large prematurely, make a further order under section 41(1) of the Mental Health Act 1983 subjecting him to special restrictions as compared with other patients for a period

[11] Hoggett, *op. cit.* pp. 182–183.

specified in the order or without limit of time. This order is known as a restriction order.

The 1982 Mental Health (Amendment) Act added the limitation *serious harm* to the prerequisites applicable to the making of a restriction order under the Mental Health Act 1959. This followed a recommendation of the Butler Report to exclude from the scope of the order such as the "petty recidivist because of the virtual certainty that he will persist in similar offences in the future."[12] Equally, a "social nuisance" such as the defendant in *Toland* (1973) 58 Cr.App.R. 453 should no longer be subject to this order.

A restriction order may not be made unless the psychiatrist, whose evidence was taken into account by the court when making the hospital order has given evidence orally before the court (M.H.A., s. 41(2)). A restriction order ought to be coupled with a hospital order where any issue relating to the public arises (*Higginbotham* [1961] 1 W.L.R. 1277; *Gardiner* [1967] 1 W.L.R. 464). Further, unless the medical advice is that the patient will recover from the disorder within a definite period, restriction orders should be unlimited as to time (*per* Lord Parker C.J., *Gardiner*, at p. 469). In *Haynes* ((1981) 3 Cr.App.R.(S.) 330), the Court of Appeal stated that it was wrong to determine the length of a restriction order by reference to the term of imprisonment which would have been otherwise appropriate for the offence. It is finally for the court and not the medical specialists to decide if a restriction order is required, and the court is not bound to accept medical evidence for or against restricting discharge where a hospital order is made (*Royse* (1981) 3 Cr.App.R.(S.) 58). A defendant should be represented if the court is considering a restriction order (*Blackwood* (1974) 59 Cr.App.R. 170).

Only a Crown Court may make a restriction order. A magistrates' court may, if it is satisfied as required under section 37(1) of the Mental Health Act that a hospital order is appropriate, but considers a restriction order should also be made, commit any offender over 14 years to the Crown Court, with a view to a restriction order being made (M.H.A., s. 43).

EFFECT OF A RESTRICTION ORDER

A patient admitted to hospital under the authority of a hospital order with an order restricting discharge may not be discharged, transferred or granted leave of absence from the hospital without the consent of the Secretary of State (M.H.A., s. 41(3)(c)). During the period of a restriction order, the patient has the right to make an

---

[12] Butler Report, note 4 above, para. 14.24.

application to a Mental Health Review Tribunal in the second six month period of the hospital order, and thereafter at yearly intervals (M.H.A., s. 70). The Secretary of State may refer the case of a restricted patient at any time to the Tribunal (M.H.A., s. 71(1)). Further the Act imposes a duty on the responsible medical officer in the hospital to examine and report directly to the Home Secretary at least once per year about every patient who is subject to a restriction order (M.H.A., s. 41(6)).

DURATION AND TERMINATION OF A RESTRICTION ORDER

Where an order restricting discharge is attached to a hospital order, then the hospital order does not terminate after six months as in the ordinary case unless it is renewed, but continues as long as the order restricting discharge is in force. The Secretary of State may release a patient subject to a restriction order at any time and either discharge conditionally or absolutely (M.H.A., s. 42(1)(2)). Where the patient is conditionally discharged, the restriction order is still in force and the patient may be recalled by the Secretary of State. The Secretary of State in considering the periodic reports on restricted patients required by section 41(6) of the Mental Health Act, and in considering whether to release will take into account the judgment of the European Court of Human Rights in *X* v. *United Kingdom* (1981) 4 E.C.H.R. 181.[13] The effect of this decision is that it would be a breach of the European Convention on Human Rights, Article 5 which protects the right to liberty to continue a restriction order if the patient's mental condition does not warrant it. Therefore, continued danger to the public alone, if a patient no longer requires hospitalisation, would not be sufficient grounds for continuing a restriction order (*Kynaston* v. *Secretary of State for Home Affairs* (1981) 73 Cr.App.R. 281). If a patient who is under a restriction order is released subject to a conditional discharge, and is recalled, he or she and relatives are entitled to be informed of the reasons and the Secretary of State must refer the case to a Mental Health Review Tribunal within one month (M.H.A., s. 75). In this case and in any other application involving a restricted patient, the Tribunal has independent powers to discharge the patient absolutely or on conditions. In the former case, the patient is no longer liable to be detained or recalled to the hospital (s. 73). In the latter case, the patient will be subject to

---

[13] See also *Legal Protection of Persons suffering from mental disorder placed as involuntary patients*, Recommendation No. R(83)2 adopted by the Committee of Ministers of the Council of Europe, February 22, 1983 (1983 Strasbourg).

supervision in the community. These provisions are also effects of the European Court of Human Rights judgment in *X* v. *United Kingdom*.

OTHER POWERS OF THE COURTS TO DEAL WITH MENTALLY DISORDERED OFFENDERS

PROBATION AND SUPERVISION

A court may include a requirement in a probation order or supervision order that the person submits to psychiatric treatment (P.C.C.A., s. 3; C.Y.P.A. 1969, s. 12(4)(5)). The requirement may be included only on the evidence of one approved doctor who must state that the person's mental condition is susceptible to treatment but does not warrant detention by means of a hospital order. The requirement may be for in-patient treatment at any specified hospital (other than a special hospital) or mental nursing home, or for out-patient treatment, or treatment under the direction of a specified doctor. (See also pp. 23–24 and 72, above.)

REMANDS

Section 35 of the Mental Health Act introduces a new power to remand a person before trial to hospital for a report on his mental condition. Remands may be continued under the conditions prescribed in the section for a maximum of 12 weeks. If an accused person absents himself from the hospital, he may be arrested without warrant and brought before the court which remanded him, which may terminate the remand to the hospital. An accused, remanded for a report, may obtain at his expense an independent assessment of his mental condition (M.H.A., s. 35(8)). This section came into force on October 10, 1984. Section 36 of the Mental Health Act empowers the Crown Court only to remand an accused person actually suffering from mental disorder to a hospital for treatment. The court must only exercise this power on the evidence of two registered medical practitioners that the accused person is suffering from a mental disorder that requires treatment by means of detention in hospital, and that a bed is available. The maximum period of a remand is 12 weeks (s. 36(6)). Absconding is dealt with as under section 35 above.

These new options are intended as alternatives to remands to prison for medical reports and should not prejudice the use of bail. The presumption in favour of bail applies (Bail Act 1976, s. 4(4)), and a condition of the bail can be to co-operate in the making of a psychiatric report.[14] A magistrates' court may remand an accused, whom they are satisfied committed the act or made the omission charged, for a report on his mental condition prior to sentence. The court in such a case should adjourn the case, for not more than three weeks at a time if the defendant is remanded in custody, or four weeks at a time if he is on bail (M.C.A., s. 30). A condition of the bail should be the imposition of a condition to undergo psychiatric examination in terms of the Bail Act 1976, s. 3(6)(*d*) as the court directs. A Crown Court may adjourn the case for medical examination of the offender before passing sentence (see p. 235, below).

PERSONS FOUND UNFIT TO PLEAD OR NOT GUILTY BY REASON OF INSANITY

Where the accused is found by a jury to be unfit to plead, the court shall order the accused to be admitted to hospital and in such a case, he will be treated as having been admitted in pursuance of a hospital order subject to a restriction order without limitation as to time (Criminal Procedure (Insanity) Act 1964, s. 5, Sched. 1). As soon as a person found unfit to plead ceases to require treatment for mental disorder the Secretary of State may remit him to prison for trial at the next Crown Court or discharge him (s. 5(4)). Any person remitted to prison by reason of unfitness to plead, has the same right of access as any other person who is subject to an order restricting discharge to the Mental Health Review Tribunal (M.H.A., s. 73). Where an accused is found not guilty by reason of insanity he will be admitted to hospital and treated as having been admitted in pursuance of a hospital order and a restriction order without limit of time (Criminal Procedure (Insanity) Act 1964, s. 5(1), Sched. 1).

APPEALS

Where a hospital order, guardianship order, interim hospital order, or order restricting discharge has been made by a court of summary jurisdiction or a Crown Court in respect of a person convicted before it, he may appeal against that order in the same manner as against a conviction.[15]

Similarly, in the rare case that a magistrate's court under section 37(3) of the Mental Health Act makes a hospital or guardianship order *without* conviction, the person has the same appeal rights as if

---

[14] Under s. 3(6)(*d*) of and Sched. 1 to the Bail Act 1976, a condition of bail may also be that the person take up residence in a hospital for purposes of the report.
[15] See note 5 above.

any such order was made following conviction (M.H.A., s. 45).[16] An appeal against a hospital or guardianship order in the case of a child or young person, or an appeal against the finding on which it was based, may be brought either by the child or young person or a parent or guardian (M.H.A., s. 45).

Where an order is appealed from the Crown Court and the Court of Appeal allows the appeal, it may impose any sentence which the Crown Court could have imposed. Where the appeal is against a hospital order, it is possible that the Court of Appeal or Crown Court if the order was made by a magistrates' court may find that the order was rightly made and, in addition, it may add an order restricting discharge (C.A.A. 1968, s. 10).

Where an appeal is made against a restriction order, the appeal court may treat it as being an appeal against the hospital order also and it may quash both and deal otherwise with the appellant for the offence in respect of which they were imposed.

The Criminal Appeal Act 1968, s. 15 provides a right to appeal against a finding that an accused is unfit to plead. A person found not guilty by reason of insanity may appeal to the Court of Appeal against that verdict (C.A.A. 1968, s. 12).

[16] C.A.A. 1968, s. 50(1). M.H.A., Sched. 4, para. 23(1).

PART VI

SENTENCING PROCEDURES AND SENTENCING PRINCIPLES

SENTENCING PROCEDURE

PLEA BARGAINING

The sentencing process may commence prior to the trial in a pre-trial review—a procedure commonly known as "plea bargaining"—in which counsel for the prosecution and the defence may confer about the plea. It is the law in the United Kingdom that the trial judge is never a party to these negotiations. Exceptionally, however, the defence may consult the judge about his sentencing intentions depending on the plea entered by the defendant. Prosecuting counsel should be present during such consultations.

Alternatively, a defendant may contemplate changing his plea during the course of the trial. A related situation, arises where, under section 6 of the Criminal Law Act 1967, a defendant seeks to plead not guilty of the offence specifically charged in the indictment but guilty of another offence of which he might be found guilty on that indictment (see *Archbold*, §4–59 and 4–60).[1] While it is true that a plea of guilty may have a mitigating effect in relation to sentencing (see "Sentencing Principles," *post*), the Court of Appeal has been at great pains to strictly limit and regulate this "plea bargaining" procedure. The leading case on the subject is *Turner* [1970] 2 Q.B. 321 which laid down the principles to be followed:

(1) Counsel must be completely free to do what is his duty, that is, to give the accused the best advice he can and, if need be, in strong terms. It will often include advice that a guilty plea, showing an element of remorse, is a mitigating factor which might enable the court to give a lesser sentence than would

---

[1] In this situation "it is for prosecuting counsel to make up their own minds what pleas to accept. If the judge does not approve, he can say so in open court, and then the prosecution will have to decide what course to take. It is bad practice for counsel as a matter of course to go to see the judge behind the scenes in order to get advice about pleas." (*Per* Lawton L.J., *Coward* (1980) 70 Cr.App.R. 70, at p. 76.)

The dangers of going to see the judge are illustrated by *Emmanuel* (1982) 74 Cr.App.R. 135. The applicant was charged on count 1 with attempted rape and on count 2 with unlawful sexual intercourse. Counsel for the defence and the Crown saw the judge in chambers who approved the proposal of the prosecution to offer no evidence on count 1, but to accept a plea of guilty on count 2. On arraignment the applicant pleaded not guilty to count 1 and guilty to count 2. The prosecution then proceeded to outline the facts which led the judge to withdraw his approval of the Crown not offering evidence on count 1. He ordered the trial to proceed on both counts and the applicant was convicted of attempted rape. The Court of Appeal dismissed his application for leave to appeal on the ground that there had been a material irregularity in the course of the trial.

otherwise be the case. Counsel, of course, will emphasize that the accused must not plead guilty unless he has committed the acts constituting the offence charged.

While the responsibility of pleading guilty or not guilty is that of the defendant himself, the Court of Appeal did state in *Hall* [1968] 2 Q.B. 787 that it is the clear duty of defending counsel to assist the defendant to make up his mind by putting forward the pros and cons of a plea, if need be in forceful language, so as to impress on the defendant what the result of a particular course of conduct is likely to be.

(2) The accused, having considered counsel's advice, must have a complete freedom of choice whether to plead guilty or not guilty.

It should be stressed that to put pressure on an accused to plead guilty is impermissible and that the effect of this is to make the plea a nullity (*Barnes* (1971) 55 Cr.App.R. 100; *Peace* [1976] Crim.L.R. 119).

In *Inns* [1975] Crim.L.R. 182 a new trial was ordered where a plea of guilty was made under pressure. In *Ryan* [1978] Crim.L.R. 306 the Court of Appeal granted leave to appeal ordering a *venire de novo* where the applicant pleaded guilty under pressure when he would not have done so had it not been for his counsel's statement following discussion with the judge that the outcome would be other than an immediate custodial sentence if he admitted his guilt.

(3) There must be freedom of access between counsel and judge. Any discussion, however, must be between the judge and both counsel. If a solicitor representing the accused is in court he should be allowed to attend the discussion if he so desires.

In *Eccles* [1978] Crim.L.R. 757 the Court of Appeal stated that it was plainly irregular for the judge to hold discussions in his private room with the prosecuting solicitor (the prosecution were refusing to accept a guilty plea to a lesser charge).

This freedom of access is important because there might be matters calling for communication or discussion of such a nature that counsel cannot in his client's interests mention them in open court. For example, counsel may, by way of mitigation, wish to tell the judge that the accused has not long to live, is suffering maybe from cancer of which he should remain ignorant. Again, counsel on both sides may wish to discuss with the judge whether it would be proper, in a particular case, for the prosecution to accept a plea to a lesser offence.

It is, of course, imperative that so far as possible justice must be administered in open court. Counsel should, therefore, ask to see the judge only when it is felt to be really necessary, and the judge must be careful only to treat such communications as private where, in fairness to the accused person, this is necessary.

Discussion between counsel and the judge should, where possible, take place in open court in the absence of the jury (*Llewellyn* (1978) 67 Cr.App.R. 148). This point was reiterated in *Coward* (1980) 70 Cr.App.R. 70, where the Court of Appeal stated that the practice of counsel going to see the judge behind the scenes is bad practice and must be confined to really exceptional cases as the public are entitled to be informed and to know the reasons behind the sentence. In *Winterflood* (1979) 68 Cr.App.R. 291, the Court of Appeal stated that such discussions were also undesirable during the trial unless absolutely necessary, and should take place in open court in the absence of the jury with a shorthand note or tape-recording being made.

(4) "The judge should, subject to . . . one exception . . . , never indicate the sentence which he is minded to impose. A statement that on a plea of guilty he would impose one sentence but that on a conviction following a plea of not guilty he would impose a severer sentence, should never be made. This could be taken to be undue pressure on the accused, thus depriving him of that complete freedom of choice which is essential . . .

The only exception to this rule is that it should be permissible for a judge to say, if it be the case, that whatever happens, whether the accused pleads guilty or not guilty, the sentence will or will not take a particular form, *e.g.* a probation order or a fine, or a custodial sentence.

Finally, where any such discussion on sentence has taken place between judge and counsel, counsel for the defence should disclose this to the accused and inform him of what took place."

Thus a judge may indicate the type of sentence he is minded to give but he should not disclose the length of a sentence of imprisonment or the amount of a fine (*Quartey* [1975] Crim.L.R. 592). In *Bird* (1977) 67 Cr.App.R. 203 the Court of Appeal allowed an appeal against sentence where the trial judge imposed immediate imprisonment following conviction by the jury having indicated earlier that a suspended sentence would be imposed if the defendant pleaded guilty (see also *Atkinson* [1978] 1 W.L.R. 425 and *Howell* [1978] Crim.L.R. 239). In *Cullen* [1985] Crim.L.R. 107 the trial judge asked to see counsel in his room before the trial commenced and indicated that in no circumstances would a custodial sentence be imposed. The Court of Appeal in quashing a suspended sentence which the judge subsequently imposed, reiterated that the *Turner* guidelines should be followed faithfully. The court emphasised that a third party should be present at such discussions to take a note to be kept with the papers. It also stated that the initiative for such discussions should come from counsel and not from the judge.

THE FACTUAL BASIS FOR DETERMINING SENTENCE

A problem which frequently confronts a sentencer is that of establishing the factual basis of the offence on which to assess the appropriate sentence. As the sentence imposed should not be more severe than the offence merits, it is important that the facts of the offence are accurately established before sentence is passed. Where there has been a guilty plea, the factual basis of the offence may not be apparent, or the defendant may have pleaded guilty on the basis of his own view of the offence which may not coincide with that of the prosecution. Even in cases where there has been a full trial and a conviction, the factual basis of the offence may not be clear from the evidence and the jury verdict. For example, a verdict of guilty of manslaughter on an indictment for murder, could be arrived at in one of several ways. If the judge is to pass the appropriate sentence, he must be able to arrive at some conclusion as to the facts of the offence (see, *e.g. Wheeler* [1967] 1 W.L.R. 1531; *Hudson* (1979) 1 Cr.App.R.(S.) 130; *Campbell* [1980] Crim.L.R. 248). Similarly, where an offender is convicted of a strict liability offence, it is important to know whether he acted intentionally, recklessly, negligently or without fault (see *Lester* (1976) 63 Cr.App.R. 144). A body of case law is gradually building up in relation to how this factual basis may be established and what evidence may be taken into consideration in establishing it.

(a) Sentencing for the correct offence
Where an accused is convicted of an offence the sentencer must pass sentence solely in relation to that offence, ignoring all evidence which would have supported other offences (whether or not they were charged on the indictment). Seven situations may arise:

(i) *More serious offence*
Even if the evidence tends to indicate that the offender is guilty of a more serious offence than the offence of which he stands convicted, the sentencer must ignore this. In *Foo* [1976] Crim.L.R. 456, the appellant pleaded guilty to attempting to possess heroin and possession of cannabis but the judge sentenced him as a trafficker on the basis of evidence tendered by the prosecution. The

Court of Appeal reduced the sentence as he had not been charged with possession with intent to supply.[2]

(ii) *More instances of same offence*

Where the sentencer is of opinion that the offender has committed more instances of the offence of which he stands convicted than are charged in the indictment, he cannot take this into account when passing sentence (see *Wishart* (1979) 1 Cr.App.R.(S.) 322). In *Morgan* [1981] Crim.L.R. 56, the appellant's sentence was reduced as the Court of Appeal was of opinion that the judge gave the impression that he had sentenced him on the basis of two acts of supplying cannabis when he had pleaded guilty on the basis of only one act of supply. By contrast, in *Russen* (1981) 3 Cr.App.R.(S.) 134, a differently constituted Court of Appeal took the view that the sentencer could sentence the appellant on the basis that he was a drugs dealer although only one count of possession with intent to supply was charged on the indictment. The trial judge formed this view on the basis of the appellant's statement to the police. The correct procedure however, would seem to be to charge an accused with these offences or for him to be asked whether he wishes further offences to be taken into consideration. These points were affirmed in *Connor* (1981) 3 Cr.App.R.(S.) 225, where the appellant pleaded guilty to two counts of handling, and was sentenced on the basis that he was a commercial and professional receiver on a large scale, following admissions in his statements to the police. The Court of Appeal took the view that the sentencer was influenced to a considerable extent by the statements made by the appellant, because the two incidents which gave rise to the counts for handling could hardly be said to constitute receiving on a large scale. The court reduced his sentence, reasserting that

> "However suspicious a court may be, it ought not, in the view of this court, ever be tempted to sentence defendants for crimes of which they have not been convicted."[3]

The relevance of an offender's previous statements suggesting other offences would appear to be limited to two matters: first, to show the nature or gravity of the current offence, *e.g.* that it was a planned offence calculated to make profit; or secondly, to rebut some suggestion put forward by the offender or his counsel in mitigation. Any suggestion by the sentencer that he is sentencing to take into account these other offences will lead to a reduction of the sentence on appeal.

---

[2] See also *Chadderton* (1980) 2 Cr.App.R.(S.) 272.
[3] See also *Ayensu and Ayensu* [1982] Crim.L.R. 764; *Johnson* [1984] Crim.L.R. 691.

(iii) *Plea of guilty to some counts on the indictment*

In *Clutterham* (1982) 4 Cr.App.R.(S.) 40, the appellant was indicted in count one for assault occasioning actual bodily harm and in count two with possession of an offensive weapon. It was alleged that he had assaulted the proprietor of a cafe with his fists and then lunged at him with a knife. He pleaded guilty to count one and not guilty to count two, the pleas being accepted. However, in sentencing him, the recorder referred to the alleged offence involving the knife. His sentence was reduced by the Court of Appeal which took the view that the recorder had failed to eliminate from his mind, when he should have done so, the allegations relating to the incident with the knife.[4]

In *Booker* (1982) 4 Cr.App.R.(S.) 53, the Court of Appeal reluctantly (as it was of opinion that the sentence imposed was appropriate to the offence) reduced the appellant's sentence as it appeared that the judge had sentenced him on the basis of attempted arson with intent to endanger life, the more serious count included on the indictment, when he had pleaded guilty only to the less serious count of attempted arson.

(iv) *Plea of guilty to lesser offence not charged*

Offenders regularly plead guilty to a lesser offence not charged on the indictment and are encouraged to do so because of the benefits they may reap from saving the court's time and sparing witnesses the ordeal of giving evidence. Having done this they must not be penalised by being sentenced for the offence to which they pleaded not guilty. In *Rogina* (1977) 64 Cr.App.R. 79,[5] the appellant pleaded not guilty to a single count charging him with incest with his 15 year old daughter, but pleaded guilty to the lesser offence of indecent assault, which was not contained in the indictment. In reducing his sentence the Court of Appeal emphasized that as the judge had accepted a plea of not guilty to incest he had to be careful

> "not to sentence or appear to sentence for incest when in fact the offence with which we are dealing is the lesser one of indecent assault."

(v) *Trial and acquittal on some charges*

Where the defendant is acquitted on some charges but convicted on others, the sentencer must ignore the allegations relating to the offences of which he has been acquitted when sentencing him for those offences of which he stands convicted. In *Worsfold,* un-

---

[4] See also *Denniston* (1977) 64 Cr.App.R. 119.
[5] See also *Fisher* (1981) 3 Cr.App.R.(S.) 313.

reported, April 29, 1975,[6] the appellant was convicted of attempted burglary having been acquitted of assaulting an officer with intent to resist lawful apprehension. His sentence was reduced on appeal as the trial judge appeared to sentence him as if he had been found guilty on all counts.

(vi) *Conviction by jury of lesser offence*

Where the jury acquit the defendant of a more serious offence but convict of a lesser one, the sentencer must give effect to their verdict when passing sentence even though it is difficult, in terms of logic, to explain the jury's verdict. In *Ajit Singh* [1981] Crim.L.R. 724, the appellant was convicted of unlawful wounding on an indictment which also charged wounding with intent to do grievous bodily harm. The appellant's defence had been self-defence but the jury clearly disbelieved this. Having rejected his defence it was difficult to explain why they did not convict him of the more serious offence. The trial judge sentenced him on the basis that it was a serious and pre-meditated attack. The Court of Appeal, while expressing their sympathy with the trial judge in his predicament of trying to give effect to the jury's somewhat illogical verdict, felt obliged to reduce the appellant's sentence. They stated that

> "[O]ne had to look at it from the point of view that one was punishing an unpremeditated unlawful wounding, somewhat artificial in effect in this case, but that was the approach that had to be made."

(vii) *Sample counts*

Often the prosecution charge an offence in one count on an indictment as a representative or sample count, contending that it is only one example of a course of conduct. The question to arise in such a situation is whether the sentencer may sentence the accused on the basis that he is guilty of these other offences. In *Huchison* [1972] 1 W.L.R. 398, a father pleaded guilty to a single count of incest with his daughter. Her deposition alleged more than one instance of intercourse, and the judge heard evidence from both father and daughter on this issue. He sentenced Huchison on the basis that there had been more than one act of intercourse. The Court of Appeal reduced the sentence as the approach adopted by the trial judge deprived the father of his right to trial by jury in respect of the other alleged acts of intercourse. The right course would have been for the judge either to allow the prosecution to prefer a voluntary bill of indictment charging the other instances or

---

[6] See Thomas, *Current Sentencing Practice*, L2.1(b).

to have given leave to amend the existing indictment (this approach was confirmed in *Jackson* [1972] Crim.L.R. 325). However, the Court of Appeal went on to state that the prosecution may put forward a count as a sample count and the judge may deal with the matter on the basis that the offence was repeated more than once or that there were similar incidents provided the defence are notified in advance.

This approach has been followed in several cases (see *Price* [1979] Crim.L.R. 468 and *Singh and Singh* [1981] Crim.L.R. 509). The problem is that a jury verdict does not make it clear whether they found the accused guilty of the offence charged or whether they also thought him guilty of these other offences. Further, it is not possible for the accused to defend himself fully against allegations not contained in the indictment, nor is it possible for him to obtain an acquittal on these unspecified charges. As Thomas so rightly states:

> "To allow a judge to impose sentence on the basis that the accused is guilty of offences which have not been charged against him, not proved beyond reasonable doubt (or indeed at all), and are not admitted, is to undermine the whole foundations of the criminal law and criminal procedure."[7]

This approach contradicts the trend of the cases in the preceding six sections, and in particular the principle stated by Lawton L.J. in *Wishart*, that an accused should be sentenced only for those offences which have been proven against him or which he has admitted. The Court of Appeal in *Wishart* expressed itself to be following the principle stated by Lord Diplock (and approved by the other Law Lords) in *Anderson* v. *D.P.P.* [1978] A.C. 964, that

> "where sample counts are used it is, in my view, essential that the ordinary procedure should be followed for taking other offences into consideration in determining sentence. The accused should be given an opportunity after verdict to consider the schedule of other offences which he is alleged by the prosecution to have committed and should be asked by the judge which of them he admits and whether he wishes them to be taken into consideration. Only if he agrees to that course may such an offence be included in calculating the amount of a criminal bankruptcy order."

In this case the appellant had been indicted on what were described as sample counts of obtaining by deception about £7,000;

---

[7] Commentary to *Singh and Singh*.

evidence of other obtainings involving over £22,000 was introduced at his trial, but these offences were never specifically charged or admitted by the appellant. The sentencer made a criminal bankruptcy order on the basis of all the alleged offences. Lawton L.J., in *Wishart*, took the view that this dictum applied to sentencing generally. It is submitted that this is the correct view as it makes for consistency in the approach to sentencing in the seven situations outlined.

(b) The factual basis of the offence

Having established the offence of which the offender stands convicted, the judge must next determine the factual basis of that offence for the purpose of sentencing. In other words, he must form a view as to the gravity of the offence of which the offender stands convicted, by drawing conclusions as to its nature and the circumstances surrounding its commission. In some cases the factual basis of the offence is implicit in the verdict of the jury. Where this is the case, the sentencer is bound to accept this and sentence accordingly. In *Hudson* (1979) 1 Cr.App.R.(S.) 130, the Court of Appeal made it clear that the sentence passed must be consistent with the verdict. Hudson had been charged with murder, but the jury convicted him of manslaughter. The prosecution case was that he knocked the deceased to the ground and then kicked him, whereas the defence claimed he had struck the deceased in self-defence and he had fallen on the ground striking his head on the pavement. The Court of Appeal concluded that:

> "the jury by finding the appellant guilty of manslaughter, but not guilty of murder, must be taken to have accepted the less violent of the two alternative versions of the struggle."[8]

In *Whittle* [1974] Crim.L.R. 487, the Court of Appeal stated that where the verdict of the jury is consistent with more than one version of the facts, the sentencer may reach his own conclusion on the evidence and he is not bound to conclude that the jury convicted on the version of the facts most favourable to the defendant; he may make his own findings of the facts consistent with the verdict of the jury.[9] Such a finding must be supported by evidence (*Browne* [1950] N.I. 20). The principle in *Whittle*, however, is qualified by the decision in *Stosiek* (1982) 4 Cr.App.R.(S.) 205 where the Court of Appeal stated that in cases where the conviction could be on one of several bases "the court has to be extremely astute to give the

---

[8] See also *Jama* (1968) 52 Cr.App.R. 498.
[9] See also *Solomon and Triumph* [1984] Crim.L.R. 433; *Wilcox* (1984) 6 Cr.App.R.(S).

benefit of any doubt to a defendant."[10] The principle, therefore, seems to be that the sentencer may make his own findings as to the factual basis of the offence consistent with the verdict of the jury, but the benefit of any doubt must be given to the defendant.

Where a defendant pleads guilty to a charge the court, while not being bound to accept his account of the circumstances of the offence (*Newall,* unreported, June 20, 1972, *Current Sentencing Practice,* L2.1(g)), should form the best picture it can of the circumstances of the offence unless it chooses to hear the conflicting evidence of each side on the point (*Depledge* (1979) 1 Cr.App.R.(S.) 183). Where there is a substantial conflict between the version put forward by the Crown and that put forward by the defence, it is incumbent upon the judge, unless he goes on to hear evidence, to take the more lenient view, accepting the defence version as far as possible (*Newton* (1982) 4 Cr.App.R.(S.) 388). If the defence give evidence which the prosecution is not in a position to contradict, the judge is not bound to accept the version put forward by the defence, provided he comes to a conclusion supported by the evidence in the case (*Kerr* (1980) Cr.App.R.(S.) 54). Where the prosecution put forward a version of the facts which is not contested by the defence, the judge, while not being bound by this view of the facts, should not sentence the defendant on the basis of a graver view of the facts than is put forward, unless there is a substantial basis in evidence for doing so (*Pearce* (1979) 1 Cr.App.R.(S.) 317).

In cases where there is more than one defendant and an assessment of the respective degrees of culpability of the defendants is necessary, the judge must do this in relation to each defendant only by reference to evidence which has been given against that defendant and which he has had an opportunity to challenge. The judge must disregard evidence given by a co-defendant in his own defence when passing sentence on another co-defendant, whether that evidence has been given in the same trial or in separate proceedings (see *Wishart,* above). The judge must also ignore evidence given against the co-defendant (*Michaels and Skoblo* [1981] Crim.L.R. 725), evidence given by the co-defendant in mitigation of his own sentence (*Lee* [1972] Crim.L.R. 319) and statements made by the co-defendant out of court alleging involvement by the other co-defendant in offences of which he has either pleaded "not guilty" or not been charged (*Craine* [1981] Crim.L.R. 727).

---

[10] The court discouraged judges from asking juries upon what basis they have reached their conclusions. The court also emphasised that the prosecution could largely obviate these sentencing dilemmas by more careful drafting of the indictment, including more counts relating to the same incident (see also *French* [1982] Crim.L.R. 380).

(c) Procedure

Where the defendant pleads guilty, prosecuting counsel will describe the circumstances of the offence on the basis of the evidence which would have been called had there been a trial. The prosecution may also call evidence after conviction (whether following a guilty plea or a jury verdict) to clarify issues of fact which have not been resolved by the plea or trial and which are relevant to sentence (*Robinson* (1969) 53 Cr.App.R. 314). If this evidence relates to matters not in issue in the trial, the prosecution must serve notice on the defendant of their intention to call it, sufficiently particularising the evidence so that he may challenge it. The witness giving this evidence must be able to speak from first hand knowledge. Allegations which are incapable of proof should not be made (*Van Pelz* [1943] K.B. 157; see also *Wilkins* (1977) 66 Cr.App.R. 49). In addition the defendant may either call evidence himself (*Evans*, unreported, December 19, 1974; *Cross*, unreported, July 1, 1975, both in *Current Sentencing Practice* L2.2(d)).

(i) *Conviction following a jury verdict*

Where a conviction results from a jury trial and the basis of the verdict is unclear, the question arises whether the judge may question the jury to clarify the basis upon which they arrived at their verdict. This practice has been adopted in the case of murder trials where a verdict of guilty of manslaughter has been returned and the factual basis for this verdict is not immediately apparent (see *Doherty* (1887) 16 Cox C.C. 306). The practice has, however, been criticised on the ground that the jury may not have been unanimous and that the foreman may misstate the reason for their verdict (*Larkin* [1943] K.B. 174). The questions put to the jury in *Larkin* were, however, particularly badly phrased and undoubtedly would have caused confusion. In *Matheson* [1958] 1 W.L.R. 474, Lord Goddard C.J. stated *per curiam* that

> "if, on an indictment for murder, the defence ask for a verdict of manslaughter on the ground of diminished responsibility and also on some other ground such as provocation, and the jury return a verdict of manslaughter, the judge may, and generally should, then ask whether their verdict is based on diminished responsibility or on the other ground or on both."

More recently, in *Frankum* [1984] Crim.L.R. 434, the appellant raised the defence of diminished responsibility on an indictment for murder. He alleged that the abnormality of mind from which he suffered was temporary, arising as a side effect of taking a drug prescribed for the treatment of a peptic ulcer. The Crown disputed this view contending that the abnormality of mind was due to inherent causes which made him a danger to the public. The jury were directed that if they found the appellant guilty of manslaughter, they would be asked to indicate whether the abnormality arose as a result of inherent causes or was induced by injury from the toxic effect of the drug, or by both. The jury returned a verdict of guilty of manslaughter by reason of diminished responsibility, indicating that the abnormality arose from inherent causes. The appellant was sentenced to life imprisonment. This case provides a good example of the situation in which it is appropriate to ask a jury to indicate the basis of their verdict. If that verdict arose from a view that the abnormality was due to the effect of the drug a sentence of imprisonment would probably not have been appropriate. The case also provides a good illustration of the procedure to be adopted in that the jury were asked to consider the basis for a verdict of manslaughter (should they arrive at such a conclusion) when they retired. Should the jury be unable to agree on the basis of their verdict then on the basis of the principles in the previous section, it would seem that the defendant should be given the benefit of any doubt (see also *McGrath and Casey* (1983) 5 Cr.App.R.(S.) 460).

Questions of a jury relating to the factual basis of their verdict should be put only in exceptional cases; the usual and proper practice is to refrain from inviting juries to explain their verdicts (*Stosiek*). Thus, generally, the judge must determine the factual basis of the verdict on the basis of the evidence he has heard in accordance with the principles stated above, although a straightforward question as to the basis for a verdict of manslaughter on a murder indictment is permissible.

(ii) *Conviction following guilty plea*

Where the defendant pleads guilty and a dispute arises as to the factual basis of the offence, the sentencer must clarify the issue and establish a version of facts upon which basis sentence may be assessed (*Campbell* [1980] Crim.L.R. 248). In some cases it may be possible to resolve the issue by amending the charges or adding additional charges so that the disputed circumstances become an ingredient of one of the offences charged which will lead to a conclusion of the issue by plea or verdict (see *Newton* (1982) 4 Cr.App.R.(S.) 388). Where this is not feasible there are two ways in which the factual basis may be established on a plea of guilty (see *Milligan* (1982) 4 Cr.App.R.(S.) 2 and *Newton*). First, the judge may determine the circumstances of the offence on the basis of the submissions of counsel. However, if he does this he is required to come down on the side of the defendant where there is a conflict between the prosecution and defence (*Newton*). If the judge is inclined to adopt a view of the facts adverse to the accused, which has not been articulated by the prosecution when stating their version of the factual basis of the offence, he should indicate to counsel what his provisional view is, and allow the defendant to call evidence on this issue (*Lester* (1976) 63 Cr.App.R. 144). Where there is a conflict the judge must indicate the basis upon which he has assessed the sentence. If he fails to do so, the Court of Appeal, on an appeal, will consider the appropriateness of the sentence passed in light of the version of facts put forward by the defence (*Brown* (1981) 3 Cr.App.R.(S.) 250).

Secondly, the judge may hear evidence on the factual basis of the offence from both sides and come to his own conclusions (*Newton*; see also *Gravell* [1978] Crim.L.R. 438; *Gortat and Pirog* [1973] Crim.L.R. 648; *Ball* [1983] Crim.L.R. 198; *Parker* [1984] Crim.L.R. 763. In such a hearing counsel on both sides will call witnesses and examine them in the normal way (see *McGrath and Casey* (1983) 5 Cr.App.R.(S.) 460; but *cf. Connors* [1984] Crim.L.R. 507). Where the judge does hear evidence he should decide the issue on the basis of the normal burden of proof (*Gortat and Pirog* and *Brassell*, unreported, February 11, 1977, *Current Sentencing Practice* L2.2(f)). In addition, he should direct himself with regard to the question of corroboration in the same way in which he would direct a jury (*Gortat and Pirog*; *Long* [1980] 2 Cr.App.R.(S.) 8). Where this procedure for determining the factual basis of the offence is followed, the determination of the trial judge is open to review on an appeal against sentence. However, provided the hearing has been properly conducted, and the trial judge has not misdirected himself, the Court of Appeal will not readily disturb his findings as he has had the advantage of seeing and assessing the witnesses (*Parker* (1984) 6 Cr.App.R.(S.) 444). The court will only interfere in exceptional circumstances such as where it is satisfied that no reasonable jury could have reached the conclusion which the judge reached (*Ahmed* [1985] Crim.L.R. 250).

In *Taggart* (1979) 1 Cr.App.R.(S.) 144, the Court of Appeal stated that where a plea of guilty is tendered on a factual basis substantially different from that contained in the evidence to be tendered by the prosecution, the judge may direct that the case be tried on a plea of not guilty, so that the evidence may be called and witnesses cross examined (see also *Michaels and Skoblo*, above). In *Milligan*, above, the Court of Appeal disapproved of *Taggart*, stating that the correct approach on a plea of guilty where there is a dispute is for the judge to hear the witnesses and draw his own conclusions. This approach is much preferable, as trying the case before the jury will not necessarily lead to a resolution of the dispute as the basis of the jury's verdict may not be clear.

Where the conflict between the two versions of facts put forward by the prosecution and the defence is such that whichever version is accepted will not materially affect the sentence the judge proposes to pass, the judge should accept the defendant's version and pass sentence on that basis, rather than conduct a hearing which will have no effect on the result (*Hall* [1985] Crim.L.R. 54).

Where the defendant changes his plea to guilty after the trial has begun, and witnesses for the prosecution have given evidence, but the plea is made on the basis of facts differing from the version put forward by the prosecution, the judge should not impose sentence without allowing the accused to give his account of the offence (*Mottram* (1981) 3 Cr.App.R.(S.) 123).

THE PREVIOUS CHARACTER AND CONVICTIONS OF THE DEFENDANT

Before a court sentences an offender it may inquire into any matter which might assist it in determining the sentence to be passed. This has developed into a practice whereby an officer dealing with the case will be called to give evidence of the offender's antecedents. A proof of the antecedents evidence should be drawn up by a police officer (*Practice Direction* [1966] 1 W.L.R. 1184). Prosecuting counsel should receive a copy of this proof either with his brief or at the outset of the case. A copy of this proof must also be given to counsel for the defendant when the jury retire to consider their verdict or, in the case of a plea of guilty, as soon as the plea is entered.[11] The antecedents statement should contain particulars of the prisoner's age, education and employment, the date of arrest, whether the prisoner had been on bail, and a statement summarising any previous convictions and any previous findings of guilt[12] (including findings of guilt when the offender was under 14 which, in proceedings against a person who has attained the age of 21, are, under C.Y.P.A. 1963, s. 16(2) disregarded for the purposes of evidence relating to previous convictions).[13] The antecedents

---

[11] Details of previous convictions must always be supplied by the police to the defending solicitor on request as, in order that the defence may be properly conducted, the prisoner's advisers must know whether they can safely put his character in issue (*Practice Direction* [1966] 1 W.L.R. 1184, para. 1).

[12] Convictions which are "spent" under the Rehabilitation of Offenders Act 1974 must be included on the offender's record, but in the *Practice Direction* June 30, 1975, Lord Widgery C.J. recommended that spent convictions should be marked as such and no reference to them should be made in open court without the authority of the judge and such authority should only be given where the interests of justice so require. The judge himself should make no reference to a spent conviction unless it is necessary for the purpose of explaining the sentence he has passed.

[13] See *Practice Direction* [1966] 1 W.L.R. 1184, para. 3.

statement should also set out the date (if known) of the last discharge from prison or other place of custody and it may also contain a short and concise statement as to the defendant's domestic circumstances.[14] The officer, in giving evidence, will be taken through his antecedents statement, often by means of leading questions, as the normal rules of evidence are relaxed at this stage.

In *Marquis* (1951) 35 Cr.App.R. 33, Lord Goddard C.J., stated that "after conviction, any information which can be put before the court can be put before it in any manner which the court will accept." In *Marquis* this involved accepting hearsay evidence as to the offender's character where this was favourable to him. However, where the offender challenges evidence given at this stage the judge should either direct that proper proof of it be given or he should, failing that, ignore it. This principle derives from *Campbell* (1911) 6 Cr.App.R. 131, where Lord Alverstone L.C.J. stated

> "If the prisoner challenges any statement, it is the duty of the Judge to inquire into it; if necessary he should adjourn the matter, and if it is of sufficient importance he may require legal proof of it. Or he may ignore it, and if he does so he should state that he is not taking it into consideration."

Counsel for the prosecution should ensure that a police officer giving antecedents evidence does not make allegations, prejudicial to the offender, which are incapable of proof, and which he has reason to think will be denied by the offender (*Van Pelz* [1943] K.B. 157). The officer should confine his evidence to matters that are within his own knowledge (*Crabtree* (1952) 36 Cr.App.R. 161). If allegations are to be made in the antecedents which the defendant is likely to dispute, notice should be given to the defence of that evidence so that they have the opportunity to consider it and prepare to challenge it if they wish (*Robinson* (1969) 53 Cr.App.R. 314).[15] In addition police officers giving antecedents should refrain from making general observations of a derogatory nature about a defendant (*Bibby* [1972] Crim.L.R. 513). The practice is for prosecuting counsel to give defending counsel the opportunity of making representations about any matter in the antecedents report which is disputed. If there are matters in dispute prosecuting counsel must decide whether to call admissible evidence to prove the disputed facts, or to omit them from evidence (see *Sargeant* (1975) 60 Cr.App.R. 74).[16]

The antecedents officer should, in addition to the above, be

---

[14] Attached to the antecedents is a form giving details of the defendant's criminal record but excluding findings of guilt covered by C.Y.P.A. 1963, s. 16(2).

[15] See also *Wilkins* (1978) 66 Cr.App.R. 49.

[16] See also *Coughlan and Young* (1976) 63 Cr.App.R. 74.

prepared to give relevant information (*i.e.* sentences passed, ages, previous convictions and such matter as work record) about any accomplices dealt with by another court or on an earlier date. Similarly, if the offender is subject to a conditional discharge, probation order, suspended sentence, community service order or parole licence which is likely to be dealt with when sentence is passed, the officer should have such information ready to hand and be prepared to prove the previous conviction and sentence should the offender deny it.

REMANDS AND REPORTS

Before passing sentence on an offender a court may wish to, or may be obliged to, consider reports on the mental, physical, social and personal condition of the offender in order to assist it in selecting the appropriate sentence. If these reports are not available the court may adjourn the case to enable the inquiries to be made by a probation officer, doctor or psychiatrist. In some parts of the country it is the practice for probation officers not to prepare reports in advance of arraignment where it is expected that the accused will plead not guilty.

The powers of magistrates' courts to adjourn for reports to be made on an offender are contained in sections 10 and 30 of the Magistrates' Courts Act 1980. Section 10(3) provides that a magistrates' court may adjourn a case after convicting the accused for the purpose of enabling inquiries to be made or of determining the most suitable method of dealing with the case. If remanded on bail the adjournment may not be for more than four weeks at a time; if the accused is remanded in custody the adjournment may not be for more than three weeks at a time.

Where a magistrates' court is trying an offence punishable on summary conviction with imprisonment, and it is satisfied that the accused committed the actus reus of the offence but is of opinion that an inquiry ought to be made into his physical or mental condition before it sentences him, the court may adjourn the case and remand him to enable the medical examination and report to be made (M.C.A., s. 30(1)). The same time limits apply as for section 10(3). Under section 3(6)(*d*) of the Bail Act 1976 it shall be a condition of his bail where he is so remanded, that the accused

    (a)   undergo medical examination by a duly qualified medical practitioner or, where the inquiry is into his mental condition and the court so directs, two such practitioners; and

    (b)   for that purpose attend such an institution or place, or on such practitioner, as the court directs and, where the inquiry is into his mental condition, comply with any other

directions which may be given to him for that purpose by any person specified by the court or by a person of any class so specified.
(M.C.A., s. 30(2).)[17]

(a) Medical reports

A magistrates' court may adjourn a case for the preparation of medical reports (see above). Likewise the Crown Court, following a conviction on indictment or prior to sentencing on a committal for sentence from the magistrates' court, may adjourn for medical reports to be made, in which case the offender will be remanded in custody or on bail. A third option has been created by section 35 of the Mental Health Act 1983. This empowers the Crown Court and magistrates' courts to remand an accused or an offender to a hospital specified by the court for a report on his mental condition.

A court must obtain medical reports before it can make an order for detention in a mental hospital or a guardianship order under section 37 of the Mental Health Act 1983 or before it can insert a requirement in a probation order that the offender undergo treatment for a mental condition under section 3 of the Powers of Criminal Courts Act. Where such a report is tendered in evidence the following conditions must be observed:

  (a) if the accused is represented by counsel or a solicitor, a copy of the report must be given to his counsel or solicitor;
  (b) if the accused is unrepresented, the substance of the report must be disclosed to him or, where he is a child or young person, to his parent or guardian if present in court; and
  (c) the accused may require that the practitioner by whom the report is signed be called to give oral evidence, and evidence to rebut the evidence contained in the report may be called by or on behalf of the accused.

(M.H.A., s. 54(3).)

---

[17] Magistrates are not required to record a conviction under s. 30 before adjourning a case for medical reports. As a result s. 30 may be combined with M.H.A. 1983, s. 37(3) to deal with the problem of the person who, if he was tried on indictment, would be found unfit to plead. Under s. 37(3) if the magistrates are satisfied that the accused committed the *actus reus* of an imprisonable offence, and there are medical reports showing him to be suffering from mental illness or severe mental impairment, they may order him to be detained in a mental hospital without recording a conviction against him. The procedure to be followed could be to order a not guilty plea to be entered on behalf of an accused who appears to have mental problems; hear sufficient evidence to be satisfied he committed the *actus reus* of the offence; and then adjourn under M.C.A., s. 30 for medical reports; if these show mental illness or severe mental impairment, a hospital order may then be made without any conviction being recorded.

(b) Social inquiry reports

A court is generally under an obligation to obtain a social inquiry report on an offender before it may pass a sentence of youth custody or make a detention centre order in respect of him (C.J.A. 1982, s. 2(2)), or before it may pass a sentence of imprisonment on a person who has not previously been sentenced to prison (P.C.C.A., s. 20A(1) as inserted by C.J.A. 1982, s. 62). The obligation to obtain a social inquiry report, however, does not apply if, in the circumstances of the case, the court is of opinion that it is unnecessary to obtain one (C.J.A., s. 2(3) and P.C.C.A., s. 20A(2)). The obligation will not apply presumably where sufficient information about the offender and his circumstances, etc., has come out during the course of the trial to enable the judge to make an educated assessment of the sentence appropriate to the offender. The fact that there would be difficulties in obtaining a report or that a custodial sentence seems virtually inevitable because of the seriousness of the offence, would not appear to be sufficient reasons for acting without a report (see *Massheder* [1984] Crim.L.R. 185 and Commentary thereon). Where a magistrates' court is of opinion that it is unnecessary to obtain a social inquiry report it must state its reasons in open court (C.J.A. 1982, s. 2(6) and P.C.C.A., s. 20A(3)). For the purposes of section 2 of the Criminal Justice Act 1982 a social inquiry report means a report about a person and his circumstances made by a probation officer or by a social worker of a local authority social services department (s. 2(10)), and for the purposes of section 20A of the Powers of Criminal Courts Act it means a report made by a probation officer (P.C.C.A., s. 20A(7)). Failure to comply with the requirement to obtain a report will not invalidate the sentence (C.J.A. 1982, s. 2(8) and P.C.C.A., s. 20A(5)), but any other court on appeal from the court which sentenced the offender must obtain a social inquiry report if none was obtained in the court below, unless it is of opinion that in the circumstances of the case it is unnecessary to do so (*ibid.*).

A community service order in respect of an offender, cannot be made by a court unless it has considered a report by a probation officer or by a social worker of a local authority social services department about the offender and his circumstances (P.C.C.A., s. 14(2)). By contrast there is no rule that a report must be considered before an offender is put on probation although a court may consider it expedient to do so before making such an order.

Where a social inquiry report is received, a copy of it must be given by the court to the offender or his counsel or solicitor (P.C.C.A., s. 46(1)). If the offender is under 17 years of age and is not represented by counsel or a solicitor, a copy of the report must be given to his parent or guardian if present in court (P.C.C.A., s. 46(2)).

This provision means that the offender is made aware of the contents of any report and therefore is able to challenge any facts stated therein. In cases of dispute the probation officer may be called and examined in relation to the contents of the report (*Kirkham* [1968] Crim.L.R. 210). The probation report should not be read in open court though it may be referred to (*Smith* [1968] Crim.L.R. 33). The report must be read before defence counsel speaks in mitigation (*Kirkham*) so that he may refer to, or make submissions in relation to, any points made in the report. If counsel is not supplied with a copy of the report he should apply to the court for a copy and not to the probation officer (*Adams* [1970] Crim.L.R. 693).

A social inquiry report is designed to assist the court in deciding upon the most appropriate method of dealing with the offender. Guidance on the preparation of reports may be found in Home Office Circulars 17/83 (dealing with the contents of reports), 18/83 (dealing with the inclusion of recommendations relevant to sentencing), and 118/77 (dealing with reports in cases involving Not Guilty pleas). Home Office Circular 17/83 suggested that the following information should be included in reports:

"i   an assessment of the offender's personality, character and family and social background which is relevant to the court's assessment of his culpability;

ii   information about the offender and his surroundings which is relevant to the court's consideration of how his criminal career might be checked (including his record while at any educational training or residential establishments where he has recently been, other than institutions controlled by the Prison Department of the Home Office);

iii   his employment or prospects of obtaining employment, and his attitudes and habits as known to his most recent employer, if any;

iv   information about the circumstances of the offence in question, and the offender's attitude towards it;

v   an opinion of the likely effect on the offender's criminal career of probation or some specified sentence."

In addition a report may contain a recommendation from the probation officer as to the form of sentence he considers most suitable to the offender. This will be based on the probation officer's opinion of the offender's likely reaction to a particular sentence and whether such sentence is likely to help prevent the offender from re-offending. The court, however, is not bound to accept the probation officer's recommendation as it takes into account broader issues, such as the public interest or the need to deter others from offending, when deciding on the appropriate sentence. The perspective of the probation officer and the sentencer, accordingly, differ. The probation officer's perspective is directed towards assessing the likely response of the offender to particular measures, whereas the sentencer will take into account the public interest which may demand a severe sentence to express society's disapproval of the conduct engaged in by the offender and to deter others from engaging in such behaviour. The fact that the court's disposition of an offender differs from the disposition recommended by the probation officer does not mean that either the probation officer was wrong or the court is wrong; the difference in perspective means that each must pay regard to differing, and sometimes conflicting, considerations. However, in several recent cases the Court of Appeal has criticised probation officers for making unrealistic recommendations without recognising this difference in perspective (see *Smith and Woollard* [1978] 67 Cr.App.R. 211; *James* [1982] Crim.L.R. 59). Such criticisms are unfounded; as Thomas states:

> "Obviously the probation officer has a duty to the court not to make a suggestion which is unrealistic in the sense that it rests on a naive assessment of the offender's character or intentions; but it is not the probation officer's duty to balance the competing claims of the offender to a sentence which will help him to conform in the future, and the public to a sentence which by deterrence or denunciation will tend to minimise the incidence of the offence in the future. The task of balancing these competing claims is the primary responsibility of the court, and a probation officer who arrogates to himself the decision whether a probation order (or whatever other measure he may consider to be needed in the offender's own interest) is a realistic possibility in the light of the gravity of the offences is usurping the decision of the judge and, by withholding information which is necessary to the judge to make his decision, preventing him from discharging his judicial responsibility."[18]

Where a court is considering whether to impose a specific form of non-custodial sentence but there is no suitable social inquiry report available, it may adjourn the case so that the suitability of the offender for such a measure may be assessed. Where the report recommends that the offender is suitable for such a non-custodial

---

[18] Commentary to *James* [1982] Crim.L.R. 60.

measure, the court should not impose a custodial sentence but should make such an order (see *Gillam* [1981] Crim.L.R. 55; *Moss* [1983] Crim.L.R. 751).[19] The decision to adjourn to obtain such a report specifically in relation to the offender's suitability for a non-custodial sentence, such as probation or a community service order, should not be made unless the sentencer is satisfied that he will be able to make such an order if the report is favourable to the offender, bearing in mind the nature of the offence and any other relevant circumstances. Where the sentencer simply adjourns to obtain a report to enable him to gain a fuller picture of the offender and his circumstances, without indicating whether he has any particular form of sentence in mind, he will not be taken to have given any express or implied indication of his intentions and will not be bound as in *Gillam* (see *Moss*). However, it may be wise, where the sentencer is adjourning for a report because he is considering a custodial sentence, for him to indicate this to avoid the risk of any misunderstanding.

(c) Juvenile court

Section 9(1) of the Children and Young Persons Act 1969 places a duty on local authorities, unless they consider it unnecessary, to make investigations and provide courts before whom care or criminal proceedings are heard "with such information relating to the home surroundings, school record, health and character of the person in respect of whom the proceedings are brought as appear to the authority likely to assist the court." The authority is also under a duty to make investigations and provide further information if requested to do so by the court (s. 9(2)).

Where a child is found guilty of an offence in a juvenile court the court is under an obligation to

"take into consideration such information as to the general conduct, home surroundings, school record and medical history of the child or young person as may be necessary to enable it to deal with the case in his best interests and, in particular, shall take into consideration such information ... which is provided in pursuance of s. 9 of the Act of 1969."

(Magistrates' Courts (Children and Young Persons) Rules 1970, r. 10(1)(*b*), S.I. 1970 No. 1792.)

Generally a court will be presented with two reports: a social inquiry report prepared by a social worker or probation officer and

---

[19] See also *Kinsman and Harthill* [1981] Crim.L.R. 264; *Ward* [1982] Crim.L.R. 459.

a report from the defendant's school.[20] If the necessary information is not available the court may remand the child or young person for such inquiry as may be necessary (r. 10(1)(c)). A report may be received and considered by the court without being read aloud (r. 10(1)(d)), and if the court considers it necessary in the interests of the child or young person, it may require him or his parent or guardian, if present, to withdraw from the court (r. 10(1)(e)). The rules go on to provide

> "Where, in pursuance of paragraph (1)(d), a report has been considered without being read aloud or where the child or young person, his parent or guardian has been required to withdraw from the court in pursuance of (1)(e), then—
>
> (a) the child or young person shall be told the substance of any part of the information given to the court bearing on his character or conduct which the court considers to be material to the manner in which the case should be dealt with unless it appears to it impracticable so to do having regard to his age and understanding, and
>
> (b) the parent or guardian of the child or young person, if present, shall be told the substance of any part of such information which the court considers to be material as aforesaid and which has references to his character or conduct or to the character, conduct, home surroundings or health of the child or young person;
>
> and, if such a person, having been told the substance of any part of such information desires to produce further evidence with reference thereto, the court, if it thinks the further evidence would be material, shall adjourn the proceedings for the production thereof and shall, if necessary in the case of a report, require the attendance at the adjourned hearing of the person who made the report."

While this is intended to enable the child, young person, parent or guardian to challenge any facts contained in the report this may not be possible because of the information which the court chooses to disclose to them and the way in which it is disclosed. The disclosure of information also hinges upon what the court considers material; the court can, therefore, avoid the obligation to disclose the substance of a report simply by declaring it was not a material consideration in arriving at its ultimate decision.[21]

---

[20] For a critical examination of the use of such reports and the interpretation of the rules, see Ball, "School Reports in the Juvenile Court", (1983) 147 J.P. 808.

[21] See Ball, *loc. cit.* p. 809.

TAKING OFFENCES INTO CONSIDERATION

The practice of taking offences into consideration is a convention without statutory basis although it has received statutory recognition in relation to compensation, restitution and criminal bankruptcy orders.[22] Under this practice the accused may ask the judge when he is passing sentence on him for the offence or offences of which he stands convicted, to take into consideration other offences committed by him for which he has not been tried or convicted. A court cannot take into consideration offences which it would, itself, have no jurisdiction to try nor should it take into consideration offences where the prosecution objects (presumably because it intends to prosecute the offender separately for these offences). In exercising its discretion the court will not take into consideration offences which are dissimilar from the offence of which the defendant has been convicted unless it considers it proper to do so in all the circumstances (*Syres* (1909) 1 Cr.App.R. 172).[23] Where the offences which the offender wishes to have taken into consideration are offences under the Road Traffic Acts which may involve disqualification from driving or endorsement of a driving licence, these are offences which should not be taken into consideration when sentence is being passed for a different class of offence (*Collins* [1947] K.B. 560; *Simons* [1953] 1 W.L.R. 1014). However, the court may take into consideration an offence of the same class where the offender is convicted of an offence for which he is liable to be disqualified (*Jones* [1970] 1 W.L.R. 1494). The reason for this limitation is that the sentencing powers of the court are limited to those it possesses in respect of the offence(s) of which the offender stands convicted.

In sentencing the offender "the court can...give a longer sentence than it would if it were dealing with him only on the charge mentioned in the indictment" (*Batchelor*); but a sentence beyond the maximum allowed by law for the offence of which he stands convicted cannot be imposed simply because other offences have been taken into consideration (*Tremayne* (1932) 23 Cr.App.R. 191; *Hobson* (1944) 29 Cr.App.R. 30).

Although an offence may have been taken into consideration, this does not count as a conviction in respect of that offence. Accordingly, the offender cannot plead *autrefois convict* if he is subsequently prosecuted for that offence (*Nicholson* [1947] 2 All

---

[22] See P.C.C.A., ss. 35 and 39 and C.J.A. 1982, s. 6 and C.J.A. 1972, s. 6. In Northern Ireland the practice has a statutory basis under s. 4 of the Criminal Justice Act (N.I.) 1953.

[23] See also *McClean* [1911] 1 K.B. 332; *Davies* (1912) 7 Cr.App.R. 254; *Smith* (1921) 15 Cr.App.R. 172; *Batchelor* (1952) 36 Cr.App.R. 64.

E.R. 535). However, the Court of Appeal went on to state where an offence had been taken into consideration the offender should not be tried again for it as a person should not be punished twice for the same offence. In *Metcalfe* [1968] Crim.L.R. 626, it was held that where a person has taken into consideration an offence committed during the operational period of a suspended sentence, this did not count as a conviction which would give the court power to activate the suspended sentence.[24] A breach of a probation order, however, should not be taken into consideration but should be dealt with separately and a separate sentence imposed in respect of it (*Webb* [1953] 2 Q.B. 390).

Where offences are to be taken into consideration a list is drawn up by the police. The defendant's solicitor should go through the list with him to ensure that he admits each of the offences listed; any which he denies should be deleted. The defendant then signs each sheet. After a guilty plea or a conviction the defendant will be asked if he has received a copy of the list and whether he admits the offences specified therein and wishes them to be taken into consideration (*Anderson* v. *D.P.P.* [1978] A.C. 964). The consent of the offender personally, and not by his counsel, should be obtained in open court (*Davis* [1943] K.B. 274). Where a person has been committed for sentence to the Crown Court after admitting other offences before the magistrates' court and asking for them to be taken into consideration, it is imperative that the Crown Court inquires before sentencing him whether he still wishes to have the offences taken into consideration; if he does not then the offences should be ignored (*Davies* (1981) 72 Cr.App.R. 262).

When sentencing one co-defendant a judge cannot take into consideration offences which his co-defendant admitted and asked to be taken into consideration alleging that these offences were also committed by the other co-defendant. A judge must sentence a co-defendant only on the basis of those offences of which he has been convicted and which he himself admits and asks to be taken into consideration (*Craine* [1981] Crim.L.R. 727).

A compensation order or restitution order may be made in respect of an offence taken into consideration (P.C.C.A., s. 35(1); T.A., s. 28(1)). In the case of criminal bankruptcy orders the amount of loss or damage suffered by the victim of an offence which is taken into consideration may be added to that deriving from the offence of which the defendant is convicted and if the aggregate exceeds £15,000 a criminal bankruptcy order may be made in respect of those offences (P.C.C.A., s. 39).

---

[24] The offence of which Metcalfe was convicted had been committed prior to the offence for which he had received a suspended sentence.

PLEA IN MITIGATION

A defendant, or his advocate if he is represented, must be allowed the opportunity to plead in mitigation before the court passed sentence. The Court of Appeal stated in *Jones* [1980] Crim.L.R. 58, that even where the offender has put forward a lying defence attacking the character of police officers, counsel still has a duty to mitigate and the judge should permit him the opportunity to do so, listening patiently and not interrupting. There are several factors to which counsel making a plea in mitigation may wish to direct the court's attention:

(1) Those circumstances of the offence of a mitigating nature such as the impulsive nature of the offence, the presence of provocation, the fact that the defendant was led into trouble by older and more experienced offenders, the fact that he was entrapped, or the limited role he played in the commission of the offence.

(2) Those circumstances subsequent to the offence which indicate contrition such as the fact that the defendant made a full and frank confession to the police, his co-operation with the police, the fact that he has made restitution to the victim. If the police officer in charge of the case can be called to give evidence on these points this will strengthen the effect of the plea.

(3) Those factors in his personal life, character and conduct which indicate an ability to reform such as the fact that this is his first offence or that he has kept out of trouble for a substantial period since his last conviction, that he has been in regular employment or has obtained employment since committing the offence, that he has a stable home and family background. If imprisonment might have an adverse effect on his health or family this should also be mentioned. If possible character witnesses should be called to add substance to these factors.

In some cases it may be appropriate to call the offender himself to give evidence if his personality and desire for reform are likely to impress the court. If counsel desires to do so the judge should not discourage him from this course (*Cross* [1975] Crim.L.R. 591).

Paragraph 157 of the *Code of Conduct for the Bar of England and Wales* states

"Defence Counsel should not, in a plea in mitigation, make any allegation which is merely scandalous or calculated to vilify or insult any person. In any case, the naming in open court of third parties, whose character would thereby be impugned, should if possible be avoided. Where necessary, names, addresses or other such details should be written down and handed in to the Court."

SENTENCING CO-DEFENDANTS

When several defendants are jointly indicted and one or more plead guilty while the others plead not guilty, the correct procedure is to postpone sentencing those who have pleaded guilty until the others have been tried when all the defendants can be sentenced together (*Payne* [1950] W.N. 35).[25] The judge in his discretion, however, may deal with a defendant at the time he pleads guilty if he is of opinion that he is in possession of the material facts and is able to assess the relative degree of guilt between this defendant and the others. This course should be followed very rarely (*Weekes* (1982) 74 Cr.App.R. 161). The danger is that further facts may come out during the trial which reveal that the defendant who pleaded guilty was more culpable than the judge believed. In such a case the judge must sentence the defendants who pleaded not guilty in accordance with their own culpability even though this may lead to the anomalous situation that they receive more severe sentences than the more culpable defendant who pleaded guilty and received a lenient sentence on the basis of the facts as the judge then believed them to be (see *Hair and Singh* [1978] Crim.L.R. 698).

Where a defendant pleads guilty and the prosecution intend to call him to give evidence against a co-defendant, it was the custom to sentence him before he gave evidence to avoid the suggestion that he was under any inducement to give evidence which would result in him receiving a lighter sentence than might otherwise have been the case. In *Weekes* the Court of Appeal declared that this was not a sufficient reason for deviating from the normal practice. The court stated:

"[T]his Court has said on numerous occasions that it should be left to the judge who may sentence those who have pleaded not guilty, to sentence all. There may be exceptions but generally it is clearly right, it is clearly fairer, and it is better for both the public and all the defendants concerned, that all are sentenced at the same time by the same Court whenever that is possible. . . ."

The fact that a defendant who has been sentenced before giving evidence against a co-accused changes the account he originally put forward does not justify a judge bringing him back to increase his

[25] See also *Weekes* (1980) 2 Cr.App.R.(S.) 377; *Weekes* (1982) 74 Cr.App.R. 161.

sentence (*Stone* [1970] 1 W.L.R. 1112). If a defendant is to give evidence for a co-defendant he ordinarily should not be sentenced until the end of the case (*Coffey* [1977] Crim.L.R. 45).

Where sentence is postponed the judge must sentence the defendant who pleaded guilty only on the basis of the admissible evidence against him and not on evidence which may have come out in the course of the trial of the other defendants.[26] If the judge, after the trial of the other defendants is disinclined to accept the version of the facts on the basis on which the defendant pleaded guilty, a post-conviction hearing should be held so that the defendant can give evidence or call witnesses and cross-examine any witnesses whom the judge may call (see *Gravell* [1978] Crim.L.R. 438 and Commentary to *Hair and Singh* [1978] Crim.L.R. 698).

Where there is a risk of disorder in the dock, judges have, on occasions sentenced separately co-defendants who have been tried together. If a judge contemplates that this may be necessary he should nonetheless allow counsel to mitigate and cross-examine on the antecedents in the presence of all the defendants, unless very exceptionally it is anticipated that serious violence will occur in the dock if the defendants (or any combination of them) are there together (see *Hall, Vary and Gregory*, unreported, January 1, 1982, noted in *Archbold*, §4–484).

LEGAL REPRESENTATION AND LEGAL AID

The following sentences, orders or powers may not be passed or made or exercised by a court on or in respect of an offender who is not legally represented before that court:

(a) a sentence of imprisonment on a person who has not previously been sentenced to that punishment by a court in any part of the United Kingdom (P.C.C.A., s. 21(1))[27];

(b) a detention centre order (C.J.A. 1982, s. 3(1)(*a*));

(c) a youth custody sentence (C.J.A. 1982, s. 3(1)(*b*));

(d) a sentence of custody for life under section 8(2) of the Criminal Justice Act 1982 (C.J.A. 1982, s. 3(1)(*c*));

(e) an order for detention under section 53(2) of the Children and Young Persons Act 1933 (C.J.A. 1982, s. 3(1)(*d*));

(f) a care order (C.Y.P.A. 1969, s. 7(7A) as inserted by C.J.A. 1982, s. 24);

---

[26] See *Wishart*; *Michaels and Skoblo*; *Lee*; *Craine*, p. 228 above.

[27] A sentence of imprisonment includes a suspended sentence; but for the purposes of deciding whether an offender has previously been sentenced to imprisonment any suspended sentence which has not been activated shall be disregarded (P.C.C.A., s. 21(3)).

(g) the addition under section 21(2) of the Child Care Act 1980 of a residential condition to a care order (C.Y.P.A. 1969, s. 20A(4) as inserted by C.J.A. 1982, s. 22);

unless either:

(a) he has applied for legal aid and the application was refused on the ground that it did not appear his means were such that he required assistance; or

(b) having been informed of his right to apply for legal aid and had the opportunity to do so, he refused or failed to apply. (P.C.C.A., s. 21(1); C.J.A. 1982, s. 3(1); C.Y.P.A. 1969, s. 7A(1); C.Y.P.A. 1969, s. 20A(4)).

In all cases a person is to be treated as legally represented in a court if, but only if, he has the assistance of counsel or a solicitor to represent him in the proceedings in that court at some time after he is convicted or found guilty and before the sentence is passed or the order made or power exercised (P.C.C.A., s. 21(2); C.J.A. 1982, s. 3(2); C.Y.P.A. 1969, ss. 7A(2) and 20(8)). "Legal aid" means legal aid for the purposes of proceedings in that court, whether the whole proceedings or the proceedings on or in relation to sentence, the making of the order or the exercise of the power (*ibid.*). Failure to comply with this requirement will render the sentence a nullity (*McGinlay and Ballantyne* (1975) 62 Cr.App.R. 156) but such non-compliance by the sentencing court does not affect the powers of the appeal court to pass such sentence as they think appropriate which the court below had power to pass.

REASONS

A court when passing sentence on an offender is generally not required to give any reasons for its decision. However, in *Newman and Newman* (1979) 1 Cr.App.R.(S.) 252, the Court of Appeal stated that where sentences of some severity are imposed, it would not be out of place for the judge to indicate the basis on which he thinks the sentences are justified.

There are certain cases, however, where a court must state its reasons for passing a particular sentence. Where a magistrates' court (but not the Crown Court) imposes a sentence of imprisonment on a person who has not previously been sentenced to imprisonment, it must state the reason for its opinion that no other method of dealing with him is appropriate (P.C.C.A., s. 20(2)). Likewise where a magistrates' court is dealing with an offender under the age of 21 and makes a detention centre order in respect of him or passes a youth custody sentence on him it must state in open court the reason for its opinion that no other method of dealing with him is appropriate (C.J.A. 1982, s. 2(4)). Where the Crown Court passes a sentence of youth custody it must state in open court the reasons for its opinion that the only appropriate method of dealing with the offender is to pass a custodial sentence (C.J.A. 1982, s. 6(1)(*b*)).

Where a court for "special reasons" exercises its discretion not to order disqualification from driving or endorsement or orders disqualification for a shorter period than would otherwise be required, it must state the grounds for doing so in open court, and if it is a magistrates' court it shall cause them to be entered in the register of its proceedings (R.T.A., s. 105(1)). The same requirement, that reasons be stated and, if appropriate, recorded, applies if for mitigating circumstances a court does not disqualify under section 93(3) of the Road Traffic Act or disqualifies for a period shorter than six months (s. 105(1)).

VARIATION OF SENTENCE

Under section 47(2) of the Supreme Court Act 1981 (which replaces s. 11(2) of the Courts Act 1971, which was in the same terms), a sentence imposed, or other order made, by the Crown Court may be varied or rescinded by the Crown Court within 28 days of the day on which it was passed. Where two or more persons are jointly tried on an indictment, the sentence or other order on any one of them may be varied or rescinded within 28 days of the conclusion of the joint trial or 56 days of the date on which the particular sentence was imposed or order made, whichever is the lesser. The court must be constituted as it was when the original sentence or order was imposed or made (s. 47(4)), but there is no need for the same judge to be sitting (*R.* v. *Dudley Crown Court, ex p. Smith* (1974) 58 Cr.App.R. 184). Where a judge intends to make a variation he should do so in open court, in the presence of the offender and his legal representatives, and the accused or his counsel should be given the opportunity to mitigate in relation to the proposed variation (*May* [1981] Crim.L.R. 729). Where a sentence is varied it will take effect from the beginning of the day on which it was originally passed, unless the court otherwise directs, but, for the purposes of an appeal, the time begins to run from the date on which the sentence was varied (s. 47(5)).

There has been some uncertainty as to the type of variation which may be made. While the wording of the section is wide enough to allow an increase or decrease in sentence, the Court of Appeal in *Grice* (1977) 66 Cr.App.R. 167 stated:

> "In our view that section [s. 11(2) of the Courts Act 1971] was included in order that slips by the judge can be corrected, be

they slips of memory, and it was necessary to have such a provision to enable that to be done. It was quite wrong, in our view, that it should be used as it was in this case, for a fundamental change of mind making a sentence which had been suspended into one which was not."[28]

The court did state that a variation making a sentence more severe may be permitted in exceptional cases; for example in *Newsome and Brown* [1970] 2 Q.B. 711, a sentence was varied from six months to seven months when the judge found that the former had to be suspended. The authority of *Grice* has, however, been substantially affected by three subsequent decisions.

In *Sodhi* (1978) 66 Cr.App.R. 260, the Court of Appeal upheld a judge's decision to vary a sentence of six months imprisonment imposed on May 16 to a hospital order and restriction order under sections 10 and 65 of the Mental Health Act 1959, made on June 10. Shortly after his trial the appellant was found to be suffering from a mental condition which made him dangerous. In effect the court held that "varied" bore its ordinary meaning and that there was no limit as a matter of law upon the variation which might be made in the circumstances of a particular case. In *Menocal* [1980] A.C. 598 it was stated *obiter* by the House of Lords (as the variation had been made out of time and therefore was invalid) that a forfeiture order, including an order made under section 27 of the Misuse of Drugs Act 1971, could be added to an offender's sentence under the powers to vary sentence. Three of their Lordships also stated that section 11(2) should be given a wide interpretation and not be restricted as it was in *Grice*, and accordingly the court has jurisdiction to change the type or nature of the sentence imposed. This approach has been followed by the Court of Appeal in *Reilly* [1982] Q.B. 1208, where the court held that the power to vary or rescind a sentence was not restricted to minor amendments and it upheld the judge's variation of sentence which involved the addition, after an adjournment, of a criminal bankruptcy order to a sentence of imprisonment. *Grice*, however, may continue to be authority for the proposition that events which occur after sentence has been passed, should not be used as a reason for varying the sentence. A case which is, however, clearly suitable for the exercise of the power conferred by section 47(2) is that of an offender who receives a lenient sentence on the basis of facts put forward in

[28] In this case the court originally passed a suspended sentence on the offender in relation to a charge of unlawful sexual intercourse with his daughter. Upon hearing that he had contacted her, contrary to an undertaking which he had given to the court, he was recalled and his sentence varied to one of immediate imprisonment.

mitigation which are subsequently shown to be untrue (see *Hart* (1983) 5 Cr.App.R.(S.) 25).

A magistrates' court, within 28 days, may vary or rescind a sentence or other order imposed or made by it (M.C.A., s. 142(1) and (4)). This power includes replacing a sentence or order which for any reason appears to be invalid by another which the court has power to impose or make (s. 142(1)). The court which makes the variation in sentence must consist either of all the magistrates who made up the original court, or if that original court comprised three or more magistrates, a majority of them (s. 142(4)). A sentence which is varied takes effect from the beginning of the day on which it was originally passed unless the court otherwise directs (s. 142(5)).

Apart from statute it has been held that the Crown Court has an inherent jurisdiction to rectify insubstantial errors in its record and an omission from an order should be rectified if it is of such a character that if it had been mentioned before the order had been entered the omission would have been supplied as a matter of course without further argument (*Saville* [1981] Q.B. 12, adopting the judgment of Judge Rubin in *Michael* [1976] Q.B. 414 at p. 419).

COMMENCEMENT OF SENTENCE

A sentence imposed by the Crown Court takes effect from the beginning of the day on which it is imposed, unless the court otherwise directs (S.C.A., s. 47(1)). The court, however, cannot order the sentence to commence on a day earlier than the day on which it was pronounced (*Gilbert* [1975] 1 W.L.R. 1012), but the court may order it to begin at the conclusion of a sentence which is imposed at the same time or which the offender is already serving (see also M.C.A., s. 133(1)).

APPEALS

A person convicted on indictment may appeal to the Court of Appeal against any sentence passed on him on his conviction or in subsequent proceedings, unless the sentence is one fixed by law (C.A.A. 1968, s. 9). "Sentence" includes any order made by a court when dealing with an offender (including a hospital order under Part III of the Mental Health Act 1983, with or without a restriction order, and an interim hospital order under that Part) and also includes a recommendation for deportation (C.A.A. 1968, s. 50(1)). A bind over to come up for judgment falls under the definition of a "sentence" against which an appeal lies (*Williams* [1982] 1 W.L.R. 1398). An appeal will lie against an order that an accused convicted on indictment should pay the whole or part of the costs of the prosecution (*Hayden* [1975] 1 W.L.R. 852). However, an order that the accused make a contribution to his own legal aid costs does not fall under the definition of "sentence" as it is not an order contingent upon a conviction (*Hayden; Raeburn* (1982) 74 Cr.App.R. 21). An order revoking a parole licence is a "sentence" within the meaning of section 50(1) (*Welch* [1982] 1 W.L.R. 976). A recommendation under section 1(2) of the Murder (Abolition of Death Penalty) Act 1965 as to the minimum period a person convicted of murder should serve in prison, is not a "sentence" and therefore no appeal lies against the recommendation (*Aitken* [1966] 1 W.L.R. 1076; *Bowden and Begley* (1983) 77 Cr.App.R. 66).

Section 66(1) of the Criminal Justice Act 1982 inserted a new subsection (1A) into section 50 of the Criminal Appeal Act 1968 as follows

> "Section 13 of the Powers of Criminal Courts Act 1973 (under which a conviction of an offence for which a probation order or an order for conditional discharge is made is deemed not to be a conviction except for certain purposes) shall not prevent an appeal under this Act, whether against conviction or otherwise."

Thus an offender who has been made the subject of a probation order, or an absolute or conditional discharge, may now appeal against his sentence and against any ancillary orders made in conjunction with a probation order or discharge. Further amendments to the Powers of Criminal Courts Act prevent a court which has power to do so, from amending or discharging the order while an appeal is pending.

There is also a right of appeal under section 10 of the Criminal Appeal Act against sentences passed by the Crown Court (otherwise than on appeal from a magistrates' court) for an offence of which he was not convicted on indictment (C.A.A. 1968, s. 10(1)). An appeal lies in the following cases where an offender convicted of an offence by a magistrates' court

> "(a) is committed by the court to be dealt with for his offence before the Crown Court; or
>
> (b) having been made the subject of a probation order or an order for conditional discharge or an attendance centre order or given a suspended sentence, appears or is brought before the Crown Court to be further dealt with for his offence."[29]

---

[29] s. 10 contains a lacuna in that no right of appeal is provided where a person originally committed for sentence to the Crown Court is ordered to do community service and subsequently has that order revoked under P.C.C.A., s. 17(3) and has a prison sentence substituted (see *Harding, The Times*, June 15, 1984).

The right to apply for leave in the circumstances covered by section 10(2) is restricted to the following cases:

    (a) where the offender has been sentenced to a term of imprisonment or youth custody for six months or more;

    (b) where the sentence is one which the convicting court had no power to pass;

    (c) where in dealing with him for his offence, the Crown Court made a recommendation for his deportation, an order disqualifying him from holding or obtaining a driving licence, or an order dealing with a suspended sentence.

(s. 10(3).)

Where a Crown Court has passed two or more sentences in the same proceedings, being sentences against which an appeal lies under section 9 or 10, an appeal or application for leave to appeal against any one of those sentences is treated as an appeal or application in respect of both or all of them (s. 11(2)).

A person convicted by a magistrates' court may appeal to the Crown Court against his sentence. Under section 108(3) of the Magistrates' Courts Act "sentence" includes any order made on conviction, not being:

    (a) an order for the payment of costs;

    (b) an order under section 2 of the Protection of Animals Act 1911 (which enables a court to order the destruction of an animal); or

    (c) an order made in pursuance of any enactment under which the court has no discretion as to the making of the order or its terms.

With the exception of appeals against orders to pay costs this definition section is as wide as section 50(1) of the Criminal Appeal Act. Section 66(1) of the Criminal Justice Act inserts a new subsection (1A) into section 108 of the Magistrates' Courts Act making like provision to that inserted in the Criminal Appeals Act for appeals where a probation order or conditional or absolute discharge is made.

A person sentenced by a magistrates' court for an offence in respect of which a probation order or an order for conditional discharge has been previously made may appeal to the Crown Court against the sentence (s. 108(2)).

Procedure

Court of Appeal

An appeal against sentence imposed by the Crown Court lies only with leave of the Court of Appeal unless the judge who passed sentence grants a certificate that the case is fit for an appeal against sentence without the leave of the Court of Appeal (C.A.A. 1968, s. 11(1) and (1A) as inserted by C.J.A. 1982, s. 29(2)(*a*)). Even if the sentence is one which the trial court did not have power to pass for the offence, no appeal lies as of right as being a point of law alone, but a certificate of leave is required (*Briggs* (1909) 1 Cr.App.R. 192). Notice of application for leave to appeal must be served on the Registrar within 28 days from the date on which sentence was passed or an order made (C.A.A. 1968, s. 18) or 28 days from the date on which the sentence was varied under section 47 of the Supreme Court Act 1981 (S.C.A., s. 47(5)). The Court of Appeal has power to extend the time limit for giving notice (C.A.A. 1968, s. 18(3)). Such an application must be accompanied by substantial reasons for the delay (*Rhodes* (1910) 5 Cr.App.R. 35; *Cullum* (1942) 28 Cr.App.R. 150). The power of the court to extend time is unrestricted. An application for leave to appeal and an application to extend time must specify the grounds of the application (C.A.R., rr. 2(2)(*a*) and 2(3)(*b*)).

The powers of the Court of Appeal to give leave to appeal or to extend time are exercisable by a single judge of the court (C.A.A. 1968, s. 31(1)), but an applicant who is aggrieved by the decision of the single judge is entitled to have the application determined by the full court provided he served the Registrar with notice within 14 days, or such longer period as a judge of the court may fix, from the date on which notice of refusal was served on him by the Registrar (C.A.R., r. 12(1)).

Crown Court

Where sentence is imposed by a magistrates' court, an appellant has 21 days from the day on which sentence was passed to give written notice of his appeal to the clerk of the magistrates' court and to the prosecutor (Crown Court Rules 1982, r. 7). The Crown Court has power to extend the time for giving notice of appeal either before or after the time expires (r. 7(5)). An application for extension of time must be in writing specifying the grounds of the application and must be sent to the appropriate officer of the Crown Court.

Bail pending appeal

The Court of Appeal may grant an appellant bail pending the determination of his appeal (C.A.A. 1968, s. 19(1) as substituted by C.J.A. 1982, s. 29(2)(*b*)). The appellant indicates that he is applying for bail on the notice of his application for leave to appeal and, in addition, serves on the Registrar a form giving details of the application (C.C.R., r. 3(1)). In addition, where a Crown Court judge certifies that a case is fit for appeal he may grant an appellant bail pending the determination of his appeal (S.C.A., s. 81(1)(*f*) as amended by C.J.A. 1982, s. 29(1)). However, the granting of bail pending appeal will be rare; "the question is, are there exceptional circumstances, which would drive the court to the conclusion that justice can only be done by the granting of bail?" (*per* Geoffrey Lane L.J., in *Watton* (1978) 68 Cr.App.R. 293). These would probably exist where the appeal seems likely to succeed or where the appellant is serving a short custodial sentence which otherwise is likely to be completed before the appeal would be heard.

The Court of Appeal may revoke bail or vary the conditions of bail where it has been granted by the Crown Court (C.A.A. 1968, s. 19(1)(*b*) and (*c*)). All the powers of the Court of Appeal under section 19(1) may be exercised on the application of either the appellant or the Registrar of Criminal Appeals (s. 19(2)).

Where a person is appealing against a custodial sentence passed on him by a magistrates' court, the magistrates' court may grant him bail (M.C.A., s. 113(1)). If the magistrates' court refuses to grant bail the appellant may apply to the Crown Court (S.C.A., s. 81(1)(*b*)). Alternatively he may apply to the High Court which has power to grant bail or vary conditions imposed by the magistrates (C.J.A. 1967, s. 22(1)).

Powers of the court dealing with appeal against sentence

Court of Appeal

On an appeal against sentence the Court of Appeal, if it thinks that a different sentence or order should have been passed or made, may quash the sentence or order passed or made by the Crown Court and in its place pass such sentence or make such order as they think appropriate which the court below had power to pass or make provided that, taking the case as a whole, the appellant is not more severely dealt with on appeal than he was dealt with by the court below (C.A.A. 1968, s. 11(3)).[30] There are several cases which give guidance as to what does or does not amount to being "more severely dealt with on appeal." A sentence of imprisonment for a fixed term of years cannot be varied on appeal to a life sentence (*Whittaker* [1967] Crim.L.R. 431; *Rose* [1974] Crim.L.R. 266). Certifying a sentence to make it an extended sentence makes it more severe than an ordinary

---

[30] The power of the court under s. 11(3) to pass a sentence which the Crown Court had power to pass for an offence, includes the power to sentence the appellant for an offence in respect of which the sentence was suspended and the Crown Court when dealing with the appellant in relation to the offence from which the appeal arises, made no order under P.C.C.A., s. 23(1) in respect of the suspended sentence (C.A.A. 1968, s. 11(4)).

term of imprisonment of the same length (*Duncuft* (1969) 53 Cr.App.R. 495), but if on appeal a suitable reduction is made in the term of the sentence, then it may be made an extended sentence (*Jones* [1970] Crim.L.R. 356; *Bourton* [1985] Crim.L.R. 165). An immediate term of imprisonment is more severe than a suspended sentence even where the immediate term is much shorter than the suspended term (*Thompson* (1977) 66 Cr.App.R. 130).

"Taking the case as a whole" in section 11(3) of the Criminal Appeal Act means taking the totality of the matters in respect of which the appellant was dealt with in the court below. As the Court of Appeal not infrequently substitutes for two consecutive sentences a lesser or equivalent term concurrent on each of two counts, the same could be done with regard to disqualification from driving (*Sandwell*, [1985] R.T.R. 45).[31]

The Court of Appeal also has power to alter sentence where the appeal is against conviction. Where the court allows an appeal in respect of part of an indictment but the appellant remains convicted under other counts the court may, in respect of any count on which the appellant remains convicted, pass such sentence, in substitution for any passed thereon at the trial, as they think proper and is authorised by law for the offence of which he remains convicted, provided that the appellant's sentence on the indictment as a whole, will not be of greater severity than the sentence which was passed at the trial in respect of all the offences of which he was convicted on the indictment (C.A.A. 1968, s. 4). Thus the sentence on an individual count may be increased provided the total sentence on the indictment is not of greater severity (*Craig* [1967] 1 W.L.R. 645).

Where, on an appeal against conviction, the Court, instead of quashing the conviction, substitutes a conviction for another offence, it may pass such sentence in respect of that offence as is authorised by law provided it is not of greater severity than the sentence passed at the trial (C.A.A. 1968, s. 3(2)).

The Crown Court

The Crown Court, on an appeal against conviction or sentence, may award any punishment, whether more or less severe than that

---

[31] In this case consecutive periods of disqualification totalling 30 months had wrongly been imposed. The Transport Act 1981 had removed the power to impose consecutive disqualifications. The court substituted a period of 12 months disqualification on the first count, two years on the second and 12 months under the Transport Act 1981, s. 19(4)(*b*) (penalty points disqualification) all being concurrent.

awarded by the magistrates' court, which that court might have awarded (S.C.A., s. 48).[32]

In hearing an appeal against sentence the Crown Court proceeds by way of rehearing. All the evidence relevant to sentence, the facts, the antecedents and mitigation, will be presented and in cases of disputes relating to the facts of the case the principles in *Newton* (1982) 4 Cr.App.R.(S.) 388 are to be followed (*Williams* v. *Another* (1983) 5 Cr.App.R.(S.) 134).

Computation of sentence on appeals

The time pending an appeal during which the appellant is released on bail does not count as part of any term of custody to which he has been sentenced (C.A.A. 1968, s. 29(3); C.J.A. 1948, s. 37(6); M.C.A., s. 113(4)). The time during which an appellant is in custody pending the determination of his appeal does count as part of any sentence to which he is, for the time being, subject, unless the Court of Appeal gives directions, stating reasons, to the contrary (C.A.A. 1968, s. 29(1) and (2)). The Court of Appeal cannot give any such direction where it grants leave to appeal (C.A.A. 1968, s. 29(2)(*a*)).[33]

The role of the Divisional Court in appeals[34]

An appeal against sentence imposed in the magistrates' court may go on to the Divisional Court of the Queen's Bench Division by one of two routes. There may be an appeal by way of case stated on the ground that the decision of the magistrates' court (or the Crown Court, if it has already heard an appeal from the magistrates' court) was wrong in point of law or in excess of jurisdiction (S.C.A., s. 28).[35] Alternatively there may be an application for judicial review on the grounds that the inferior tribunal has acted in excess of its

[32] For an example of a case where the Crown Court increased sentence on appeal, see *Baber* v. *Chief Constable of Gwent* (1983) 5 Cr.App.R.(S.) 121.

[33] See *Howitt* (1975) 61 Cr.App.R. 327, and *Practice Direction* (1980) 70 Cr.App.R. 186. An applicant for leave to appeal whose application is based on the determination of the trial judge of the factual basis of the offence, is at risk of losing time if the trial court has proceeded properly, particularly in those cases where the prosecution was made aware of the different factual basis on which it was intended to make a plea only after the plea had been made (*Ahmed* [1985] Crim.L.R. 250).

[34] See Wasik, "Sentencing and the Divisional Court" [1984] Crim.L.R. 272; Thomas, "Sentencing in magistrates' courts—a lack of judicial guidance" (1981) 145 J.P.N. 467.

[35] See for example *Miller* v. *Lenton* (1981) 3 Cr.App.R.(S.) 171, where a recommendation for deportation was set aside where the magistrates' court and the Crown Court on appeal had failed to apply the guidelines laid down in *Nazari* [1980] 1 W.L.R. 1366.

jurisdiction, as occurred in *R.* v. *Uxbridge JJ., ex p. Fisc* (1980) 2 Cr.App.R.(S.) 112, where *certiorari* was granted to quash sentences of imprisonment for default made consecutive to another sentence passed on the same occasion.[36] In *St. Albans Crown Court, ex p. Cinnamond* [1981] Q.B. 480, the Divisional Court went even further by declaring that it would grant judicial review where a sentence, while not being unlawful, was:

"either harsh and oppressive or ... so far outside the normal discretionary limits as to enable this Court to say that its imposition must involve an error of law of some description, even if it may not be apparent at once what is the precise nature of that error.... [T]he jurisdiction which this Court is empowered to exercise in this field can be considered analogous to the jurisdiction which it exercises in relation to the Crown and Government departments where, on *Wednesbury*[37] tests, it examines a decision and says that no reasonable authority could have reached that decision without a self-misdirection of some sort and therefore is satisfied that there has been some misdirection." (*per* Donaldson L.J. at p. 484.)

The dividing line between cases appropriate for appeal by way of case stated and those appropriate for judicial review is not a clear one and in *Cinnamond* Donaldson L.J. considered that the case could just as properly have come before the court by way of case stated when the same principles would have applied.[38] Judicial review was chosen in order to minimise delay. The Divisional Court reduced to six months a disqualification from driving for 18 months for careless driving as it went so far beyond the normal range of disqualifications imposed in such cases.

In pursuing an appeal against sentence an appellant should go to the Crown Court first of all. Judicial review may be denied an appellant if he has not exhausted his right of appeal to the Crown Court (*Battle Justices, ex p. Shepherd* (1983) 5 Cr.App.R.(S.) 124). If appeal to the Crown Court does not lead to the result desired and a further appeal is being considered, case stated is to be preferred if the case is factually complex as then it will be heard more fully (see *Ipswich Crown Court, ex p. Baldwin* [1981] 1 All E.R. 596) rather than relying on affidavits as in judicial review (see, *e.g. Tottenham Justices, ex p. Joshi* [1982] 1 W.L.R. 631). However, an appeal by way of case stated may be taken direct to the Divisional Court from the magistrates' court on the issue of a harsh and oppressive

[36] See also *Teeside Crown Court, ex p. Clarke* (1983) 5 Cr.App.R.(S.) 92.
[37] *Associated Provincial Picture Houses* v. *Wednesbury Corporation* [1948] 1 K.B. 223.
[38] This has been confirmed in *Universal Salvage Ltd.* v. *Boothby*, *The Times*, December 14, 1983.

sentence, but if an applicant does this he loses his right of appeal to the Crown Court (M.C.A., s. 111(4)).[39]

When will sentence be reduced because it is unduly harsh or oppressive? In *Cinnamond* it was reduced because the disparity from the normal range was so great "as to constitute an error of law." In *Joshi* Lord Lane C.J. stated:

> "The only basis upon which an appeal to this court can be made is if it can be shown that the justices, in purporting to exercise their discretion ... have acted on some improper principle, have taken into consideration something they ought not to have taken into consideration or have failed to take into consideration something which they should. It is not enough that the fines were more than this Court would have imposed. We have to ask ourselves this question: has there been an error of law? Has there been a purported exercise of discretion based upon some wrong principle or assumption? Could any reasonable bench of magistrates have reached this decision without having misdirected themselves?"

In *Universal Salvage* v. *Boothby*, (1983) 5 Cr.App.R.(S) 428, a maximum fine imposed on the defendant company by the magistrates' court for road traffic offences involving the use of a motor vehicle on the road without recording equipment, was reduced to a conditional discharge as they had given no weight to the crucial mitigating factor that they had relied on a letter from the Department of Transport which had caused them reasonably to believe that they were acting lawfully. The Divisional Court concluded that such a sentence in the circumstances was "so far outside the normal discretionary limits" that the justices must have erred in law. In *Joshi* the procedure provided a means of appealing against an order to pay the costs of the prosecution; such an order is excluded from the definition of sentence in section 108(3) of the Magistrates' Courts Act, so there could be no appeal to the Crown Court. The court made it clear that the order could be challenged only if it could be shown that the magistrates in exercising their discretion, had acted on some improper principle, taking into consideration something which they ought not to have taken into consideration or failing to take into consideration something which they should.

---

[39] The right of appeal to the Crown Court against sentence will not be lost, however, where the case stated is in respect of a matter affecting conviction rather than sentence (*Winchester Crown Court, ex p. Lewington* [1982] 1 W.L.R. 1277).

SENTENCING PRINCIPLES

THE TARIFF PRINCIPLE[1]

The first decision a sentencer must make relates to the type of sentence he should impose on an offender. The sentencer is generally faced with two alternatives: he may impose a "tariff sentence" (fine, imprisonment, detention in a detention centre or youth custody) or he may choose an individualised measure (probation, absolute or conditional discharge, community service order, hospital order, discretionary life sentence, etc.). In general the objectives of these two types of measures are in conflict. A tariff sentence is a punitive measure reflecting the gravity of the offence and is designed to deter; whereas individualised measures are designed to help the offender to conform with the law by providing him with treatment, guidance or supervision, and tend not to provide general deterrence nor to reflect the gravity of the offence. A tariff sentence may provide no assistance to an offender to conform to the law, and may actually increase the likelihood of him offending in the future by exposing him to corrupting influences and damaging his prospects. The sentencer generally has to make a choice between these two competing and often conflicting alterna- tives. Occasionally both objectives may be achieved in one and the same measure, for example, by imposing a suspended sentence or by imposing a term of imprisonment where treatment is the objective. A Northern Irish case illustrates this point. In *Winchester* [1978] N.I.J.B. the appellant on a plea of guilty was convicted of the manslaughter of her father who for many years had subjected her to incestuous and perverted sexual abuse and physical beatings. In refusing leave to appeal against a sentence of imprisonment for seven years, Lowry L.C.J. stated that there were two main points to be considered in relation to the sentence:

(1) how it relates to the gravity of the crime and
(2) (which was very much to the fore in the mind of the learned trial judge) how the rehabilitation of the applicant could best be promoted.

He concluded:

> "The applicant had been cut off from life in society and, apart from the self-imposed task of caring for [her brother and sister]

[1] See generally Cross, *The English Sentencing System* (3rd ed., 1981); Thomas, *Principles of Sentencing* (2nd ed., 1979).

had no normal human contacts. She had benefitted from prison pending her trial and was thought likely to benefit further from a period in the same atmosphere.... It seems that she really had to be re-educated as a member of society. Therefore from both points of view we are quite clear that the learned trial judge was right in principle in imposing a custodial sentence and that having regard to all the circumstances the period of 7 years was not manifestly excessive."

The conflict which often confronts the sentencer was highlighted by Kelly J. in another Northern Irish case, *Magee* [1975] 6 N.I.J.B., a drugs case where he stated:

"Sentencing offenders for drug offences is not always easy. It is recognised that drug taking and drug dependence are complex phenomena. And offenders are invariably young people, usually of good character. Frequently they are students, showing ability and well set on course to professional or technical achievement. Deterrent custodial sentences imposed in such cases mean the interruption and sometimes the end of a career of promise.

While those considerations alone may point to an individualised sentence, and in many cases to a non-custodial one, there are clearly other matters to be weighed and given effect to in sentencing ... Undoubtedly there is a community rejection of drug-taking and a public will that it should be firmly discouraged ... These factors—the antagonism of the community to drug-taking and the increase or prevalence of drug-abuse in a particular community will generally outweigh in my opinion, the personal considerations of the individual offender ... and invariably lead to custodial sentences ... Of course there will be cases where a non-custodial sentence may achieve the near certainty of permanent abandonment of drug-taking by a drug dependent and other cases where the personal claims of the individual offender are so outstanding that a non-custodial sentence is justified—but these will be exceptional cases although I have encountered some."

The difference in the ultimate outcome of a case depending on which approach is adopted is illustrated by the case of *Heather* (1979) 1 Cr.App.R.(S.) 139. The appellant pleaded guilty to robbery at a chemist's shop where he had obtained drugs after threatening the assistant with a knife. He was originally sentenced to five years imprisonment which the Court of Appeal considered was well justified as a deterrent sentence for a grave offence and a reduction of it would be wrong. However, by adopting a different philosophy, that of treatment of the offender, the court decided to quash the sentence and replaced it with a probation order.

The decision, however, to impose a tariff sentence is often virtually automatic. In *Roberts and Roberts* [1982] 1 W.L.R. 133, the Court of Appeal stated that rape is always a serious offence, and, save in the most exceptional circumstances, calls for an immediate custodial sentence. The situation is the same in relation to the other serious offences, such as robbery, wounding with intent to do grievous bodily harm, serious drugs offences, perjury, arson and blackmail. In these cases it is the gravity of the offence which dictates the imposition of a deterrent sentence. In other cases the position of the offender as a person in a position of trust or authority who abuses that position may dictate the imposition of a tariff sentence (see *Dimsey* (1981) 3 Cr.App.R.(S.) 32; *Usher* (1980) 2 Cr.App.R.(S.) 123).

Whatever the reason for choosing a tariff sentence, the sentencer must decide on the appropriate length of the sentence. Various factors will be taken into consideration before arriving at the quantum.

In *Bibi* [1980] 1 W.L.R. 1193, Lord Lane C.J. made a policy statement on sentencing encouraging the courts to impose shorter terms of imprisonment for certain types of crime. He stated

> "Many offenders can be dealt with equally justly and effectively by a sentence of six or nine months' imprisonment as by one of 18 months or three years. We have in mind not only the obvious case of the first offender for whom any prison sentence however short may be an adequate punishment and deterrent, but other types of case as well.
>
> The less serious types of factory or shopbreaking; the minor cases of sexual indecency; the more petty frauds where small amounts of money are involved; the fringe participant in more serious crime: all these are examples of cases where the shorter sentence would be appropriate.
>
> There are, on the other hand, some offences for which, generally speaking, only the medium or longer sentences will be appropriate. For example, most robberies; most offences involving serious violence; use of a weapon to wound; burglary of private dwelling-houses; planned crime for wholesale profit; active large scale trafficking in dangerous drugs. These are only examples. It would be impossible to set out a catalogue of those offences which do and those which do not merit more severe treatment. So much will, obviously, depend upon the circumstances of each individual offender and each individual offence.

What the court can and should do is to ask itself whether there is any compelling reason why a short sentence should not be passed. We are not aiming at uniformity of sentence; that would be impossible. We are aiming at uniformity of approach."

SELECTING THE SENTENCING RANGE

Each criminal offence is characterised by typically recurring factual situations of varying degrees of gravity and, accordingly, the severity of the sentence to be imposed must reflect these degrees of wickedness.[2] Ranges of sentence appropriate to each level of gravity have been developed over the years and can be identified from the decisions of the Court of Appeal. The maximum sentence available for a particular offence is reserved for the worst form of that offence (*Byrne* (1975) 62 Cr.App.R. 159; *Smith* [1976] Crim.L.R. 468). Using their experience and knowledge of the decisions of other judges and of the Court of Appeal, particularly cases where the court seeks to give guidelines,[3] judges must first allocate the offence to the appropriate sentence range. There is a normal bracket of terms of years within which the sentence for an offence is to be assessed. This bracket forms the starting point for determining the appropriate sentence. From this starting point the final sentence will be calculated by taking into account any aggravating factors which lead to a sentence towards the upper end of the bracket. If appropriate, the court will also consider any mitigating factors which may lead to the imposition of a lesser sentence. In some circumstances the court may consider it inappropriate to give a discount for mitigating circumstances in order to achieve some other penal objective such as deterrence, but the sentence must be proportionate to the facts of the case, and generally must not exceed that range for that type of offence.

The evolution of a pattern of sentencing in relation to causing serious explosions or conspiring to commit such offences is

---

[2] See Thomas, *op. cit.*, p. 33.

[3] See, *e.g. Mohammed* (1974) 60 Cr.App.R. 141; *Taylor, Simons and Roberts* [1977] 1 W.L.R. 612; *Aramah* (1982) 4 Cr.App.R.(S.) 407; *Wood* [1984] Crim.L.R. 305; *Clarke* (1982) 4 Cr.App.R.(S.) 197.

The Court of Appeal emphasised in *de Havilland* (1983) 5 Cr.App.R.(S.) 109 that decisions on sentencing are not binding authorities but are no more than examples of how the court has dealt with a particular offender in relation to a particular offence. As such they may be useful as an aid to uniformity of sentence for a particular category of crime, but they are not authoritative in the strict sense. Even in relation to guideline cases the sentencer retains his discretion within the guidelines and even may depart from them if the particular circumstance of the case justifies departure.

illustrated by *Fell* [1974] Crim.L.R. 673, *Ladd, The Times*, October 15, 1984 and *Byrne* (1975) 62 Cr.App.R. 159.

In arriving at a final determination of the sentence certain recurring factors are given considerable importance by the courts. These will be examined in more detail.

(a) Exemplary or deterrent sentence

An exemplary or deterrent sentence will be imposed as a warning to others not to engage in similar criminal activity. In such cases the sentence will be based solely on the facts of the case with little or no discount being given for mitigating factors. In *Bradley* [1970] Crim.L.R. 171, the Court of Appeal stated that "when a court finds that its duty is to pass a deterrent sentence, considerations of the particular prisoner's past good character . . . are of much less moment than normally would be the case."[4] In *Turner* (1975) 61 Cr.App.R. 67, where a gang of bank robbers was convicted of a series of armed robberies, the court emphasised that it was imposing deterrent sentences with the result that it declined to take into account variations in the defendants' records. However it did make reductions in some sentences to reflect variations in the offenders' respective degrees of involvement and responsibility.[5]

There are several reasons for imposing exemplary sentences.

(i) *Type of offence or its prevalence*

The prevalence of an offence in a certain locality or the frequency with which it is committed generally may lead to the imposition of a deterrent sentence. In *Wilson and Tutt* (1981) 3 Cr.App.R.(S.) 102, the Court of Appeal described sentences of three years' imprisonment imposed on two pickpockets convicted of attempted theft, as an entirely proper deterrent to this offence which was very prevalent on the London Underground where it was committed.[6] The prevalence of obtaining unemployment benefit by deception justified exemplary sentences in *Boyle* (1981) 3 Cr.App.R.(S.) 13.[7]

Whether or not an offence is particularly prevalent, its gravity may be regarded as justification for an exemplary sentence. In *McCay* [1975] N.I. 5, the Northern Ireland Court of Appeal upheld exemplary sentences imposed on the appellants who had been convicted of supplying dangerous drugs. Lowry L.C.J. stated that "severe sentences are of assistance in signifying the community's rejection of drug-trafficking and its hostility to traffickers in drugs."

---

[4] See also *Inwood* (1974) 60 Cr.App.R. 70.
[5] See also *Boyle* (1981) 3 Cr.App.R.(S.) 13.
[6] See also *Elvin* [1976] Crim.L.R. 204; *McMenemy and Murray* [1971] N.I.J.B.
[7] See also *Bogle* [1975] Crim.L.R. 726; *O'Connor* (1981) 3 Cr.App.R.(S.) 154.

Even stronger sentiments were expressed by the Court of Appeal in *Poh and To* [1982] Crim.L.R. 132, where the appellants aged 64 and 58 respectively, were sentenced to the maximum of 14 years' imprisonment for fraudulently importing heroin with a street value of £5 million. The Court of Appeal stated that the appellants had "forfeited any rights to humanitarian consideration."[8]

(ii) *Organised criminality*

The fact that an offence results from organised criminal activity will lead to the imposition of a severe sentence because such offences are planned and present a serious threat to society. In the Great Train Robbery case of *Wilson* [1965] 1 Q.B. 402, the Court of Appeal stated that:

> "severely deterrent sentences were necessary, not only to protect the community against these men for a very long time, but also to demonstrate as clearly as possible to others tempted to follow them into lawlessness on this vast scale that, if they are brought to trial and convicted, commensurate punishment will follow; and that being so, ... minor differences in age and record between these men become ... irrelevant."[9]

In the Northern Irish case of *McKellar* [1975] 4 N.I.J.B. which involved armed robbery, McGonigal L.J. stated:

> "Those who plan or take part in such offences, must do so with the knowledge that the sentences which the Courts will impose are sentences based, not on the norm, but severer sentences, longer terms of years than would fall within the norm, designed as a deterrent to stay the hands of others who may contemplate the commission of such an offence and also give to the public the protection it requires and is entitled to."

(iii) *The position of the offender*

The position of the offender may lead to the imposition of an exemplary sentence. In *Dimsey* (1981) 3 Cr.App.R.(S.) 32, in affirming a sentence of imprisonment on an accountant convicted of conspiracy to defraud in connection with an asset stripping scheme, the Court of Appeal stated that a great deal of trust is reposed in accountants, and when a member of that profession falls from grace it is almost inevitable that he is sentenced to a term of imprisonment

---

[8] See also *Ashraf and Hug* [1982] Crim.L.R. 132. In *Campbell* (1979) 1 Cr.App.R.(S.) 12, the Court of Appeal stated that where an offence of violence was committed against a public servant an exemplary sentence would be imposed.

[9] See also *Wilde* (1978) 67 Cr.App.R. 339; *Turner* (1975) 61 Cr.App.R. 67.

as a deterrent to others.[10] A sentence of imprisonment rather than any other sentence will also be imposed where persons in positions of trust steal from their employers, but the length of the sentence will vary depending on the amount involved and may not be unduly long as the deterrent effect is achieved by the fact of imprisonment itself.[11] In such cases, depending on the circumstances, part of the sentence may be suspended.[11a]

The Court of Appeal has also stated that where a person abused a position of trust for the purpose of sexual gratification an exemplary sentence is appropriate. In *Taylor* (1977) 64 Cr.App.R. 182, the court stated that "a man in a supervisory capacity who abuses his position of trust for his sexual gratification ought to get a sentence somewhere near the maximum."[12]

(b) Discretionary life sentences and the dangerous offender

The major offences for which discretionary life sentences are available are outlined above (see pp. 93–94). The courts normally reserve life sentences for the dangerous offender who for one reason or another cannot be dealt with under the provisions of the Mental Health Act. Life imprisonment will be appropriate where the offender is suffering from some personality disorder or instability of character and commits a grave offence or an offence of lesser gravity but there is evidence that it is likely that he will commit similar offences in the future, and if the offences are committed again the consequences to others could be specially injurious. The principles involved in sentencing the dangerous offender are gradually becoming clearer although there have been many contradictory dicta in earlier cases. The implementation of the principles, however, sometimes presents difficulties.[13]

In *Picker* [1970] 2 Q.B. 161, the court highlighted the reasoning behind the imposition of life sentences when it stated:

"[W]here the nature of the offence and the make-up of the offender are of such a nature that the public require protection for a considerable time unless there is a change in his

[10] See also *Coleman* (1967) 51 Cr.App.R. 244; *Jacob* [1982] Crim.L.R. 135; *Grundy* (1982) 4 Cr.App.R.(S.) 234; *Milne* (1982) 4 Cr.App.R.(S.) 397.
[11] See *Sumners* (1979) 1 Cr.App.R.(S.) 13; *Wearn* (1980) 2 Cr.App.R.(S.) 295; *Smedley* (1981) 3 Cr.App.R.(S.) 117; *Satterthwaite and Satterthwaite* [1981] Crim.L.R. 657; *Tonks* [1982] Crim.L.R. 193; *Eagleton* [1982] Crim.L.R. 322; *Jacob* [1982] Crim.L.R. 135; *Routley* [1982] Crim.L.R. 383; *Noden* [1983] Crim.L.R. 637; *Kelly* (1983) 5 Cr.App.R.(S.)1; *Black* (1984) 6 Cr.App.R.(S) 455.
[11a] See *Carr* [1985] Crim.L.R. 166 and *Dixon* [1985] Crim.L.R. 167.
[12] See also *Usher* (1980) 2 Cr.App.R.(S.) 123; *Pornomansy* (1980) 2 Cr.App.R.(S.) 373; *Simpson* (1981) 3 Cr.App.R.(S.) 345.
[13] See, *e.g. Gray* [1983] Crim.L.R. 691.

condition ... it is right for the judge to impose a life sentence. This will enable some authority to ascertain from time to time whether the condition has changed and it is safe for the offender to be released."

More recently in *Blogg* (1981) 3 Cr.App.R.(S.) 114, where the offender was committed to the Crown Court for sentence after pleading guilty before a magistrates' court for a minor offence of arson, the Court of Appeal asserted:

"... it cannot be overemphasised that in cases of this kind it is very often far more merciful to the offender to impose upon him a sentence of life imprisonment than to do what we are asked to do, namely to impose a fixed term, which in this case would have to be in our view a very long term....

[L]ife imprisonment sentences in cases of this kind are generally preferable to long fixed term sentences if the offender is likely to represent a continuing danger in the future....

Passing a term of life imprisonment upon him will enable the Home Secretary to keep him under constant surveillance with a view to his release at such time as those who advise the Home Secretary deem it safe to allow him to go outside prison again.... It may very well be that by that means he will leave prison far sooner than he would do if a fixed term of imprisonment were to be imposed upon him."

However, in several other cases the Court of Appeal has attempted to limit the use of life imprisonment. In *Pither* (1979) 1 Cr.App.R.(S.) 209, the court, taking the view that life sentences were not always merciful, stated:

"It may well be that a man who is sentenced to life imprisonment may be released fractionally earlier than one who is sentenced to a fairly long determinate sentence. He may be; but he may not. What this court has to bear in mind is the anguish which must be felt, even by the most hardened young thugs, if they are in prison sentenced to life imprisonment, and have no idea, as the years go by, when (if at all) they will be released."

The court expressed a similar view in *Hercules* (1980) 2 Cr.App.R.(S.) 156, stating that life imprisonment is a severe sentence which should be avoided whenever possible. Views on the desirability of imposing life sentences accordingly vary. However, it is the indeterminacy of a life sentence which is regarded by some judges as one of its good points over a long determinate sentence. The powers of the Home Secretary to implement the indeterminacy of the life sentence should not be restricted by the imposition of a long determinate sentence to run concurrently which is disproportionate to the gravity of the offence or offences for which it was passed (*Middleton* (1981) 3 Cr.App.R.(S.) 273). However, it is perfectly proper to impose determinate sentences to run concurrently with a life sentence provided they are proportionate to the offence(s) and if consecutive to each other, have been made consecutive in accordance with the correct principles *Daniels* (1984) 6 Cr.App.R.(S) 8 *Nugent* (1984) 6 Cr.App.R.(S) 93. In assessing whether determinate sentences do fetter the discretion of the Home Secretary, it is permissible to pay regard to the date on which the offender would become eligible for release on licence in respect of the determinate sentence (*Griffiths* (1983) 5 Cr.App.R.(S) 365).

The overriding principle in deciding whether a life sentence is appropriate is that

> "life imprisonment is really appropriate and must only be passed in the most exceptional circumstances. With few exceptions . . . it is reserved . . . for offenders who for one reason or another cannot be dealt with under the provisions of the Mental Health Act, yet who are in a mental state which makes them dangerous to the life or limb of members of the public." (*Per* Lord Lane C.J., *Wilkinson* (1983) 5 Cr.App.R.(S.) 105, at pp. 108–109.)[14]

In the absence of such evidence of mental instability and continuing dangerousness to the public, a life sentence is inappropriate (see, *e.g. Headley* (1979) 1 Cr.App.R.(S.) 158; *Blackburn* (1979) 1 Cr.App.R.(S.) 205; *Owen* (1980) 2 Cr.App.R.(S.) 45; *Laycock* (1981) 3 Cr.App.R.(S.) 104). The cases do not make it entirely clear how much importance is attached to the gravity of the offence. In *Hodgson* (1968) 52 Cr.App.R. 118, the Court of Appeal stipulated that a life sentence was appropriate only where the offence or offences are in themselves grave enough to require a very long sentence.[15] However, this requirement appears to have been moderated by other cases. In *Ashdown* [1974] Crim.L.R. 130, the real possibility of violent sexual offences in the future was held to justify a life sentence where the appellant was convicted of armed robbery where he stole £2 from a man whom he threatened with an air pistol. In *Blogg* a life sentence was imposed by the Crown Court after a conviction before a magistrates' court for a minor offence of arson as the offender had a history of arson over a period of 30 years and there was evidence that he was a real danger to the public. In similar circumstances the Court of Appeal stated in *Thornton* [1975]

---

[14] See also *Pither* (1979) 1 Cr.App.R.(S.) 209.
[15] See also *Williams* [1974] Crim.L.R. 376; *Herples* (1979) 1 Cr.App.R.(S.) 48; *Gordan* [1982] Crim.L.R. 240.

Crim.L.R. 51, that when considering the appropriateness of a life sentence, the gravity of the offence need not be so serious in a case where the likelihood of repetition is high as it must be in a case when the likelihood is remote." Accordingly, the decision to impose a life sentence seems to be based on balancing the gravity of the instant offence against the dangerousness of the offender. Thus where the offence is not particularly serious it would appear that a life sentence can be imposed where there is substantial evidence that the offender represents a danger to the public.

Generally there must be psychiatric evidence that the offender is sufficiently dangerous to warrant the use of a life sentence,[16] but it is not necessary to show that he is suffering from mental illness. The important consideration is not whether the offender suffers from a recognisable mental condition but whether he represents a danger to the public for the foreseeable future (see *Laycock* (1981) 3 Cr.App.R.(S.) 104). A life sentence is appropriate in such cases as it is indeterminate and subject to review. Thus in *Thornett* [1979] 1 Cr.App.R.(S.) 1, the Court of Appeal described it as a classic case for the life sentence where the offender had been convicted of three rapes with violence. The offender was described as an emotionally unstable and immature person who was likely to use violence to achieve his aims. There was hope that he might mature and that eventually it would be safe to release him, but the fundamental consideration was the protection of the public.[17] In some cases a life sentence may be imposed with little prospect of the offender ever being safe to be released (*Chaplin* [1976] Crim.L.R. 320); or it may be imposed for the safety of the public even though there is evidence that the offender might respond better to a fixed term sentence and a life sentence might make his eventual rehabilitation more difficult (*Waight* [1979] Crim.L.R. 538). However, a life sentence should not be imposed if there is no evidence to suggest that the offender represents a continuing danger to the public and sufficient protection could be provided by a fixed term sentence proportionate to the gravity of the offence.[18]

A problem arises, however, in relation to several recent decisions of the Court of Appeal. In *Green* (1981) 3 Cr.App.R.(S.) 144, a sentence of 18 years for unlawful sexual intercourse with a girl of 10 was imposed on a man of 40 to keep him out of the public's way for

---

[16] See *Spencer* (1979) 1 Cr.App.R.(S.) 75; *Blackburn* (1979) 1 Cr.App.R.(S.) 205; *Pither* (1979) 1 Cr.App.R.(S.) 209; *Owen* (1980) 2 Cr.App.R.(S.) 45; but *cf. de Havilland* (1983) 5 Cr.App.R.(S.) 109, where the judge imposed the sentence without hearing psychiatric evidence.

[17] See also *Waight* [1979] Crim.L.R. 538; *Watson* [1980] Crim.L.R. 247.

[18] See *Hutchinson* [1979] Crim.L.R. 190; *Spencer* (1979) 1 Cr.App.R.(S.) 75; *Mottershead* (1979) 1 Cr.App.R.(S.) 45.

a long time. This was approved by the Court of Appeal even though a life sentence could have been passed and might have had the effect of keeping him out of the way for much longer. The problem with this decision is that the sentence was disproportionate to the gravity of the offence. In the earlier case of *Rose* [1974] Crim.L.R. 266, where a sentence of 18 years was imposed on an offender suffering from a severe personality defect which made him dangerous, the Court of Appeal stated that the appropriate sentence would have been life imprisonment. The court took the view that a tariff sentence is subject to the principle of proportionality and should not be considered in the light of criteria appropriate to individualised measures. It stated:

> "Once the judge had decided to pass a determinate sentence this Court has to consider whether in all the circumstances the sentence was of appropriate length, and it has come to the conclusion that it was not."[19]

The problem with *Green* is that the principle of proportionality seemed to be well established. In those cases where a life sentence cannot be imposed or where it is not appropriate in the circumstances,[20] the cases seemed to establish that the sentence passed on a dangerous offender must be proportionate to the gravity of the offence.[21] This principle is now in some doubt. In *Corner* [1977] Crim.L.R. 300, the Court of Appeal approved a disproportionate sentence for trivial homosexual assaults because there was medical evidence that the offender might become extremely violent.[22] In *McCauliffe* [1982] 4 Cr.App.R.(S.) 13, the court accepted a plea of guilty to burglary with intent to rape on an indictment which charged aggravated burglary (for which a life sentence may be imposed which is not available for simple burglary). The Court of Appeal upheld a sentence of 10 years imprisonment, expressing its regret that the trial judge had accepted the plea to the lesser offence. The case seems to approve a disproportionate sentence where the offender is dangerous.

The total inconsistency of the decisions in this area is highlighted by the decision in *Ashe* [1982] Crim.L.R. 134. In *Gouws* [1982] Crim.L.R. 187, the Court of Appeal approved of a disproportionate sentence of six years imprisonment for a comparatively minor example of criminal damage, where the offender was regarded as

---

[19] See also *Handoll* [1978] Crim.L.R. 637.
[20] *e.g. Hutchinson* [1979] Crim.L.R. 190.
[21] See *Rose* [1974] Crim.L.R. 266; *Coombs* [1973] Crim.L.R. 65; *Slater* (1979) 1 Cr.App.R.(S.) 350.
[22] See *Gouws* [1982] Crim.L.R. 187; *Gordan* [1982] Crim.L.R. 240; *Chadbund* [1983] Crim.L.R. 48.

dangerous.The court on this occasion included Lord Lane C.J. (as it did in *Gordan* [1982] Crim.L.R. 240). Lord Lane was also a member of the court in *Ashe* which reduced to three years the sentence of four years imprisonment imposed on an 18 year old offender who had pleaded guilty to assault occasioning actual bodily harm and to causing grievous bodily harm. The court felt that although an immediate sentence of imprisonment was inevitable, it was too long even for the unprovoked and serious attack involved in the case, despite the fact that the offender had a serious personality disorder and the sentencer feared that there might be some future outbreak of violence leading to serious injury or even death.

Accordingly, for the present, this area is left in some doubt. Where available a life sentence is preferable to a fixed term which is disproportionate to the gravity of the offence. Where a life sentence is not available for the offence or where it is not appropriate, as where the offence is a minor example of a serious offence and the evidence of the offender's danger to the public is not overwhelming, a determinate sentence will be imposed and whether this need be proportionate to the gravity of the offence is uncertain. Where a court decides to impose a tariff sentence on a dangerous offender, however, it may ignore mitigating factors (*King and Simpkins* (1973) 57 Cr.App.R. 696; *Wren* [1974] Crim.L.R. 322).

(c) The mentally disordered offender

(i) *Mental Health Act*
See Part V above.

(ii) *Offenders with personality disorders*
This type of offender presents problems to the courts; while the personality disorder may create difficulties for social services agencies or hospitals, the offender is not sufficiently disturbed for the court to make a hospital order nor are the offences sufficiently serious to carry life sentences or long determinate sentences. As in the previous section the cases in this area are in conflict. This is not entirely surprising as a wide range of offenders fall into this category, such as those with behavioural difficulties associated with mental handicap, the socially inadequate who are generally of low intelligence, those with psychiatric disorders and a history of intermittent stays in mental institutions, the institutionalised who commit offences in order to obtain refuge in prison, those suffering from alcoholism or drug addiction and those with unstable personalities who verge on the dangerous.

In *Clarke* (1975) 61 Cr.App.R. 320, a woman suffering from a psychopathic disorder committed criminal damage to a flower pot valued at £1. The Court of Appeal held that a sentence of 18 months imprisonment was wholly inappropriate. While she was a social nuisance the court declared that it would not send people to prison to fill a gap in the welfare system which failed to make adequate provision for such people. The punishment should be proportionate to the offence (*Tolley* (1978) 68 Cr.App.R. 323; but see *Arrowsmith* [1976] Crim.L.R. 636). These points were re-emphasised in *Coombes* [1982] Crim.L.R. 188, where the court was made up of Lord Lane C.J., Roskill L.J. and Skinner J.[23]

However, there are cases where the court has upheld sentences which are disproportionate to the gravity of the offence because of the offenders' personality disorders. In *Arrowsmith* a disproportionate sentence was approved on the basis that the public needed protecting from the offender and the sentence might help to alleviate her condition. The offender was disturbed, impulsive and aggressive, prone to suicide attempts and made a nuisance of herself with hospitals and social services agencies. The court sentenced her to three years imprisonment for criminal damage to her boyfriend's flat by flooding. Only £18 worth of damage was done. The offence was committed while she was on probation for a previous criminal damage offence. Disproportionate sentences were also approved in *Walsh* [1982] Crim.L.R. 247, and *Scanlon* (1979) 1 Cr.App.R.(S.) 60, in relation to offenders who verged on the dangerous and required hospital treatment but no hospital would accept them. Similarly, in *Rouse* [1981] Crim.L.R. 120, a court which included Lord Lane C.J., reluctantly approved a sentence of imprisonment on an offender with psychiatric disorders because there were no other suitable facilities and the court had to consider the safety of the people against whom he had a grudge and whose property he had damaged. The report does not make it clear, however, whether the court considered the sentence of 18 months imprisonment as particularly severe in relation to the gravity of the offence.

As it is doubtful whether disproportionate sentences can be imposed on dangerous offenders such sentences should not be imposed on offenders who suffer from personality disorders. If *Rouse* is interpreted as a case illustrating the factors a court should consider when deciding whether to impose an individualised sentence or a tariff sentence rather than a case approving disproportionate sentences, and is combined with the views expressed by highly prestigious courts in *Clarke*, *Coombes* and *Ashe*, the authority of cases such as *Walsh* and *Scanlon* is considerably weakened.

---

[23] See also *Fisher* [1981] Crim.L.R. 578; *Slater* (1979) 1 Cr.App.R.(S.) 350; *Judge* [1981] Crim.L.R. 60; *Tunney* [1982] Crim.L.R. 699 (where the court was made up of Lord Lane C.J. and Skinner J.).

(d) Persistent offenders

The fact that an offender has a long record of offences does not justify the imposition of a sentence disproportionate to the facts of the case. In *Re Moore* (1938) 73 I.L.T.R. 143, Andrews L.C.J., in the Court of Criminal Appeal for Northern Ireland, stated:

> "... it is clearly established that when one is dealing with a relatively minor case a previous bad record does not warrant the imposition of an unduly severe sentence."

This principle has been restated and acted on in numerous English cases.[24] In *Skidmore* (1983) 5 Cr.App.R.(S.) 17, the court sought to remove the offender from society for six years by passing sentences of two years imprisonment on each of three counts of obtaining money by deception and making them consecutive. The Court of Appeal varied the sentence to make the terms concurrent as the principle of proportionality applied when a court was aggregating sentences and thus the total had to be proportionate to the type of offences involved. Peter Pain J. spoke out against the temptation to use prison as a dustbin for social nuisances stating

> "Prison is meant, amongst other things, for the punishment of the offender and not as a convenient sort of hostel where you can tuck away people for making social nuisances of themselves, as this man undoubtedly has."

However, the previous record of the accused may justify the court in ignoring mitigating factors and the possibility of an individualised sentence in favour of a sentence of imprisonment (see *Queen* [1982] Crim.L.R. 56).[25] (See also "Extended Sentences," pp. 95–99 above.)

(e) Imprisonment for the offender's benefit

The general principle appears to be that it is wrong to impose a disproportionate sentence in order that the offender may receive treatment.[26] Some offenders, for example, drug addicts, may derive

---

[24] See, *e.g. D.P.P.* v. *Ottwell* [1970] A.C. 642; *Harrison* [1979] Crim.L.R. 262; *Hall* (1979) 1 Cr.App.R.(S.) 27; *Galloway* (1979) 1 Cr.App.R.(S.) 311; *Loosemore* (1980) 2 Cr.App.R.(S.) 72; *McPherson* (1980) 2 Cr.App.R.(S.) 4; *Queen* (1981) 3 Cr.App.R.(S.) 245; *Skidmore* (1983) 5 Cr.App.R.(S.) 17; *Cooper* (1983) 5 Cr.App.R.(S) 295.

[25] But see *Maher* (1979) 1 Cr.App.R.(S.) 52, where the fact that the appellant had a long record of convictions which had made him "institutionalised" combined with the "social nuisance" factor of his alcoholism, was regarded as justification for a sentence of two years imprisonment for a very minor theft. This must be regarded as a bad decision which should not be followed by any court.

[26] See *Moylan* [1970] 1 Q.B. 143; *Ford* [1969] 1 W.L.R. 1703; *Grimes*, unreported, November 14, 1974, *Current Sentencing Practice*, A7.4(a); *Goodall*, unreported, April 22, 1977, *Current Sentencing Practice*, A7.4(a).

some benefit from a prison sentence. In *Moylan* [1970] 1 Q.B. 143 the Court of Appeal stated that the sentencing court must first determine the proper sentencing bracket for the offence but it could, within that bracket, increase the sentence in order to enable a cure to be undertaken while the offender is in prison.

In *Maguire and Enos* (1957) 40 Cr.App.R. 92, the Court of Appeal stated that as a general rule a court should not take possible remission of a sentence into account, but should pass the sentence which it thinks the gravity of the offence deserved. An exception to this principle was established in *Turner* (1967) 51 Cr.App.R. 72, where the Court of Appeal approved a sentence of five years imprisonment in order that the offender could receive necessary mental treatment for three years. The court expressed the view that where reform or treatment is being considered rather than punishment the court should take remission into consideration. It is submitted, however, that the sentence must remain within the appropriate bracket. In *Roote* [1981] Crim.L.R. 189, the Court of Appeal gave the following guidance to sentencers:

> "save in exceptional circumstances, a sentencer should not pass a sentence of imprisonment outside the range appropriate for the offence and for the particular offender on the grounds that the additional term of imprisonment will be of benefit to the offender in helping him overcome some addiction such as an addiction to alcohol or drugs."

The appellant was a heroin addict. A sentence of five years imprisonment was imposed for possession of morphine, forgery of a prescription and demanding drugs on a forged instrument. The judge had received a medical report (after a period of deferment at the end of which the appellant failed to appear, having been taken to hospital with an overdose) which stated that the appellant had a very tenuous hold on life and a longer sentence would probably save her life. The Court of Appeal reduced the sentence to three years. The implication from this decision is that exceptional circumstances will be found to exist very rarely and thus the proportionality principle will be applied in virtually all cases.

MITIGATION

Unless there are grounds for ignoring mitigating factors the sentencer, having chosen the sentence range appropriate to the offence will next consider whether the sentence appropriate to the gravity of the offence should be reduced to reflect the presence of mitigating factors. Mitigation may be found to exist in the character and past history of the offender, pressures which led to the commission of the offence such as emotional distress or provocation, and the consequences of a conviction on the offender such as loss of profession or a marriage break-up. The amount of reduction to make is very much in the discretion of the judge.

(a) Age, character and history of the offender

(i) *Age*
Youth is a strong mitigating factor and generally the courts will choose individualised measures in the case of offenders under 21. Where a custodial sentence is considered necessary a shorter sentence will generally be imposed than would be imposed in the case of an older offender (see, *e.g. Pinnock* (1979) 1 Cr.App.R.(S.) 169).

As the offender becomes progressively older, the relevance of age as a mitigating factor decreases. However, age may be relevant in relation to an older offender where the court out of mercy may reduce the sentence, especially if the offender has a limited life expectancy or ill health. In *Wilkinson*, unreported, November 14, 1974,[27] the appellant was convicted of various sexual offences committed with his young grandnieces. In reducing his sentence Roskill L.J. stated:

> "When one looks at the details of this case it is about as bad of its kind as one could imagine ... [but] on the other hand this man is 60, and no court willingly sentences a man of 60 to spend a large part of the remainder of his life in prison. In the circumstances, as an act of mercy, this Court thinks the right thing will be to reduce the sentences. ... "[28]

However, in *Waterfall* [1976] Crim.L.R. 203 two years imprisonment for forgery of a will by a man of 70 was upheld by the Court of Appeal despite his age and ill health as it was a serious case (see also *Poh and To* [1982] Crim.L.R. 132).

(ii) *Good character and past history*
The previous good character of the offender can act as a mitigating factor leading to a reduction of the sentence. In *Vinson* [1982] Crim.L.R. 192, the Court of Appeal (made up of Lord Lane

[27] See *Current Sentencing Practice*, C2.2(b).
[28] In the "Kincora Sex Scandal" case in Northern Ireland of *Semple*, unreported, 1982, the age, heart condition and plea of guilty of one of the offenders, McGrath, influenced Lord Lowry C.J. in imposing a much more lenient sentence than might otherwise have been expected for a series of homosexual offences committed against boys in care.

C.J. and Skinner J.) reduced a sentence of two years imprisonment to three months where the offender pleaded guilty to two counts of indecent assault. Two factors were of importance in arriving at this decision. First, insufficient credit had been given for the guilty plea, and secondly, "for a man of good character undergoing his first prison sentence, conviction and a prison sentence are in themselves a substantial punishment" (see also *Lewis* (1980) 2 Cr.App.R.(S.) 62). This idea that the fact of a prison sentence itself may be a sufficient punishment to the offender and sufficient deterrence to others has been relied on by the Court of Appeal in a number of cases, particularly breach of trust cases. The court frequently refers to the effect "the clang of the prison gates" has on these offenders. While it was stated above that breach of trust cases arising out of an offender's employment or the office he holds would be met with prison sentences, the courts have come to recognise that the deterrent effect can be achieved by fairly short sentences as the people involved are generally of good character and they usually suffer further consequential loss, such as the loss of their employment, and even the loss of a professional career.[29] However, reduction of sentence on the basis of the "clang of the prison gates" principle will not apply where the offender has previous convictions (*Osborn* [1982] Crim.L.R. 322): nor will it apply where substantial sums of money are involved (*Tonks* [1982] Crim.L.R. 193; *Jacob* [1982] Crim.L.R. 135; *Mian* (1984) 6 Cr.App.R.(S) 10).

Related to the "clang of the prison gates" principle are cases where the Court of Appeal has reduced sentences imposed on offenders because, by the time of the appeal, the sentence has served its purpose by providing a sufficient shock to the offender to make him never want to offend again.[30]

While an offender may have a previous record and therefore not be a person of good character, he may be given credit for making the effort to keep from crime if there is a sufficient gap between his previous offences and the current one (see *Brighton* [1963] Crim.L.R. 64; *Davey* [1980] Crim.L.R. 388). Alternatively, if the offence is out of character with his past record an offender may be treated as a person of good character (*Rackley*, unreported, March 26, 1974, *Current Sentencing Practice*, C2.2(f)). A sentencer may even take into account meritorious conduct in the offender's past as in *Keightley* [1972] Crim.L.R. 262 where sentence was reduced for rescuing a child from drowning; and in *Playfair* [1972] Crim.L.R.

---

[29] See *Wearn* (1980) 2 Cr.App.R.(S.) 295; *Smedley* (1981) 3 Cr.App.R.(S.) 117; *Hulme* [1981] Crim.L.R. 62; *Lalor* [1982] Crim.L.R. 60; *James* [1982] Crim.L.R. 62; *Smith* [1982] Crim.L.R. 469.

[30] See *Blake* [1979] Crim.L.R. 735; *Brotherton* [1981] Crim.L.R. 59; *Skinner* [1981] Crim.L.R. 59; *Lafranceshina* [1980] Crim.L.R. 390; *Smith* [1980] Crim.L.R. 391.

387, sentence was reduced for assisting a wounded police officer; and in *Reid* (1982) 4 Cr.App.R.(S.) 280 a sentence of detention was varied to a conditional discharge where the appellant had attempted to rescue three children from a burning house.

(b) The circumstances of the offence

Some mitigation may be found in the circumstances leading to the commission of the offence. In relation to crimes of violence, provocation has a mitigating effect (see *Blake* [1979] Crim.L.R. 735).[31] In other cases the offences may ensue from emotional stress or depression or domestic tension. In *Lewis* (1980) 2 Cr.App.R.(S.) 62, a mitigating factor on a charge of wounding with intent was that the offence arose from an emotional quarrel when the appellant's common law wife deserted him for another man and refused to let him have their baby.[32] However in *Buchanan* (1981) Cr.App.R.(S.) 13, where the appellant pleaded guilty to wounding with intent and the victim was his common law wife, the offence arising from a quarrel which resulted in the victim leaving the appellant, the Court of Appeal stated that the fact that an offence of violence was committed against a domestic background did not mean that it was a matter of purely domestic concern. The court upheld a sentence based on the gravity of the offence ignoring this mitigating factor. As a result this area is left in some doubt, but it is submitted that there are more cases favouring mitigation in these situations than there are against it.

Frequently sexual offences are committed in periods of emotional stress, for example, where a marriage is breaking down (*Moores* (1980) 2 Cr.App.R.(S.) 317). Financial anxiety (*Weeks* (1979) 1 Cr.App.R.(S.) 239) or depression (*Lindley* (1980) 2 Cr.App.R.(S.) 3) may also amount to mitigating factors in relation to sexual offences. Financial difficulties may also result in offences of dishonesty. Where these difficulties are not of the offender's own making, they may amount to mitigating factors (*Murray* (1980) 71 Cr.App.R. 379).

In at least one case mitigation has been found to exist in the character of the "victim" of the offence. In *Moores* (1980) 2 Cr.App. R.(S.) 317, where a father committed incest with his daughter aged 15 on many occasions over a period of eight months, the Court of Appeal found the fact that the daughter was sexually experienced and promiscuous before incest began was a strong mitigating factor.

Drunkenness, it would appear, will not be regarded as a mitigating factor (*Paton* [1982] Crim.L.R. 58), and has been described as an aggravating factor (*Lindley* (1980) 2 Cr.App.R.(S.) 3; *Bradley* (1980) 2 Cr.App.R.(S.) 12).

---

[31] See also *Heyfron* [1980] Crim.L.R. 663; *Knight* [1980] Crim.L.R. 253.
[32] See also *Blair* [1980] Crim.L.R. 317; *McPhillips* [1980] Crim.L.R. 450.

The fact that the offender has been entrapped into committing the offence of which he has been convicted, may operate to mitigate the penalty. In *Sang and Mangan* [1979] 2 W.L.R. 439, the Court of Appeal stated:

> "If a court is satisfied that a crime has been committed which in truth would not have been committed but for the activities of the informer or police officers concerned, it can, if it thinks right to do so, mitigate the penalty accordingly."

This view was confirmed by the House of Lords in *Sang* [1980] A.C. 402, and the Court of Appeal relied on this principle in *Underhill* (1979) 1 Cr.App.R.(S.) 252. Before entrapment may be considered as a mitigating circumstance it seems that it must be clear that the offence would not have been committed but for the entrapment. Prior to *Sang* and *Underhill* the "possibility" that the offence might not have been committed but for the activities of the informer or police officers appeared to be sufficient to justify mitigating the penalty (see *Birtles* [1969] 1 W.L.R. 1047; *McCann* (1971) 56 Cr.App.R. 359). Accordingly entrapment will operate as a mitigating factor only very rarely as it will be very difficult to show that the offence definitely would not have been committed but for the activities of an *agent provocateur*.

(c) Mitigating consequences of the offence

Various consequences resulting from the offence, conviction or sentence of imprisonment may amount to mitigating factors justifying a reduction in sentence. The normal hardships caused to a wife or family as a result of the offender's imprisonment are not mitigating factors. However, illness on the part of a wife or children requiring the husband's assistance may operate as mitigating factors (*Sumners* (1979) 1 Cr.App.R.(S.) 13).

Where a single parent or a mother with young children commits an offence the needs of the family may lead to the suspension or reduction of the sentence (*Franklyn* (1981) 3 Cr.App.R.(S.) 65).[33]

---

[33] See also *Regan* [1979] Crim.L.R. 261; *Haleth* (1982) 4 Cr.App.R.(S.) 178; *Vaughan* (1982) 4 Cr.App.R.(S.) 83. In *Hamouda* [1982] Crim.L.R. 460, the Court of Appeal refused to quash a sentence of two years imprisonment imposed on an Egyptian woman who was convicted of fraudulently importing cannabis. She committed the offence in order to raise the necessary money for an operation on her sick child. The court took the view that those who planned drugs smuggling operations were always looking for couriers who, if they are caught, can tell a story which may affect their sentences. As the menace of illegal importation of drugs is so great the court took the view that those who engage in the traffic must expect severe custodial sentences. The trial judge had already mitigated the sentence by passing a sentence at a lower end of the bracket and thus the appeal was dismissed.

In some situations mitigation may be found to exist in the hardship suffered by the offender over and above that usually suffered by offenders as a result of their offences. The loss of a career or family as a result of the commission of an offence may lead to reduction in sentence (*Fell* [1975] Crim.L.R. 349).[34] In *Richards* (1980) 2 Cr.App.R.(S.) 119, 30 months imprisonment for fraud offences committed by a medical practitioner against the Health Authority was reduced to 12 months as the conviction meant the end of his career, disciplinary proceedings before the Disciplinary Committee of the General Medical Council and the probable reduction of his pension. Similarly where imprisonment has serious consequences for the offender's business or livelihood the sentence may be reduced (*Wilson* [1980] Crim.L.R. 662; *Battams* (1979) 1 Cr.App.R.(S.) 15). Serious injury suffered by the offender in the course of committing the offence may be regarded by the court as a form of punishment justifying a reduction in sentence (*Barbery* (1975) 62 Cr.App.R. 248).

Prison, itself, may involve difficulties or hardships for the offender. Where the prisoner suffers from bad health or physical disability his sentence may be reduced (*Deffley* [1972] Crim.L.R. 123).[35] In other cases the hardship suffered by the prisoners may be at the hands of other prisoners because of their previous positions (*e.g.* police officers, prison officers), or the help they may have given the police (informers), or the nature of their offences (sexual offences, especially against children) (see *Harrison* (1979) 1 Cr.App.R.(S.) 248; *Weeks* (1979) 1 Cr.App.R.(S.) 239).

(d) Other mitigating factors

(i) *Remorse, guilty plea and other behaviour subsequent to the offence*

The behaviour of the offender subsequent to the offence may be taken into account as a mitigating factor. If he voluntarily gives himself up to the police this will be a strong indication of remorse and can lead to a reduction or even suspension of a prison sentence or to the imposition of some other non-custodial measure. Alternatively, a frank admission to the police when accused of an offence may also indicate remorse (*Moores* (1980) 2 Cr.App.R.(S.) 317; *Weeks* (1979) 1 Cr.App.R.(S.) 239). Efforts to make restitution or pay compensation prior to the trial will also indicate remorse.

The most frequently arising indication of remorse is the guilty plea. While this does not always indicate remorse or repentence on

---

[34] See also *Harrison* (1979) 1 Cr.App.R.(S.) 248; *Long* (1980) 2 Cr.App.R.(S.) 8; *Vinson* [1982] Crim.L.R. 192; *Stanley* (1981) 3 Cr.App.R.(S.) 373.
[35] See also *Battams* (1979) 1 Cr.App.R.(S.) 15; *Semple*, unreported, N.I.

the part of the offender, it is given credit in sentencing (*Meade* (1982) 4 Cr.App.R.(S.) 193; *Skilton and Blackham* (1982) 4 Cr.App.R.(S.) 339) even if the offender has no possible defence to the charge (*Davies* (1980) 2 Cr.App.R.(S.) 168). The guilty plea saves time and expense (*McPhee* [1980] Crim.L.R. 445); and its mitigating effect has been particularly emphasised in cases involving sexual offences where it saves the victim the ordeal of having to give evidence (*Robertshaw* (1981) 3 Cr.App.R.(S.) 77).[36]

Where there are two or more defendants of equal culpability, the fact that one has pleaded guilty will be marked by giving him a lighter sentence (*Quirke* (1982) 4 Cr.App.R.(S.) 187; *Ross* (1983) 5 Cr.App.R(S) 318). Thus where an offender pleads guilty it will rarely be appropriate to impose upon him the maximum sentence (*Barry and Barry* (1983) 5 Cr.App.R.(S.) 11; *Stewart* [1983] Crim.L.R. 830; *Barnes* (1983) 5 Cr.App.R(S) 368).

While a plea of guilty will justify a reduction in the length of a sentence, whether it justifies a suspension of the sentence is questionable. The authorities are in conflict (see *Tonks* [1980] Crim.L.R. 59 and *Hollyman* (1979) 1 Cr.App.R.(S.) 289). *Hollyman* is the only case to suggest that suspension of a sentence may be justified where there is a guilty plea for an offence meriting imprisonment, whereas *Tonks*, following the view implicit in *Turner* [1970] 2 Q.B. 321, supports the view that a plea of guilty may justify a reduction of sentence but it does not justify a change of the type of sentence which the judge would otherwise impose on a plea of not guilty.

(ii) *Informers*

A substantial reduction in sentence will be made where the offender assists the police by providing them with information leading to the apprehension of other offenders (*James and Sharman* (1913) 9 Cr.App.R. 142). In recent times this has led to the rise of the "supergrasses" who have received substantial reductions in sentence for serious offences because of the amount of information they have supplied in relation to other serious offences (see *Lowe* (1977) 66 Cr.App.R. 122; *Davies and Gorman* (1978) 68 Cr.App.R. 319).[37] This reduction recognises the service rendered to the police, acts as an encouragement to other offenders, and reflects the risk to which these offenders expose themselves and the conditions under

[36] See also *Vinson* [1982] Crim.L.R. 192; *Hunter* (1979) 1 Cr.App.R.(S.) 7; *Barnes* (1983) 5 Cr.App.R.(S) 368. But cf. *McLoughlin and Simpson* (1979) 1 Cr.App.R.(S.) 298 and *Stabler* (1984) 6 Cr.App.R.(S.) 129, where the Court of Appeal took the view that the seriousness of the offences and the need to protect the public dictated that the fact of guilty pleas being made should be ignored in the circumstances.
[37] See *The Sunday Times*, August 28, 1977, p. 14, November 18, 1979, p. 3.

which they will serve their sentences, *i.e.* in solitary confinement for their own safety (see *Sinfield* (1981) 3 Cr.App.R.(S.) 258). However, there is no "tariff" reduction; each case will depend on its own facts, with the above factors being weighed against the criminality of the offences of which the informer is convicted, to determine the amount of reduction which should be made (see *Rose and Sapiano* (1980) 2 Cr.App.R.(S.) 239; *Sinfield*).

(iii) *Delay*

Mitigation may be found to exist in the long delay between the discovery of an offence and its prosecution (*Regan* [1979] Crim.L.R. 261; *Hockey* [1980] Crim.L.R. 594). In *Tierney* [1982] Crim.L.R. 53, there was an 18 month delay between the arrest of the appellant and his trial for burglary. Part of the delay was due to the fact that he had spent some time in hospital following a road accident. During the interval the appellant had married and settled down and had a good job. The Court of Appeal reduced his sentence of nine months imprisonment to six months suspended for 12 months, stating that the just way to deal with the appellant was to deal with him as he was at the time of the trial and not as he had been 18 months previously.

CO-DEFENDANTS AND MULTIPLE SENTENCES

(a) Sentencing co-defendants

A frequent reason for appealing a sentence is the disparity between the appellant's sentence and that of his co-defendant. Where two or more offenders are involved in the commission of an offence they should be sentenced according to their respective degrees of culpability and taking into account the mitigatory factors relating to each individually (see *Weekes* (1982) 74 Cr.App.R. 161).[38]

The following matters have been found to justify disparity in sentences between co-defendants: a plea of guilty by one offender[39]; other mitigating factors[40]; the presence of aggravating factors, such as a breach of trust, in relation to one offender.[41] Where, however, the sentencer uses an individualised measure in relation to one offender, this provides no basis for an appeal by another dealt with

---

[38] See also *O'Brien and Noonan* (1975) 61 Cr.App.R. 177; *Oxton and Neil* [1981]. Crim.L.R. 188; *Giannitto* [1980] Crim.L.R. 665; *Davey* [1982] Crim.L.R. 388.

[39] *Campbell* (1979) 1 Cr.App.R.(S.) 200; *McClurkin* (1979) 1 Cr.App.R.(S.) 67; *Ross* (1983) 5 Cr.App.R.(S.) 318; *Quirke* (1982) 4 Cr.App.R.(S.) 187.

[40] *Armstrong* [1979] Crim.L.R. 61; *Sykes* (1980) 2 Cr.App.R.(S.) 173; *Oxton and Neil* [1981] Crim.L.R. 188; *Tremarco* (1979) 1 Cr.App.R.(S.) 286.

[41] *Warton* [1976] Crim.L.R. 520; *Oxton and Neil.*

apparently more severely, as the sentences are based on different approaches (*Watson* [1979] Crim.L.R. 730). However, individualised measures should not be used for one offender if his culpability and circumstances are substantially the same as an accomplice who has received a tariff sentence (*Milburn* [1974] Crim.L.R. 434).

As a ground for appeal against sentence, disparity of sentences will be successful and lead to a reduction of sentence only if there is "such a glaring difference between the treatment of one man as compared with another that a real sense of grievance would be engendered" (*Brown* [1975] Crim.L.R. 177). The court has reduced sentences where, although looked at in isolation they are correct, inappropriately lenient sentences have been passed on co-dependants creating real and justified senses of grievance on the part of the appellants. (*McPhee* (1980) Crim.L.R. 445).[42] In the most recent case of *Okuya and Nwaobi* (1984) 6 Cr.App.R.(S.) the Court of Appeal refused to reduce sentences imposed on the appellants, on the ground of disparity, as the sentences were correct and there was, in the court's view no good reason for doing so, even though the third defendant (a woman) had received an unduly lenient sentence. This case suggests that the court may not now be as prepared to countenance undue leniency in relation to one defendant as a ground for reducing otherwise correct sentences imposed on other defendants.

(b) Concurrent and consecutive sentences

Where a person is convicted of more than one offence or where a suspended sentence is activated, or the offender is dealt with in respect of earlier offences for which he was subjected to probation or a conditional discharge, or where he is already in prison in relation to another offence, the sentencer must decide whether the sentences should run concurrently or consecutively. Two principles are of importance in relation to the exercise of this discretion.

First, *where the offences arise out of the same transaction the sentences should normally be concurrent* (*Hockey* [1980] Crim.L.R. 594; *Jones* (1980) 2 Cr.App.R.(S.) 152). A problem, however, is to define the "same transaction." A series of offences against the same victim (*e.g.* sexual offences with the same partner) can amount to the same transaction provided they are committed within a relatively short space of time.[43] Ultimately the decision whether a

---

[42] See also *Begg* [1981] Crim.L.R. 423; *Street* [1974] Crim.L.R. 264; *Weeks* (1982) 74 Cr.App.R. 161; *Wood* (1983) 5 Cr.App.R.(S.) 381; but *cf. Okuya and Nwaobi* [1984] Crim.L.R. 766.

[43] See Thomas, *Principles of Sentencing* (2nd ed., 1979), p. 54.

series of offences constitutes a single transaction is a decision for the judge. As this decision is so much dependant upon the facts of each case it is not possible to state any principles, and indeed, many of the cases appear to be in conflict.[44]

Several recent decisions have added to the confusion. In *Wheatley* (1983) 5 Cr.App.R.(S.) 417, the Court of Appeal admitted an exception to the general principle "when the circumstances demand it". Thus where the maximum sentence would be too short, in the view of the court, to reflect the gravity of the offender's conduct if the offences were treated as a single transaction, the court may treat them as separate offences and impose consecutive sentences. In *Dillon* (1983) 5 Cr.App.R.(S.) 439 and *Michel, Berry and Eade* [1985] Crim.L.R. 162, the Court of Appeal appeared to adopt a very narrow view of what constitutes a single transaction in order to impose consecutive sentences for several offences. Whichever approach is adopted it seems that the Court is becoming less inclined to reduce consecutive sentences on the basis of the single transaction principle where the maximum sentences for the offences are low and do not sufficiently reflect the actual seriousness of the offender's conduct.

Where sentences are made concurrent the court must pass the correct tariff sentence in respect of each offence, as it is wrong to impose an excessive sentence on a particular charge on the grounds that the sentence will be swallowed up by a heavier sentence in relation to one of the other offences (*Smith* [1975] Crim.L.R. 468).

Secondly, *where the offences do not arise out of the same transaction it is at the discretion of the court whether the sentences should be consecutive or concurrent.*

Consecutive sentences are generally imposed where an offence has been committed during the period of a suspended sentence and the suspended sentence is activated (*Ithell* [1969] 1 W.L.R. 272; *May* (1979) 1 Cr.App.R.(S.) 124). However, it may be inappropriate to make a suspended sentence consecutive where the operational period of the suspended sentence is almost expired (*Carr* (1979) 1 Cr.App.R.(S.) 53). Equally it may be inappropriate where the sentence for the new offence is quite severe by comparison to the period of the suspended sentence (*Christie* (1979) 1 Cr.App.R.(S.) 84). Where the court imposes a sentence of imprisonment for an offence in respect of which the offender had been subject to a probation order or conditional discharge, the sentences will normally be consecutive.

---

[44] The case of *Hancock and Swan* [1977] Crim.L.R. 367, is a good illustration of a case which could have been decided either way. The ultimate decision depended on the judge's view of the facts.

Where the sentences are ordered to be consecutive the total period of imprisonment should not exceed what is just and appropriate to the overall gravity of the law breaking (*Smith* [1972] Crim.L.R. 124; *Clarke* [1977] Crim.L.R. 430; *Skidmore* [1983] Crim.L.R. 407); nor should the sentence represent a "crushing sentence" on the offender (*Raybould,* unreported, June 1, 1970). A judge passing consecutive sentences should review the total period and if this appears excessive, an adjustment should be made,[45] usually by ordering some of the sentences to run concurrently rather than by reducing the length of individual sentences and allowing them to remain consecutive.[46] Reduction may be merited on one of two grounds. First, where, for example, the offender commits three separate offences of dishonesty which individually merit three years imprisonment, a reduction would be required if nine years imprisonment is disproportionate to the gravity of the law breaking. Secondly, when the judge is reviewing the total sentence he should pay regard to mitigating factors such as the age of the offender or the fact that it is his first term of imprisonment (*Koyce* (1979) 1 Cr.App.R.(S.) 21; *Morgan* (1972) 56 Cr.App.R. 181).

Magistrates' courts

In relation to magistrates' courts the power to impose consecutive sentences is contained in section 133 of the Magistrates' Courts Act 1980. The aggregate of the consecutive terms cannot exceed six months (s. 133(1)), except where two or more consecutive terms of imprisonment are imposed in respect of indictable offences tried summarily[47] when the aggregate of those terms cannot exceed 12 months (s. 133(2)).[48] However, if the court has power to impose a

---

[45] Thomas, *op. cit.,* p. 57 states:

  "The principle applies to all situations in which an offender may become subject to more than one sentence: where sentences are passed on different counts in an indictment or on different indictments, where the offender is subject to a suspended sentence or probation order, where he is already serving a sentence of imprisonment or makes appearances in different courts within a short space of time. In all such cases "the final duty of the sentencer is to make sure that the totality of the consecutive sentences is not excessive'." (footnotes omitted).

[46] This is an important principle as reduction of the length of the sentence for an offence may make that offence one in respect of which the offender may become rehabilitated sooner. See Appendix B.

[47] "Otherwise than in pursuance of s. 22(2)," *i.e.* summary trial of offences where the value involved is small.

[48] This does not prevent the subsequent imposition of a term of imprisonment in default of payment of a fine consecutive to a six month term which has already been imposed at the same time as the fine: *R.* v. *Stipendiary Magistrate for South Westminster, ex p. Green* [1977] 1 All E.R.353.

sentence greater than the maximum aggregate of section 133(1) or
(2) in respect of a particular offence, the provisions of section 133(1)
and (2) will not operate to reduce the sentence to that aggregate but
the maximum for that offence will become the maximum aggregate
(s. 133(3)).

APPENDIX A

SENTENCING ALTERNATIVES

Crown Court

AGE	NON-CUSTODIAL	CUSTODIAL
10 and under 14	Absolute/Conditional Discharge Bind over (child or parent) Fine (generally parent) Supervision Order Attendance Centre Order Care Order Deferment of Sentence	Detention during H.M.'s Pleasure (C.Y.P.A. 1933, s.53(1)) Detention under, C.Y.P.A. 1933, s.53(2) Hospital Order Interim Hospital Order Guardianship Order
14 and under 17	Absolute/Conditional Discharge Bind over (young person or parent) Fine (young person or parent) Supervision Order Care Order Attendance Centre Order Community Service Order (where 16) Deferment of sentence	Detention Centre Order (if male and 15 or over) Youth Custody Order (if male and 15 or over) Detention during H.M.'s Pleasure (C.Y.P.A. 1933, s.53(1)) Detention under C.Y.P.A. 1933, s.53(2) Hospital Order Interim Hospital Order Guardianship Order
17 and under 21	Absolute/Conditional Discharge Bind Over Fine Probation Order Community Service Order Attendance Centre Order Deferment of Sentence	Detention Centre Order (if male) Youth Custody Order (male or female) Custody for Life Detention during H.M.'s Pleasure (if under 18 and convicted of murder: C.Y.P.A. 1933, s.53(1)) Default Detention Hospital Order Interim Hospital Order Guardianship Order
21 and over	Absolute/Conditional Discharge Bind Over Fine Probation Order Community Service Order Deferment of Sentence	Imprisonment Suspended/Partly Suspended Sentence of Imprisonment Hospital Order Interim Hospital Order Guardianship Order

284

Magistrates'/Juvenile Court

AGE	NON-CUSTODIAL	CUSTODIAL
10 and under 14	Absolute/Conditional Discharge Bind Over (child or parent) Fine (generally parent) Supervision Order Attendance Centre Order Care Order Deferment of Sentence	Hospital Order Interim Hospital Order Guardianship Order
14 and under 17	Absolute/Conditional Discharge Bind Over (young person or parent) Fine (young person or parent) Supervision Order Attendance Centre Order Care Order Community Service Order (where 16) Deferment of Sentence	Detention Centre Order (if male and 15 or over) Youth Custody Order (if male and 15 or over) Hospital Order Interim Hospital Order Guardianship Order
17 and under 21	Absolute/Conditional Discharge Bind Over Fine Probation Order Community Service Order Attendance Centre Order Deferment of Sentence	Detention Centre Order (if male) Youth Custody Order (male or female) Default Detention Hospital Order Interim Hospital Order Guardianship Order
21 and over	Absolute/Conditional Discharge Bind Over Fine Probation Order Community Service Order Deferment of Sentence	Imprisonment Suspended/Party Suspended Sentence of Imprisonment Hospital Order Interim Hospital Order Guardianship Order

APPENDIX B

THE REHABILITATION OF OFFENDERS ACT 1974

Under the Act in certain circumstances convictions may become "spent" and a convicted person may be considered "rehabilitated" (s. 1(1)). Where a conviction becomes spent the offender is treated for most purposes as if he had never been convicted of the offence concerned.

Convictions which may become spent

The Act applies to anyone convicted of a criminal offence in civilian life, or in the Services, in Great Britain or abroad. However, not every conviction may become spent and result in rehabilitation. Section 5(1) makes all sentences subject to rehabilitation except sentences of life imprisonment or corrective training for more than 30 months, preventive detention, and equivalent detention imposed under section 53 of the Children and Young Persons Act 1933 on young offenders convicted of grave crimes, and corresponding court-martial punishment. The Act, accordingly, applies to anyone given any type of sentence, up to a maximum of 30 months in prison, including fines, probation orders, and conditional and absolute discharges.

"Conviction" includes a conviction by or before a court outside Great Britain (including foreign courts) and any finding (other than one linked with a finding of insanity) in any criminal proceedings or in care proceedings under section 1 of the Children and Young Persons Act 1969, that a person has committed an offence or done the act or made the omission charged, notwithstanding that the conviction resulted in the imposition of a probation order or a conditional or absolute discharge (s. 1(4)).

"Sentence" includes any order made in dealing with a person for his conviction other than an order for committal or any other order made in default of payment of a fine or orders dealing with a person in respect of a suspended prison sentence (s. 1(3)).

How a conviction becomes spent

Section 1(2) provides that a person will not become a rehabilitated person unless he has actually served or otherwise undergone or complied with any sentence imposed on him in respect of that conviction. If a person receives a partly suspended sentence he is to be treated as having served the sentence as soon as he completes the part which he had to serve in prison (s. 1(2A) as inserted by C.L.A., Sched. 9). Where a person is released on licence, breach of any condition of such licence will exclude rehabilitation as he will not have "undergone or complied with" his sentence. However, under section 1(2)(*b*) certain breaches of condition or requirement which render the person liable to be dealt with for his original offence do not have this effect. Thus breach of a requirement in a probation order or community service order or of a condition in an order of conditional discharge will not prevent rehabilitation, but the rehabilitation period may be extended. Nor will the fact that a person undergoing a suspended sentence of imprisonment commits another offence prevent rehabilitation. Similarly failure to pay a fine or breach of condition of a recognizance to keep the peace or to be of good behaviour will not prevent a person from becoming rehabilitated (s. 1(2)(*a*)).

Rehabilitation periods

Section 5 sets out the rehabilitation periods which vary depending on the sentence imposed. Consecutive sentences of imprisonment count as a single term and suspended sentences are treated as if they had been put into effect. The rehabilitation period is based on the sentence imposed by the court and not the time actually served in prison which may be less because of remission. The rehabilitation period runs from the date of the conviction and not the date of the offence.

In relation to custodial sentences the rehabilitation period is fixed depending on the length of the sentence, while for fines, community service orders, absolute discharge and any other sentence for which specific provision is not made in the Act, there are specified fixed periods. The period in relation to probation, bind over to keep the peace and/or to be of good behaviour, conditional discharge and care and supervision orders is the date the order or bind over ceases or one year, whichever is the longer. For hospital orders under the Mental Health Act 1983 the period is five years from the date of the conviction or two years after the order expires, whichever is longer. Where, in respect of a conviction, any disqualification, disability, prohibition or other penalty is imposed the rehabilitation period lasts until the order ceases (s. 5(8)). Where the period of the disqualification, etc., is for life the offender will never become rehabilitated in relation to the offence concerned.

Where more than one sentence is imposed in respect of a conviction, and none of the sentences are excluded from rehabilitation, the rehabilitation period is the longer of the relevant periods if there is any difference in the period applicable to each of the sentences (s. 6(2)).

Subsequent convictions during the rehabilitation period

Where a person is convicted of a subsequent offence during the currency of a rehabilitation period, the rehabilitation period may be extended, or the subsequent conviction may preclude rehabilitation altogether. Where the sentence imposed on the subsequent conviction is not open to rehabilitation this conviction and the earlier conviction will never become spent (s. 1(1)(b), s. 6(4)(b)). If the subsequent conviction is for an offence which is only triable summarily, or is tried summarily in pursuance of section 22(2) of the Magistrates' Courts Act, this will have no effect on the rehabilitation period for the first offence; the rehabilitation periods in relation to each conviction will run separately (s. 6(6)(a)). The rehabilitation period for the first offence will similarly not be affected where the subsequent conviction is by a court outside Great Britain "of an offence in respect of conduct which, if it had taken place in Great Britain would not have constituted an offence under the law in force in that part of Great Britain" (s. 6(6)(c)). Where the subsequent conviction is in respect of an indictable offence, an indictable offence triable summarily, an offence triable either summarily or on indictment, a summary offence triable on indictment, or results from inservice disciplinary proceedings, the longer of the two rehabilitation periods will apply to both offences (s. 6(4) and (7)).

As the rehabilitation period for any disqualification, disability, prohibition or other penalty lasts from the date of conviction to the date on which it ceases to have effect (s. 5(8)), section 6(5) provides that such a rehabilitation period will not operate under section 6(4) to extend the rehabilitation period relating to the other conviction. However, where any other sentence is imposed in respect of the offence to which the disqualification, disability, prohibition or other penalty relates, the rehabilitation period for the other offence, where appropriate, will be extended under section 6(4) by reference to the rehabilitation period applicable to that sentence (s. 6(5)).

The effect of rehabilitation

Where a person becomes rehabilitated under the Act, he is treated, with certain exceptions, for all purposes in law as if he had never committed, been charged with, prosecuted for, convicted of, or sentenced for, the relevant offence or offences (s. 4(1)).

In proceedings before a judicial authority (as defined by s. 4(6)) no evidence is admissible to prove that a rehabilitated person committed or was tried for an offence which is the subject of a spent conviction (s. 4(1)(a)), nor may any questions concerning these matters be asked in such proceedings and, if asked, they need not be answered (s. 4(1)(b)). However, certain proceedings are excepted by section 7(2) from the provisions of section 4(1)(*a*). The most important are criminal proceedings (thus courts deciding sentence will still be able to consult the full record of the offender before them), various proceedings relating to minors (*e.g.* adoption, guardianship, wardship, etc.), any proceedings in which the rehabilitated offender is a party or witness and he consents to the admission of evidence of previous offences and convictions, and any proceedings before a judicial authority where that authority is satisfied that justice cannot be done in the case except by admitting or requiring evidence relating to a person's spent convictions or to circumstances ancillary thereto (s. 7(3)). Pursuant to the powers conferred upon him by section 7(4) the Secretary of State has extended the list of excepted proceedings by article 5 of the Rehabilitation of Offenders Act 1974 (Exceptions) Order 1975. The list of excepted proceedings is contained in Schedule 3 to that Order.

Subject to exceptions which the Secretary of State may by order make (s. 4(4)), where questions are asked otherwise than in judicial proceedings they are to be treated as not relating to spent convictions or any circumstances ancillary to spent convictions, and no penalty attaches to failure to disclose either in the answer (s. 4(2)). In addition, where any person is obliged by law, agreement or arrangement to make a disclosure, the obligation (subject to exceptions under section 4(5)) does not cover disclosure of spent convictions or ancillary circumstances; nor is a spent conviction or ancillary circumstances, or failure to disclose them, a "proper ground for dismissing or excluding a person from any office, profession, occupation or employment or for prejudicing him in any way in any occupation or employment" (s. 4(3)). Thus, in filling in most forms (*e.g.* applying for hire purchase or insurance), in interviews, writing references relating to another person, a person is not required to disclose his own or another person's convictions.

The Secretary of State has, however, drawn up a wide range of exceptions contained in the Rehabilitation of Offenders Act 1974 (Exceptions) Order 1975. These cover a wide range of offices, professions, occupations and employments specified in Schedule 1, Parts I, II and III. In completing application forms, or at interviews, relating to these exceptions a rehabilitated offender will not be protected by the Act if he fails to mention a spent conviction provided he is told at the time that, because of the Exceptions Order, spent convictions are to be mentioned (r. 3(*a*)). Under rule 3(*b*) a person may in certain cases be asked to disclose spent convictions provided he is given the necessary warning. The question must be asked by or on behalf of a person in the course of his duties as a person employed in the service of the Crown, the

United Kingdom Atomic Energy Authority, the Civil Aviation Authority, the Post Office or British Telecommunications in order to assess, for the purposes of safeguarding national security or of protecting public safety or public order, the suitability of the person to whom the question relates or of any other person for any office or employment.

Spent convictions or any ancillary circumstances, or a failure to disclose a spent conviction or ancillary circumstances, may be a proper ground for dismissing or excluding a person from an office, profession, occupation or employment, where that office, profession, occupation or employment is excepted by Parts I, II and III of Schedule 1 or where the action is taken for the purpose of safeguarding national security or protecting public safety or public order (r. 4).

Defamation actions

Section 8 is the main enforcement provision of the Act. The Act only covers actions for defamation founded on publication of an imputation that the plaintiff has committed or been tried for a spent offence where the publication took place, and the action was commenced, after the commencement of the Act (s. 8(1)). In an action for defamation covered by section 8, section 4(1) and the remaining provisions of section 8 do not apply where the publication took place before the conviction became spent. Thus section 8 applies only where the publication takes place after the conviction becomes spent. Subsections (3) to (7) of section 8 apply to these cases excluding the application of section 4(1), and thereby preserving, with some modification, the established defences to an action for defamation:

(i) *Justification*

Justification is only available as a defence where the publication was not made with malice (s. 8(3) and (5)).

(ii) *Absolute privilege*

This defence is available with one exception: a fair and accurate report of judicial proceedings will not be privileged if it contains a reference to evidence ruled inadmissible under section 4(1) (s. 8(6)). Thus the defence of absolute privilege cannot be pleaded where the only means of proving that the report is fair and accurate is to rely on the fact of the spent conviction or bringing evidence of it. However, section 8(6) does not cover every report of judicial proceedings. Section 8(7) excludes reports where there is a need to give a complete and accurate account of the judicial proceedings; this takes precedence over the protection of the rehabilitated person. Accordingly references to inadmissible evidence continue to be privileged in two situations:

(a)   in "any report of judicial proceedings contained in any bona fide series of law reports which does not form part of any other publication and consists solely of reports of proceedings in courts of law."

This class covers the various series of law reports. However, law reports contained in, *e.g. The Times* are not covered by this provision. If absolute privilege is to cover them they must depend on the second class.

(b)   in "any report or account of judicial proceedings published for bona fide educational, scientific or professional purposes, or given in the course of any lecture, class or discussion given or held for any of those purposes."

This class will protect textbooks and articles in periodicals. It will probably cover law reports in *The Times*, but it will not cover accounts of trials published simply for their news or scandal value. Reports of proceedings given in lectures etc. are covered provided the report is included for its educational value and not included gratuitously because of value as scandal designed to give added interest to the proceedings.

(iii) *Qualified privilege*

This defence may be defeated by the plaintiff proving that the defendant was actuated by malice in publishing the alleged defamatory material. The operation of section 4(1) is excluded in these cases thereby leaving the defendant unrestricted in relation to the evidence he may bring to rebut the allegation of malice (s. 8(4)).

(iv) *Fair comment*

The defence of fair comment on a matter of general public interest is preserved by section 8(3).

Unauthorised disclosure of spent convictions

Section 9 creates two summary offences. The first offence under section 9, which is additional to any offence which may be committed under the Official Secrets Act, may be committed by any person who has, in the course of his official duties, had access to any "official record" or information in it. An "official record" is one kept officially by the courts, police, government department, public authority, or the Services, which contains information about persons convicted of offences. The offence under section 9(2) is committed when, knowing or having reasonable cause to suspect that any information he has obtained in the course of his official duties is "specified information," the official discloses that information otherwise than in the course of his duties. "Specified information" is information imputing that a living, rehabilitated person committed or was tried for a spent offence. Prosecution for this offence may not be instituted except by the Director of Public Prosecutions. The maximum penalty on a summary conviction is a fine at level 4.

It is a defence to a charge under section 9(2) for the defendant to prove that the disclosure was made:

(a) to the rehabilitated person or to another person at the express request of the rehabilitated person; or

(b) to a person whom he reasonably believed to be the rehabilitated person or to another person at the express request of a person whom he reasonably believed to be the rehabilitated person.

The person who has deceived the official into disclosing the specified information may himself be guilty of an offence under section 9(4).

Section 9(4) creates the more serious offence of obtaining specified information by fraud, dishonesty or bribery and the maximum penalty for this offence is a fine at level 5 and/or imprisonment for six months.

Index

293

302